Art of Investing: Sector Rotation

Tony Pow

Highlights

Why you want to read this book

- My annuity has grown **four** times using sector rotation. I started with a position more than my annual salary then, and hence I do not boast with a tiny amount. In March, 2000, I switched out all my tech positions from this account. How many authors can say that? We can make money by spotting the market plunge and spotting the trend.

- I have **21** strategies in sector rotation while most books have only one. It ranges from simple rotation of a stock ETF and cash to finding best stocks in best sectors.

- If you follow O'Neil, our greatest chartist, you will be surprised. Do not be fooled by past performances. Just check their recent performance of the top 50 stocks selected by IBD in the last five years. The mediocre result (hopefully it will change) could be due to too many followers and/or there is no evergreen strategy. The adaptive strategy of this book shows you how to select the most profitable strategy for the current market.

- As of 4/2016, I had switched 80% of this account to cash based on the technical indicator. I switched most (if not all) my sector funds in April, 2000 from technology sectors to traditional sectors (better to money market fund). We can reduce losses by spotting market plunges (Chapter 2) and spotting the sector trend.

- As of 9/25/15, I glanced through my competing books in Kindle format. Here are my personal comments and check whether it makes sense to you.

  - ETF Rotation. 3.5 stars. **91** pages. $9.99.
  - Super Sectors. 3.5 stars. 264 pages. $26.39.
  - Profiting from ETF Rotation. 3.5 stars. **35** pages. $7.55. Must be reviewed by friends or it is very, very concisely great.
  - Standard & Poor's Sector Investing. 3 stars. 260 pages **$97.58**. Another one costs $200 with all the hard-to-understand formulae. This must be written by professors requiring their students to buy. How many professors make money in the stock market?

- Dual Momentum Investing. 5 stars. 240 pages. $34.99. After reading several of the comments and the table of contents, I only found only one chapter is useful to me. The absolute momentum and relative momentum have been described in my book.

  My book has about 250 pages (solid information and nothing on my life to fill the pages) and the Kindle version only costs $8.95 and paperback is also available.

- Most books on this topic do not consider cash or money market fund as a sector. The average loss in the last two market plunges is about 45%. When the market is plunging, cash is the best investment. If you can tolerate more risk, buy contra ETFs betting the market to go further down.

- I select proven ideas from more than 100 books besides my original ideas and experiences.

- Many 100-page books could turn into just a few pages of useful information after the narrating the story of the author's life.

- Andrew, a contributor on Sector Rotation article at Seeking Alpha, said, "Great stuff, Tony. It's great to meet experienced traders such as yourself. I had a browse through the book and think your method is a little more refined than mine."

- My articles in SeekingAlpha.com. I claim to have the best one-year performance of any articles for recommending 5 or more stocks.
http://seekingalpha.com/article/2492255-a-tale-of-2-portfolios

My motivation to write this book is sharing my experiences, both bad and good. I provide simple-to-follow techniques using the free (or low-cost) resources available to us. I have been successful in investing for decades. I am enjoying a comfortable financial life. I do not hold back my 'secrets' as my children are not interested in investing. It is my small legacy in sharing my investing ideas. If you are looking how to make 100% return overnight, there are many other books claiming to do so and this book is not for you. This book describes how to be a 'turtle' investor making fortune gradually and surely. Be warned that many books written by authors who have never make money in the stock market.

Why you trust me

All of the below are provable. I did made some blunders and both are described in this book.

- My annuity (not recommended due to my higher tax bracket during retirement) grows to **5** times mostly using Fidelity's funds for sector rotation.

- I switched most (all in my annuity) of my tech funds to other sectors (should be cash if I had a time machine) in April, 2000. It was only provable if Fidelity keeps record for the year 2000.

- I achieved 80% return in my largest taxable account in 2009.

- I recommended to buy oil when it was $30 at Seeking Alpha, a web site for investors.

- I recommended 20 stocks in an article Amazing Return in Seeking Alpha. If you bought them on the published date, you would have beaten the S&P500 index by over 100% without considering dividends as demonstrated in my other article A Tale of Two Portfolios. Search these articles.

  I challenge anyone who had better one-year performance for recommending a diversified portfolio of 15 or more stocks.

Why you invest

You will need to learn about investing sooner or later in your life. You also need to take some calculated risks.

Compare the returns of the following assets: cash, CDs, treasury bills, bonds, real estate and stocks. We start with the risk-free investments and end with the riskiest. It turns out that the average returns are in the opposite order. Cash and CDs are not risk-free as inflation eats our profits. For example, the real return is negative for the 2% return in a CD and a 3% inflation rate. In addition you have to pay taxes for the 'returns'. Our capitalist system punishes us for not taking risk.

There are two kinds of risk: blind risk and calculated risk. If you buy a stock due to a recommendation from a commentator on TV or a tip, most likely you are taking a blind risk. It would be the same in buying a house without thoroughly evaluating the house and its neighborhood. When you buy stocks with a proven strategy (i.e. when/what stocks to buy and when/what stocks to sell), you are taking a calculated risk. In the long run, stocks with calculated and educated risks are profitable.

Be a turtle investor by investing in value stocks and holding for longer time periods (a year or more). "Buy and Monitor" is a better approach than "Buy and Hold" as some could lose all the value such as in the failure of Enron.

For experienced investors, shorting, short-term trading and covered calls would make you good profits. Simple market timing would reduce your losses during market down turns. If you buy a market ETF and use my simple market timing, you should have beaten the market by a wide margin from 2000 to 2019.

With so many fraudulent and poor managed hedge funds (but many exceptions), do not trust anyone with your investing. Do not buy investing instruments that are highly marketed such as annuity and term insurance.

If you are a handy man and do not mind to satisfy the constant requests of your tenants, buy real estate in growing areas that could be very profitable in the long run.

Take advantage of the tax laws such as investing in a 401K especially the part that is matched by your company and/or a Roth IRA.

Bubbles

Bubbles have existed throughout our history. Bubbles occur due to the excessive valuation most likely driven up by the big institutional investors (fund managers, pension managers, hedge fund manager, etc.). Asset valuations are then driven even higher by the retail investors. For example in 3/2014, the market bubble was caused by the government stimulus with the injection of capital into the excessive money supply and subsidies. The first investors riding the wave made good money, and the last ones buying at the peak would lose.

From our recent history, we have the 2000 internet bubble, and then the 2007 (2008 for some) housing bubble. The chapter "Spotting Big Market Plunges" illustrates it was easy to detect the last two plunges. It could save us more than 25% of your portfolio in the next plunge.

Today most of the mentioned bubbles could be caused by pumping too much money into the economy by the government. However, the government cannot keep on injecting money into the economy, and ask our children to pay for our debts forever. When the injections stop, the market will drop fast and deep.

USD
As of mid-2020, the USD is doing quite well. It could be the other countries (EU and Japan) that are doing worse off than us, as Einstein said, "everything is relative". The strong USD is not good for exports and the global corporations would have less profits after converting them back to USD. However, the excessive printing of money and high government debts would shake the status of USD as a reserve currency. It will also be hurt if China sells the U.S. Treasury bonds which she owns.

Bond
The bond bubble will burst when the interest rates rise. Also it will as the interest rates should have bottomed by mid-2020. It is even possible that it could go negative.

Stocks

There are several bubble stocks such as FAANGs. The market was peaking in Jan., 2020 before the virus breakout. Play defense with your stop loss orders.

The record of margin debt is a big concern. When the credit is tightened with higher interest rates, this bubble will burst.

When to act

Without a time machine, no one can pin point when most of these bubbles will burst. Your market timing depends on your risk tolerance, your knowledge and your greed.

Today, we have the housing bubble (2007-2008), the gold bubble, the market bubble, the second housing bubble, the debt bubble, the bond bubble, the second market bubble, etc. It seems like we can never get out of the bubble cycle. In 2020, the world would be in a global recession if the trade war between the two largest economies continue. It would be worse for sure, if the trade war turns into a military war.

The world is economically connected better than before. When the U.S.A. sneezes, it affects our trading partners such as European countries along with China and Japan, and also their partners such as the resource-rich countries of S. America, Australia, Russia, Canada and Africa.

For me, it is safer not to try to make the last buck when the reward / risk ratio is too low. A good sleep would improve your health which is worth all the gold in the world.

#Filler: Your complaint department

Depending on your investing knowledge, the more complicated concepts are harder to understand. Some strategies even require you paper trading. It is even more complicated if you do not read this book sequentially, as this book outlines chapters for beginner, intermediate and expert investors.

Do not complain on the fillers as they just take up the blank space in the printed book and you should be glad to take a break on this lengthy book.

#Filler: My trailing stop is different from the conventional definition as described next. Periodically change the stop order based on the current stock price, when the return is positive.

Contents

Filler: A nightmare?

I got a call from Buffett asking me to lead their stock research.
I asked him why for a nobody; you may be asking the same question. No kidding.

He told me that he should have read my book Scoring Stocks to buy Apple instead of IBM in May, 2013. It would save his company millions of dollars minus $10 for my book. Not to mention the market timing technique that had worked in the last two major market plunges.

I told him, "OK, I'll beat your mediocre returns of the last 5 years."
He said, "You can do better than that and at least beat SPY. If you do so, no one will be that stupid to leave my fund and pay the hefty capital gain taxes."

I told him, "I cannot beat the market as you are the market especially after your expensive fees. In addition, I do not know how to avoid day traders from riding my wagon in trading. Also most of my big profits were made in small stocks that your fund cannot trade besides owning the company."

I woke up trembling. I'm glad it is only a nightmare.

The Main Book: Sector Rotation

Sector rotation has been proven to make good profits with the least risk if it is properly implemented. However, sectors are risky, less diversified and more volatile than the market. In the long run, this book improves your odds in making profits rather than traditional schemes in sector rotation by:

- Market Timing. When the market is plunging, do not buy any stock including sector ETFs and sector funds. This book provides a simple chart to detect market plunges. The simplest (for beginners) is a sector rotation between SPY (an ETF that simulates the market) and cash (or an ETF of short-term bonds).

- The next rotation strategy involves four ETFs in a rising market. Optionally, advance investors can include a contra ETF to time the market further. Buy the best performer from the last month of these four selected ETFs.

- Some sectors perform better in different stages of a market cycle.

- Many free sites describe the best sector performers such as Seeking Alpha and CNNfn.

- Evaluate sectors using Technical Analysis (simple charts available free from the web and Fundamental Analysis.

- You should spend one or two hours a month to determine which sector to rotate to, or move your portfolio to cash when the market is risky. The "Buy and hold" strategy has not performed since 2000.
- Subscription services of which there are many. Even if you subscribe to these services, you should read this book to evaluate their services and use this book as a second opinion. When your portfolio is over $100,000, $100 for a yearly subscription should pay for itself in the long run.
- Market timing by calendar and presidential cycle.
- My recent experiences in sector trading. Be careful with many of the books on this topic that were written by professors who may never have made a buck in the stock market. When you see a lot of equations, run as fast as you can.

- Some "best" sellers were written more than 10 years ago that do not use today's basic tools such as technical analysis and the extensive offers of so many sector ETFs. They bear little resemblance to today's market, which can be manipulated by institutional investors.

- Most large companies today are global companies. The importance with investing in foreign companies or diversifying is less important than in the past.
- When China expands, natural resource-rich countries would most likely benefit, and vice versa.
- Most likely for luck but with good reasons, I predicted correctly that a disaster would happen in China as reported in August, 2019 in my article "Disasters in 2020". The second prediction has not happened yet, but it has more impact to our economy.

The third prediction: China would not agree to pay for the damages of this pandemic and that would lead to the freezing of their debts to us (1.07T as of Dec., 2019). Eventually it could lead to cold war or even a military war. I hope it would never happen.

Besides industrial sectors, I include bonds, contra ETFs, sector mutual funds, countries, commodities, etc. Today, most sectors are covered by ETFs. For example, you do not need to buy gold coins to invest in that sector but the ETF GLD.

Important notices
© Tony Pow 2019-2021. Email ID: pow_tony@yahoo.com.

Version	Paperback	eBooks
1.00	10/19	10/19
1.04	05/21	05/21

Printed version ISBN-13: 978-1497483927 or ISBN-10: 1497483921.

Disclaimer
Do not gamble with money that you cannot afford to lose. Past performance is a guideline and is not necessarily indicative of future results. All information is believed to be accurate, but there it is not a guarantee. All the strategies including charts to detect market plunges described have no guarantee that they will make money and they may lose money. Do not

trade without doing due diligence and be warned that most data may be obsolete. All my articles and the associated data are for informational and illustration purposes only. I'm not a professional investment counselor or a tax professional. Seek one before you make any investment decisions. The above mentioned also applies for all other advice such as on accounting, taxes, health and any topic mentioned in this book. I am not a professional in any of these fields. Most of the time, I use annualized for a better comparison; 5% in a month is more than 4% in a year for example. For simplicity, most of my returns do not include commissions, exchange fees, order spread and dividends. It is the same for all the links contained in this book. Some articles may offend some one or some organization unintentionally. If I did, I'm sorry about that. I am politically and religiously neutral. I have provided my best efforts to ensure the accuracy of my articles. Data also from different sources was believed to be accurate. However, there is no guarantee that they are accurate and suitable for the current market conditions and /or your individual situations. The values of some parameters such as RSI(14) are arbitrarily set by me. My publisher and I are not liable for any damages in using this book or its contents.

Filler: CIA mistook it as a missile silo in China.

1   Sector rotation in a nutshell

How to start

I have been rotating sectors in my annuity investments for quite a long time with a sum of more than my annual salary at the time. As of 1/2020, it had increased about four times. My mutual fund employer had a lot of restrictions for me trading stocks, so rotating sector funds in my annuity was the best investment tool for me.

For a starter, I recommend that you paper trade your strategy first. Use Finviz.com, SeekingAlpha.com and/or Fidelity.com to select the best performing sector and/or use my quick analysis of ETFs. Switch it every month (or two) to the ETF corresponding to the best sector. Again, switch to cash when the market is risky. You may consider sector mutual funds which are managed, but most have restrictions such as holding periods and fees. Most if not all sector mutual funds do not have contra funds that expect the sector to go down in value. Sector mutual funds cannot be shorted.

After the basics, this book provides many features to further refine your strategy such as technical Analysis. Beginners should use Strategy 1 in Book 2. After that, start with the technical indicators such as SMA-50% and RSI(14) with a handful of sector ETFs to rotate (suggested sectors are technology, bank, health care, housing, consumer and material).

In addition, some sectors are more profitable in different phases of a market cycle. We will examine several industry sectors and country sectors in more detail. China is affecting the global economies including ours. When the interest rates are low, it would affect bonds and stocks yielding high dividends. Many books ignore market timing. It turns out to be the most important technique as the last market plunges have had an average loss of 45%!

The keys to profitable sector rotation

Sector rotation could be very profitable and less risky than most of us may expect. However, it is volatile and risky if not properly implemented. There are two ways to profit from the following:

1. Buy the sector when it is trending up and sell when the sector is trending down. It is the common approach to sector rotation.

2. Buy at the bottom or close to of a sector and sell at the peak or close to. It is hard to detect the bottom/peak.

Many investment subscriptions and free sites such as Finviz.com select favorable sectors every month. We assume the best-performing sector last month will perform better in the coming month or months. It does not always happen such as the tech sector in April, 2000 and the reversed direction of the drug sector in 2015. To protect your investments, use stops.

Alternatively, we can select them via simple charts as described in this book. Beginners should start with Single Moving Average (SMA-20 and SMA-50 for 20 sessions and 50 sessions respectively) provided by Finviz.com without charting.

Detecting the bottom of a sector

It is not easy and no one can detect the bottom or the peak of a sector consistently but easier with trends. Enter the ETF for a specific sector or the SPY for the market in Finviz. Use a short-term SMA such as SMA-20 and SMA-50 (expressed in percent), and check these two parameters every week. If both SMA-20% and SMA-50% are positive, most likely the market or a sector is trending up.

For market timing, the SMA-350 (Single Moving Average with 350 sessions) detects the market quite accurately for the last two market plunges. I have tested out the "days" with different numbers and 350 is the best fit for the last two market plunges. In recent days, 400 could be a better choice to reduce the number of false alarms.

Besides technical indicators, there are hints that indicate a sector is close to the bottom. Using the ETF for the sector and check out the fundamental metrics similar to evaluating a stock. To illustrate, enter XLE in Yahoo!Finance or Finviz.com to get the current price and other info about this sector. Sites specializing in ETFs such as ETFdb that will give you more information about ETFs.

The intangibles for stocks and ETFs should be considered too. For example in 2020, the potential decoupling with China would make a lot of U.S. chip companies less profitable.

Detecting the trend

Detecting the trend is easier than detecting the bottom/peak. To illustrate, bring up Finviz.com from your browser and enter XLE. For most sectors, I use the SMA-50 (single moving average for last 50 days), which is readily available as one of the metrics. When the stock price is 3% above this SMA, it is most likely a buy. When it is 3% below this SMA, sell. It is simple, and it has been proven many times. Currently Finviz.com provides SMA-20% and SMA-50% only for short-term averages. For other durations, you can construct charts.

You can adjust the 50-day and the 3% (some use 1% or 5%) on how long your average holding period of an ETF or a stock that also depends on how often you want to trade). If your holding period is longer, use higher number such as 90 days; use SMA-20 if it is shorter. If you want to trade more often use 2% instead of 3% (or use 5% if you want to trade less often).

Personally I use 60 days if I use charts (from Yahoo!Finance among one of the many free sites that provide charts). One of my sector fund accounts requires 60 days for a minimum holding period without incurring a fee.

To detect a market crash and when to reenter the market, I use 350 days (some use 300 or 400 days). The 'days' are actually trade sessions.

The RSI(14) indicates whether the sector is overbought or oversold. RSI oscillates between zero and 100. Traditionally, and according to Wilder, the creator, RSI is considered overbought with a value above 70 and oversold with a value below 30 as described in the article. This indicator is available from Finviz.com.

(http://stockcharts.com/school/doku.php?id=chart_school:technical_indicators:relative_strength_index_rsi)

A simple way is to buy last month's winner(s). Ensure your ETFs are not leveraged if you are conservative. Include contra ETFs when the market is risky for aggressive investors. Here are the links to the web sites that keep track of top performers varying from 1 to 3 months.

Seeking Alpha's ETF Hub.
http://seekingalpha.com/insight/etf-
hub/asset_class_performance/key_markets
Morning Star. Select the period (1 month for example).
http://news.morningstar.com/etf/Lists/ETFReturns.htm

What to buy

I prefer ETFs for specific sectors and the second choice is sector funds (check out the holding period to exit without penalties). With good analysts, most sector funds are better than ETFs in specific sectors such as banking, drug companies and mining. Compare their performances.

ETFs charge less for maintaining and they have all the advantages of a stock. However, mutual funds select the stocks within a sector selectively. Fidelity offers the most complete list of sector mutual funds. Again compare the 3 or 5 year performance between the ETF and the fund in this same sector.

The third option is a top-down approach. First, when the market is not plunging, select the most favorable sector and then the bet stocks within the sector. Many free sites provide a filter to find favorable sectors.

Here is a list of sector ETFs.
(http://www.bloomberg.com/markets/etfs/)

Here is a list of commission-free ETFs from Fidelity.
(https://www.fidelity.com/etfs/ishares)

Some funds automatically switch sectors for you. From my experience so far, they have not proved to be very profitable. You should check out their past performances.

Favorable sectors according to the market cycle
Refer to the chapter on Market Timing and Spotting a Market Plunge for specific strategies. Close and/or adjust your positions when the market is plunging.

Favorable sectors according to the interest rate
It is similar to the above. Retailing, auto and housing are usually hurt by high interest rates. An improving economy would do the opposite.

Favorable sectors according to geography
It is not an easy task. China and India had their best performing years. The trade war with the U.S. may favor India as of 2020. Japan had one of the best years in 2013 during the last two decades. For foreign countries, currency fluctuation should be considered. Most emerging countries have their ups and downs. Most ETFs and sector funds in emerging countries buy larger companies that are more trustworthy as noted with their financial statements.

Global economies have never been that tightly connected. When the U.S. economy is down, China is affected and so are the resource-rich countries that China depends on.

Favorable and unfavorable events
The EU crisis has taken more than three years as of 4/2016 and the EU stocks are still close to the bottom. I prefer to buy ETFs or mutual funds which specialize in EU stocks, when the trend is up.

When the head of our Treasury says the interest will be lower, the market and the long term bond funds will move up, and vice versa. To me, the interest rates will move up slowly from the 1/2014 bottom.

Recent favorable and unfavorable sectors
There are many sources to check which sectors performed best recently. Finviz.com is one of them. From the top menu bar, select Group, and the best and worst sectors will be displayed. Skip one day or one week unless you have a special interest on these short durations. Select the duration depending on your purpose. Personally I would use one month (or two) for my monthly rotation strategy assuming the momentum would pass to the next month.

Technical analysis would help to spot the trend. Select the Simple Moving Average. It is similar to the TA used in the chapter spotting a market crash. Instead of using SPY or another ETF market index, use an ETF that represents the sector.

Sector rotation by fund managers

We cannot beat these institutional investors. We need to follow them, or be one step ahead of them. They rotate sectors when they find another sector that has better appreciation potential, or the current favorable sector has reached its peak.

When to rotate

Rotate for the following reasons:

1. When the market is plunging, rotate the sector ETFs and/or mutual funds to cash. Aggressive investors would rotate their equities to contra ETFs. The average loss of the last two market plunges had been about 45%. This chart will not determine the peak (or bottom) as it depends on the falling data. However, it will tell you when to exit to prevent a further loss and tell you when to reenter the market.
2. When the fundamentals of the current sector you owned are turning bad.
3. When there is another sector that has better appreciation potential. Finviz.com tells you the rankings of the sectors.
4. When the sector is overbought or peaking, and / or has met our objective.

Do not forget about market timing
Do NOT buy any stocks except the contra ETFs for an aggressive investor, when the market is plunging. Playing defense usually wins the game more often than playing offense. When the market is peaking, protect your profits by placing stop loss orders.

Positions and how often to switch
It depends on the size of your portfolio and how much time you can afford to monitor your portfolio. To me, it varies from 2 to 6 positions and 20 to 90 days to monitor these switches.

Statistics show that a portfolio with 5 positions rotating in 20 days give you slightly better performance and less drawback (maximum loss for the period). I recommend 4 (2 for a portfolio of less than $20,000) and 30 days (and 60 days for Fidelity sector funds). You determine according to your portfolio size and the time available to you for investing.

Conclusion

Sector rotation is described in very basic terms here. The links in Afterthoughts provide additional information.

As a reminder, **roughly half of a stock's price movement can be attributed to the sector** it is in.

Afterthoughts

- There are many articles on this topic. They are:

  Sector rotation strategies ETF investors must know. There are many useful links.
  http://www.bloomberg.com/markets/etfs/

  Sector rotation based on performance.
  http://stockcharts.com/school/doku.php?id=chart_school:trading_stra
  tegies:sector_rotation_roc
  Fidelity on Sectors.
  https://www.fidelity.com/sector-investing/overview
  Video instruction.
  http://www.YouTube.com/watch?v=j5yYoOoATRM

- No one can consistently predict the bottom or the peak of any sector. Sometimes we move in too early and lose another 25% or so, or we leave the sector too early to lose another 25% or so potential gain. It is quite normal. Learn why we move with in the wrong time frame, and a lot of times it may be just bad luck or other events that are beyond our control.

- A free (as of this writing) service on sector rotation.
  http://www.gosector.com/

More links from YouTube
Simple sector rotation, another one, and one more.
https://www.youtube.com/watch?v=85IRL_3oR8&t=219s
https://www.youtube.com/watch?v=gu-46zcBwsl&t=177s
https://www.youtube.com/watch?v=acOMOh7Zc6c

2   Outline on how to start sector rotation

As with everything in life, there is no guarantee that this book will make you a lot of money. However, the chance of success will be substantially improved especially when you practice with most of the ideas presented in this book. Always start with paper trading first.

1. First determine your objectives. Retirees select safer strategies. Millionaires can afford to select riskier strategies for larger returns.

2. Determine your risk tolerance, how much time you have for investing, your knowledge of investing, and your desire to continue to learn about investing and your portfolio size.

    To illustrate, when the market is risky, do not buy any stock. However for investors who can tolerate higher risk, buy contra ETFs as a hedge against the market for larger returns. Retirees may be less risk tolerant unless they're rich.

    If your job is very demanding, you should spend less time in investing even if you're knowledgeable on investing and have a desire to learn about investing.

    Check your net worth (= what you own − what you owe) and cash flow (incomes − debt payments). Reserve your emergency cash equal to your expenses for at least 3 months.

    If the above is limited, SPY or any ETF simulating the market is your only sector and market timing is your primary tool (Book 2, Strategy 1, Chapter 2). You can stop here for now, and continue reading the rest of the book when the limitations change.

3. When the market is peaking, invest cautiously. Use trailing stops described in this book. The same for your sector ETFs / funds that have appreciated a lot.

4. When you have lost two trades in a row, take a break and return to paper trading until you're comfortable.

5. Test your strategies on paper. This book requires you to try out the various strategies, and select the one you are comfortable with. All theories may not always work for real trading.

6. When a strategy has been thoroughly tested out recently and the results are good, use real money slowly and gradually. Then monitor your performance.

7. When you have a new strategy or you need to test a strategy whether it works in the current market, read "Testing strategies" (Bonus. Chapter 2).

Not all of predictions (mine or others) have materialized, and no strategy is evergreen. Always use stops to protect your portfolio. Learn from your arguments for the predictions, not merely the accuracy of the predictions. Predictions are based on educated guesses, and hence hopefully more of them will materialize in the long run. Consult your financial advisor before investing with real money.

The rest of this book describes the other aspects of sector rotation such as Top-Down Investing (in case you prefer to find the stocks in the favorable sector), country sectors, specific industry sectors... Many investing ideas described here are applicable to other investing strategies.

3   Sectors

The primary sectors are: Materials, Consumer Discretionary, Consumer Staples, Energy, Financial, Real Estate, Health Care, Industrial, Information Technology and Utilities. Click the above links from Fidelity, or search from Fidelity, Investopedia and/or Wikipedia for a description of these sectors.

We can sub divide a sector into sub sectors (a.k.a. industries). For example, Information Technology can be divided into Computer and Software. When the computer industry is good, it does not mean that the software industry is also good. Some industries such as banking software can belong to more than one sector (banking and software in this example).

Fidelity has its own definition and overview as described in this link: https://www.fidelity.com/sector-investing/overview

In the above links, Fidelity describe sectors pretty well. Many vendors including IBD provide industry rankings. You may want to select the best sector or industry first and then select the best stocks in that sector or industry.

GIGS (developed by MSCI and S&P500) separates more than 29,000 stocks into 11 major sectors. It is very similar to Fidelity but GIGS's industry classification is more complicated to deploy. Most other sources do not follow GIGS's industry classification.

Here is my additional description to cover the basic sectors and some will be described in more detail in their appropriate strategies that follow.

Materials
Material should be separated into two categories: Basic (a.k.a. Industrial) Materials and Precious Metals. Basic materials such as copper and iron rise in prices when the economy is humming, and vice versa. Precious Metals such as gold and silver do not usually correlate with basic materials. Gold and silver usually rise due to high inflation, political unrest and/or falling USD.

Consumer Staples and Discretionary
Consumer Staples are food, beverages, household products and the products we buy as necessities. They are recession-proof. Our products have demonstrated high quality and safety. With the growing middle class in

developing countries such as China and India, we expect they should grow well outside the USA. In early 2020, it has not been the case due to the trade war.

Consumer Discretionary are just the opposite. For example, car sales would be down in a recession.

Energy

Energy has many sub sectors (a.k.a. industries) such as clean energy, exploring, distribution, refining and even all of the above (using the term 'integrate'). When the economy is growing, usually energy sectors rise in price. When the market and/or oil price falls, Saudi Arabia, the largest oil exporter, would dump more oil and hence it would make the oil price fall further.

Financial

The sub sectors are banks, mortgage companies, brokerages (tough industry with no commission trades today), insurance companies and many other financial institutions. This sector would plunge during a recession. In the period of 2007 and 2008, this sector had a tough time.

Real Estate

Besides housing construction, this sector is primarily made up of companies that own and/or build properties and REITs. This sector should not do well during a recession.

Health Care
It should be divided into many sub sectors: hospitals, research / development of medical equipment and drugs. In some sense, hospitals and generic drugs also belong to Consumer Staples that you need to use or buy regardless of the condition of the economy. Most likely, we do not need new equipment and new drugs in a depressed economy.

Industrial

This sector includes Boeing, construction equipment companies such as Caterpillar and defense companies. Most of GE's subsidiaries belong to this sector. With the global economies slowing down and the problems with Boeing in 2019, this sector has not been doing well in 2020.

Information technology

It is a very wide sector covering hardware companies and software companies. If Telecommunication is not a separate sector, it should be under this sector too. Microsoft, Facebook and Apple are under this sector. From 1/2010 to 1/2020, this sector is very profitable. With the decoupling with China, the profits will be reduced.

Utilities

It is a consumer staple sector. However, we use more electricity, fuels and water when the economy is humming.

Other sectors

Transportation, Services and Retail should be separate sectors but are not classified so by many institutions. Retail has had a tough time since the rise of Amazon, and now it is even worse during the pandemic of 2020.

Links

A list of sectors.
http://www.investorguide.com/sector-list.php
Check's sector analysis.
http://seekingalpha.com/article/2806655-the-stock-market-2015-a-sector-by-sector-valuation-perspective-part-1-an-overview

#Filler: My grandson

My six-year old grandson called the library about the availability of the book Mine Craft. The lady told him that only "Mine Craft for Dummies" was available. He told her it was not for him as he was not a dummy.

#Filler: My daughter's wedding banquet

How do you have a wedding banquet that the entire town will talk about and at the least cost? It is at the Burger King where they treat you like a king. All the fries are super-sized and the drinks are bottomless. The king's crown and the most popular party favor, are included. Of course, my daughter flatly refused.

4   Subsectors (i.e. Industries) and sector funds

Sectors are further divided into subsectors (same as industries). For example, Oil Energy is a sector while Oil Exploration and Oil Service are industries. Industries cover a very specialized segment of the sector, so they consist of fewer companies and sometimes smaller companies; they are more volatile and hence more risky. To illustrate, the ETF for an industry (say Oil Exploration) has less companies than the entire sector Oil Energy. Some industry ETFs such as Uranium are very small with a handful of stocks; they are highly volatile with high risk.

Sector mutual funds are managed by fund managers who select stocks instead of including most stocks in the sector. The disadvantages over ETFs are fees, restrictions of holding periods (the usual 1 to 2 months) without a penalty, offering fewer industries and you cannot short a fund.

SeekingAlpha.com has a good performance summary for each sectors including many countries and industries. Select the best ETF from the last month, use stop loss to protect momentum reversal and switch when there is a better sector or industry to buy. Aggressive investors can also short an ETF, or buy contra ETFs for the worst performed sectors or industries.

5   Selecting ETFs

Judging by the popularity, ETFs are a better way to rotate within sectors compared to sector mutual funds. Select ETFs from my ETF tables (Book 2, Strategy 3, Chapter 1). You rotate an ETF(s) from your selection of ETFs. I will explain my selection here starting from a few to about 25. It is less time-consuming to limit your selection to 4 to analyze and keep track of their performances. A larger selection gives you more choices and hence supposedly improves your performance.

The selected ETFs must have assets over 100 million. If there are two similar ETFs, check out their expense ratios. As of today, Fidelity offers commission-free for most ETFs. Check your broker for similar offerings. The corresponding sector fund is also provided in my tables; you cannot rotate ETFs within Fidelity's Annuities.

Beginners should skip subsectors (a.k.a. industries), which are riskier as they are too specialized. Skip the leveraged ETFs unless you can bear the risk.

Some sectors especially the subsectors are more volatile than others and they would be on the top and bottom performers more frequently. From Finviz.com or other sources, check out the RSI(14) to ensure the sector is not overbought (i.e. the value is greater than 65). I prefer to select the one of the top ETFs with a lower volatility and an RSI(14) between 30 and 60. From my testing using ETFReplay, it is better to use 2 months rather than 20 trade days for selecting the best-performing ETFs.

Starting with ETFs

To start, I recommend the following ETFs: SPY and GLD (in the risky 2020). Add a money market fund, or a bond ETF with a short duration when the market is risky. Beginners should NOT use SH (a contra ETF to SPY) for monthly rotation and only aggressive investors should buy SH when the market is plunging.

Add the following ETFs to broaden your selection on market cap: DIA, QQQ, SPYG, SPYV, NOBL, IWM, IWC and BOND. The market may favor very large companies (DOW), tech (QQQ), growth (SPYG), value (SPYV), NOBL (dividend), mid cap (MDY), small cap (IWM) and microcap (IWC; risky). Add a total bond (BOND) if desirable. Optionally I add buy back (PKW) and momentum (MTUM).

It is better not to include bond funds in monthly rotation. Long term bond funds rise opposite of the interest rate.

Skip foreign countries if you do not want to take the foreign exchange risk. Otherwise, I would include some foreign exposure: small cap (SCZ), Europe (VGK), China (FXI), Latin America (ILF), EFA(EAFE), global (KXI) and VWO (Emerging; risky).

If you're into specific foreign countries, add Australia (EWA), Brazil (EWZ), Canada (EWC), India (INDY), Indonesia (EIDO), Hong Kong (EWH), Japan (EWJ), Singapore (EWS), Taiwan (EWT), United Kingdom (EWU) and Vietnam (VNM; profitable if decoupling with China).

The last selection could be the only selection for some investors specialized in industry sectors (a.k.a. sub sectors). They are the industry sectors: bank (KBE), Bio (XBI), consumer discretionary (XLY), consumer staple (XLP), finance (IYF), energy (XLE), health care (IYH), house builders (ITB), industrial (IYJ), material (XME), oil (USO), oil service (OIH), oil exploration (XOP), gas (UNG), real estate (VNQ), retail (RTH), regional banking (KRE), semiconductor (SMH), software (XSW) and technology (XLK).

My summaries from testing (mainly from using ETFReplay):

- Slightly better results using relative strength of 1 month than 2 months. 1 month means 20 trade sessions (30 days - 10 weekends / holidays). Relative strength means picking the best performing ETF from your selected group of ETFs.

- There were better results not using contra ETFs (could be due to our long bull market from 2009), so I skipped them especially for beginners.

- The same for interest-sensitive ETFs, so I actually skipped them.

- Do not include the offending sectors that caused the market to crash – these sectors take longer to recover. They are internet ETF (not available then) in 2000 and banks / house construction in 2008.

6   How to find the current best-performing sectors

There are many web sites that will show you the current best-performing sectors or ETFs for sectors. Depending on the web site, some may give you the best-performed ETFs for the last month or the last 30 days for example. If you rotate among a few sectors, you can maintain a record of their performance.

Seeking Alpha's home page has further divided the ETFs into the following groups: Sector, Industry (sub sector) and country. Pick the site you use most and/or your broker's site for this information.

Fidelity

Click on "News & Research" and then "Stock Market & Sector Performance" for sector performance and weighing recommendations. Fidelity offers the most choices for sector funds plus many sector commission-free ETFs. Most sector funds have penalties if you hold them less than 30 days (60 days for most sector funds in an annuity). Check the current restrictions.

7   How to determine a reversal

This article describes two basic ways to detect a reversal of trend. For illustration purposes, I describe the reversal of an uptrend. The reversal of a downtrend follows similar logic. Volume is the confirmation. Detecting reversal is a technique and it does not always work. Hence, use stops to protect your portfolio and review the stops every week or two for rising stocks.

Simple method

When the SMA-20 (from Finviz.com) drops below SMA-50, it is an indication that the uptrend could be over. For a longer holding period, it is the SMA-50 dropping below SMA-200. If both SMA-20 and SMA-50 are negative, most likely the uptrend turns to a downtrend. You can confirm it with volume; a low volume is not a confirmation.

If it is vastly overbought (RSI(14) > 65) and the volume is low, it could mean that there are no buyers for the ETF. If the peak has occurred, do not be the last one holding that ETF.

ETFs and stocks are normally traded in a range between the resistance and the support. However, when the trend is up and the volume is high, the chance of breaking up the resistance is high. The opposite applies: When the trend is down and the volume is high, the chance of breaking up the support is high.

Complicated method

Method 1. Head and Shoulder is a reliable chart pattern to predict a trend reversal. Basically the uptrend is running out of momentum and hence the reversal (i.e. down turn) is possible. The head indicates a price peak and followed by a smaller peak.

Method 2. A Candlestick charts tell more about an ETF's or stock's movement. Basically it shows the opening price, the closing price and the price fluctuations for the day (or the week if selected). The white body means it is an up day while the black body indicates a down day.

When the candle stick is black (meaning a down day) and is larger than the previous day which is white, it could indicate the uptrend is reversing. The technical term is engulfed candlestick.

When the candle stick returns back to an uptrend, it means the trend is still up and the engulfed candle stick on the second day is a false indicator. It involves 3 candle sticks. It is a more complicated topic.

8   SMA and Volume

Bring up Finviz.com. Enter SPY for your ticket symbol. The market trend is up if both SMA-20 and SMA-50 are positive. Finviz.com uses percent to indicate how far away the current price is above the average. The daily change of volume is also displayed. It is the confirmation indicator. When the price rises with low volume, it may not indicate the trend is up.

Most use daily charts (charting is not for beginners). Weekly charts should be used if the duration of holding the stock is longer. The above also applies for stocks trending down.

Filler: Happy Mother's Day Poem
(This is my translation from a Chinese poet Yee. Made several changes due to lost in translation. The title could be "Two cries".)

I cried at two unforgettable times in my life.

The first time when I came to this world.
The second time when you left this world.

The first time I did not know but from your mouth.
The second time you did not know but from my heart.

Between these two crises, we had endless laughs.
For the last 30 years, we had joyful laughs that had been repeated, repeated...

You treasured every laugh.
I cherish every laugh for the rest of my life.

9   An example: Rotating Apple

Contrarian

I have been contrarian several times and most times I made good money. We need to have good arguments to be contrary. Otherwise, we're committing financial suicide.

Many investors commit the same error: Invest in a company because they love the company's products. We need to check out the fundamentals of the company and its prospect. I have nothing against Apple. Actually I recommended Apple before based on its great fundamentals when many institutional investors were dumping it.

Scoring Apple

When I was writing the book Scoring Stocks, first I used IBM but its low score would not be a good example. Then I switched to Apple (AAPL). It scored almost the highest. I recommended AAPL at $55.72 (split adjusted) on April 19, 2013, the date the book mentioned was published. It is another example that fundamentals work. However, when we're swimming against the tide, we need to be patient. At that time, the media and institutional investors ignored fundamentals. The best argument of not buying Apple was "Apple has turned from a growth stock to a value stock". They think they cannot get fired by thinking the same as the herd. Just garbage talk from the smartest folks!

Fundamental analysis as of 02/23/2015

	Passing grade	AAPL		Industry
Score System #1	>=15	16		
Score System #2	>=2	2		
Pow EY	>=5	6%		
Expected Earning Yield	>5 & <35	7%		5%
Debt / Equity	<.5	.30		.29
Analyst Rating	>7	9		
EB/EBIT	>5	13		
F-Score	>7	6		
ROE	>=15%	37%		27%
SMA-200%	>0%	29%		
RSI(14)	<60	78		
Price		$132.06		

Explanation
- The first scoring system incorporates many vendors' grades. The second scoring system is from my book Scoring Stocks using metrics available free from many web sites.
- Pow EY – Earning Yield (E/P) takes cash and debt into consideration.
- Expected EY, Debt/Equity, ROE, SMA-200% and RSI(14) are obtained from Finviz.com.
- Analyst Rating (now it is Equity Summary Score) is from Fidelity. Alternatively, use Recommendation from Finviz.com.
- EB/EBIT and F-Score are from GuruFocus.com.

How Apple scores

It scores fine but not spectacular. The score from my book in April, 2013 is 5 and as of this writing it is 2. Fundamentally it is not as good as before.

P/B and P/S are usually not useful for high tech companies. However, Apple's P/B at 6 is exceedingly expensive as compared to Google's 3. When most analysts like the stock, usually it will rise in the short-term. RSI(14) shows it is overbought. To conclude, its fundamental score passes but not in flying colors.

The brief Fundamental Analysis should be followed by the following:

Qualitative Analysis includes articles for Apple. First, search articles on Apple from Finviz.com and Seeking Alpha. Large companies like Apple are hard to manipulate, so most articles are not 'pump and dump'.

Technical Analysis detects the trend and overbought condition. Many investors do not buy a stock that is in its downward trend. SMA-200 is a good long-term trend indicator. Its price should be above the SMA-200 (same as SMA-200% is positive in Finviz.com).

Intangible Analysis
Apple has lost a visionary leader Steve Jobs. I hope he was not replaced by similar managers at Microsoft, who are responsible for Microsoft's lost decade with few innovative products. Apple has a lot of cash to finance new projects. High tech business is tough as they need to build a better mouse trap continuously. When the mouse trap becomes a commodity, the profit

margin would be reduced. This is the major reason that Buffett does not invest in Apple. If he read my book in May, 2013, he would buy Apple instead of IBM saving his company millions minus $10 for my book. LOL.

There are bright and bad spots for Apple:

1. Apple Text Book. Imagine all students carry iPads instead of text books. Several educational apps have been created for iPads. The competition is laptops and Chrome Book.

2. Apple TV.
   It is a loser so far with a lot of risk and potential competitors. However, the potential is great. It could give all cable companies a run for the money. Wider internet channels would make it more feasible. Will the cable companies provide these speeds to allow Apple TV and similar products to step into their turfs?

3. While the iPad and iPhone are peaking in the hardware, iTunes, software and contents for these devices to access have no limit. We have witnessed how iPad helps the folks with autism and iPhones for the blind. I can envision many other similar applications.

4. Will Apple moves into Kindle's market?

5. All the mobile phone technology is originated by the first generation (if not counting Motorola) that Apple has a lot of patents. Its lawyers will milk money from Samsung. It also prevents cheap mobile phones from coming to the USA. U.S. helps Apple by not letting Huawei's phones in.

6. Apple Pay.
   Apple has a proven history of picking up some failed products and turning them into gold. This product could be the next innovative and most profitable for Apple. Apple Pay will not make a splash in the bottom line initially.

7. Apple Watch.
   There will be cheap Chinese products flooded in our market. However, the selling point is the prestige of Apple and its integration to other Apple products. The major problem of Apple Watch is the short battery life. With the reduced urge of upgrade and competition on Apple phones, Apple Watch is a bright product for Apple.

8. The major worry is whether they can maintain the urge of upgrade. If the new enhancements would not give me reason to upgrade, I would not be the one waiting in long line in bitter cold weather to upgrade my iPhone just to satisfy my dumb ego. It accounts the majority of Apple's profit.

9. Apple has a lot of cash. Dividends usually boost the stock price and the option values granted to the management. However, it is important to plow back to development and acquiring technologies.

10. U.S. stops Huawei and Xiaomi from coming to the U.S. Apple is not the state-of-the-art phones.

#Filler: iGeneration

Almost everyone has an iPhone. Folks including myself in the lower class of the society carry imitators and/or those 'outdated' iPhones that are several months old.

My grandchild of just over one year old had a good time in playing with the iPad and it usually kept her busy for hours. Before she could say Mom, she said "I" for iPad. During my family gatherings, my cousins communicate with each other via their smart phones even when they sit next to each other. When they do not text messages, they play games with their smart phones.

Even with one pair of eyes and one pair of ears, they can play iPad, listen to iPod and text using iPhone at the same time. Thanks Apple for demonstrating what multi-tasking really is. I prefer to do one task correctly than several tasks incorrectly. Chinese and Indian students are leaving us further behind by spending more time in study. Do you believe those children spending extra 2 hours every day in games would accomplish the same later in life?

Some parents have a hard time to explain to their children that their existence was due to the blackout of the iPad and iPhone caused by the hurricanes.

10   Evaluating a sector

"Section I and Chapter 6" describes how to find the current-performing sectors via free web sites such as Seeking Alpha and Fidelity (requiring opening an account). This article describes how you can do it yourself.

The following is for illustration only. The figures are from 12/20/2020 and the sector is "XLK", the technology sector.

Determining the trend

Bring up Finviz.com from your browser. Enter "XLK" for the ticker (stock symbol).

From the graph, it shows it is in an uptrend.

Most of us use SMA50 (Simple Moving Average for the last 50 sessions). It is 6%, and hence the ETF is up. SMA20 is for average holding period of the last 20 sessions, and is 3%. The percentage gives us how the average is above the current price.

My holding period is about 30 sessions and I use the average value. In this case it is about 4.5%. If you want to be more precise, you can open a chart and specify 30 sessions for SMA.

SMA200 is for long-term hold, and most of us do not care about it for short-term sector rotation.

Other parameters

RSI(14). If it is higher than 65, watch out for oversold condition, which could indicate a higher chance to reverse the trend. Some sectors just keep on rising. The best way is to use trailing stops (you update the stops every week or so from the current prices).

P/E. It is not available in Finviz.com. Bring up dbETF.com. From the Search icon, enter XLK. It indicates a P/E of 28.57. It is a better value than the average of most sectors; it ranks 18 out of 42. For Sector Rotation, value parameters such as P/E are not that important as the trend value.

Holdings. Click on Holdings in dbETF. This ETF is weighed by Market Cap and Apple is comprised of about 24% of the Assets. The next one is Microsoft with 19% of the Assets. It is quite risky, and not as diversified as expected. These two stocks is about 43% of the total Assets of this ETF. If you have $100,000 to invest, you can invest 24% of the $100,000 in Apple and 19% of $100,000 in Microsoft. In this way, you have better control and save the management fees.

Many parameters such as Finviz's Debt/Equity, Insiders' Transactions, Short%, Quarter-to-Quarter Sales and Profits can be estimated by making the proportional averages of these parameters of these two stocks.

Other parameters from dbETF

Technicals.

SMAs are available here. I prefer the percentages from Finviz.

Beta of 1.06 in this example indicates this ETF is more volatile than the average stock. MACD, Bollinger Brands, Supports / Resistance and Stochastic are available. They are useful, but you have to fully understand these technical parameters.

Intangibles

There are other considerations that affect the performance of the sector. Apple could be a victim of the trade war with China. There are many sectors that will be affected by today's pandemic. For example, in Feb, 2020, we should know the pandemic was coming. At that time, you should unloaded ETFs and stocks related to travel such as airlines and cruise lines if you had them. The riskier investors should consider shorting them. The excessive printing of money would give rise of ETFs related to gold and gold miners.

One strategy

Find the best sectors with best values (based on P/E for example) and select the top one or two best momentum ETFs as described here.
https://www.youtube.com/watch?v=uwfrdxxtULk&list=WL&index=112

Section II: Strategies for sector rotations

Most books on Sector Rotation have one strategy so it is easy to follow. I recommend glancing thru the entire book. Then select the recommended strategy depending on your knowledge, your risk tolerance and available time for research.

We have 15 strategies in sector rotation from simple market timing to rotate between SPY and cash to the more complicated ones. You can combine the strategies such as Strategy #1 and #8. Many strategies share common topics such as ETF Analysis. Because of this, the flow of the book is not linear and appears to be more complicated. However, this edition tries to flow as linear as possible.

Besides market timing and finding last month's (or last 60 days or last 90 days) best-performed sector, some sectors reverse their trend very fast. From my limited testing, I found using 60 days is better than using last month. To limit market loss, use stop orders (i.e. when the price falls into a specific value, sell it via a market order). When the market is peaking, I prefer not to own it or am more cautious. Many learned it the hard way during the internet crash in 2000 and the recent bio tech crash.

Start with one (rotate between SPY and cash recommended) and use a virtual account from one of the free sites such as Investopedia.

 # Filler: Victims?

We're victims of our own success: A higher living standard means higher wages, more protections for our workers and more regulations for our environment. All these will make us less competitive.

#Filler: My grandson

My six-year old grandson called the library about the availability of the book Mine Craft. The lady told him that only Mine Craft for Dummies was available. He told her it was not for him as he was not a dummy.

Strategy 1: Market Timing

"The Power of Market Timing" should convince you to rotate an ETF such as SPY and cash (or an ETF for short-term bonds) would give an incredible return. If you are aggressive, replace part of the cash with a contra ETF such as SH. All other strategies should follow this strategy. When the market tanks, most stocks will tank.

1   The power of market timing

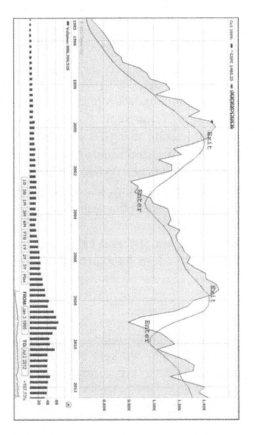

Most e-book readers allow you to select the graph to make it fit entirely on your screen. Detecting market plunges as seen in this graph indicates the exit points and reentry points also from 2000 to 9-2009 as follows.

Table: Vital Dates

Market Plunge	Peak	Bottom	Indicator Exit	Indicator Reenter
2000	08/28/00	09/20/02	10/01/00	06/01/03
2007	10/12/07	03/06/09	02/01/08	09/01/09
			08/01/11	11/01/11

As of 04/2014, my chart (from Yahoo!Finance) still indicates to invest fully in the market. For simplicity I skipped a few brief exits and reentries since 2011. You can run the simple chart once a month. When it indicates a potential market plunge is close, run the chart once a week.

This is based on stock prices so it may not identify the peaks and bottoms precisely, but so far it has never failed to avoid big losses and ensure big gains by reentering the market. I hope it will give us enough time to act when the next market plunges as the last two did.

Unbelievable return with market timing

Calculate how much you made if you followed the above exit points and reenter points from 2000 to today. I bet you would have made a good fortune.

To test the effect of market timing, I calculated the return of the S&P 500 stocks with market timing and compared it to the return of the S&P 500 without market timing from 1-2000 to 9-2013.

There are many assumptions you can make the calculations. In general, dividends are not considered. Also compounding is not considered in most cases. The return with market timing should be substantially better if we buy contra ETFs during exits and sell them during reentries.

I was shocked by the incredible return by using simple market timing when the chart tells us to exit and reenter the market only 3 times from 2000 to 2013.

Summary info:

S&P 500 1-2000 to 9-2013	With Market Timing	Without Market Timing
Better	**500%**	
Gain	1,000	167
Gain %	68%	11%
Annualized gained	5%	1%
Days	4,959	4,959

Calculations:

S & P 500	With Market Timing	Without Market Timing
1-2000	1,469[1]	1,469[1]
Exit 10/01/00	1,041[2]	1,041
Enter 06/01/03	1,041	964[4]
Exit 02/01/08	1,489[3]	1,379[4]
Enter 09/01/09	1489	1,020[5]
Exit 08/01/11	1,888	1,293
Enter 11/01/11	1,888	1,251
09/03/13	2,469	1.638
Gained	2,469 – 1,469=1,000	1,638-1,469=167
Gain %	1000/1469 = 68%	167/1469 = 11%
Annualized gained	68% * 365/4959=5%	11%*365/4959=1%
Better	(1,000-167)/167 = 500%	

Portfolio with Market Timing:

[1] Both start with S&P 500 of 1,469 on 1-3-2000.
[2] 10/01/00
The market timing portfolio exits the market and remains the same value of 1,041 until 6/1/00.
[3]   02/01/08·
The market timing portfolio exits the market and remains the same value of 1,489 until 9/1/09.

'1,489' is calculated as follows:
1,041 * (1 + Rate) = 1,041 * (1 + 1,379-964)/964) = 1,489
where the S&P 500 is 964 on 6/1/00 and 1,379 on 2/1/08.

The other calculations are based on the S&P 500 at 1,020 on 9/1/9, 1,293 on 8/1/11, 1,251 on 11/1/11 and 1,636 on 9/3/13.

Portfolio without Market Timing:

[1] Both starts with the S&P 500 of 1,469 on 1-3-2000. We could use the 9/3/13 the S&P 500 value, but it would not account for some compounded interest considerations.

[4] S&P 500 is 964 on 6/1/00 and 1,379 on 2/1/08.

[5] 02/01/08. The portfolio value is calculated to be 1,020 as follows:
    1,379 * (1 + Rate) = 1,379 * (1 + (1020-1379)/1379) = 1,020
    where S&P 500 is 1,379 on 2/1/08 and 1,020 on 9/1/09.

The other calculations are based on the S&P 500 at 1,293 on 8/1/11, 1,251 on 11/1/11 and 1,636 on 9/3/13.

I cannot believe the shocking return with market timing. I checked my calculations and there was nothing wrong that I could find. Ignore the compound rate of return that should be minor. If you find something wrong, send your findings to me (pow_tony@yahoo.com).

Even if I made a mistake somehow and got 100% instead of 500%, it still doubles the return without market timing! Ask any fund manager what it means to his or her fund performance and his / her career.

It will detect the next market plunge, but it may not give us ample time to react as the last two did. It will not detect the precise bottoms and peaks as they depend on the stock price of an ETF representing the market. I have separate statistics on market peaks and bottoms, but they have not yet been fully proven. The above may not work as effectively if there are too many followers. On the contrary it may work to be a self-fulfilling prophesy.

The stock prices of SPY are obtained from Yahoo!Finance. The entry and exit points are obtained from my simple chart from Yahoo!Finance as described and they are subject to my own interpretation.

2   Simplest market timing

Market timing depends on charts; the following describes how to use chart information without creating charts. Most charts will not identify the peaks and bottoms of the market as they depend on data (i.e. the stock prices). However, it would reduce further loses.

It is simpler than it sounds. Just follow the procedure below –the

How

The first part of this technique detects market plunges and the second part advises when to reentry the market.

How to detect market plunges without charts (a.k.a. Death Cross)

1. Bring up Finviz.com.

2. Enter SPY (or any ETF that simulates the market).

3. If SMA-200% is positive, it indicates that the market plunge has not been detected and you can skip the following steps.

4. The market is plunging if SMA-50% is more negative than SMA-200%. To illustrate this condition, SMA-200% is -2% and SMA-50% is -5%.

5. Sell most stocks starting with the riskiest ones first such as the ones with high P/Es and/or high Debt/Equity. Obtain this info from Finviz.com by entering the symbol of the stock you own.

6. Conservative investors should sell only those over-priced stocks. For aggressive investors, sell all stocks. Extremely aggressive investors should buy contra ETFs and even short stocks besides selling all stocks.

When to return to the market (a.k.a. Golden Cross)

Use the above in a reversed sense to detect whether the market has been recovering. However, when the SMA-200% is positive, I would start buying value stocks (low P/E but the 'E' has to be positive and/or low Debt/Equity).

1. Bring up Finviz.com.
2. Enter SPY (or any ETF that simulates the market).

3.   If SMA-200% is negative, the market is not recovering according to this indicator and you can skip the following steps.
4.   Start buying the best value stocks. Sell all contra ETFs if you have any. You can re-evaluate the stocks from my list in my other book, Best Stocks for 20XX, if it is available. I should have a book in the future when the market is favorable for buying stocks, but that is not a promise.
5.   Market recovery is confirmed when SMA-50% is more positive than SMA-200%. To illustrate this condition, SMA-200% is 2% and SMA-50% is 5%. Commit a larger percent (or all for aggressive investors) of your cash to stocks.

Do the above once a month. When the SPY price is closer to SMA actions percentage, perform the above once a week. The charts and data for market timing described in this book are based on SMA-350 that is more preferred than this simple procedure without using charts.

Note.
Predictions are predictions. However, the more educated that the guess is, the better chance the guess will materialize. It does not mean it will always materialize as the market changes and sometimes it is not rational. My technical indicator (SMA-350) gave me only one false alarm from 2000 to 2010. False signals happen more often after this period. The market is far more volatile than before. In most cases, false alarms will not hurt at all except for the tax consequences on taxable accounts. The false alarm tells us to exit the market and come back to the market shortly.

3   Additional hints:

Sound Advice Risk Indicator

We only invest in stocks or real estates in a crude sense. This indicator compares the allocations between these two investments has been quite successful. When we invest too much in the stock market instead of real estates, we will expect a market crash. When this index hit 2 as in 1906, 1928, 1937 and 1965, we had market crashes at all these times. Today (12/2018), we have a similar warning. Use Google to search for articles mentioning this indicator. Here is one of many.
Lazy man's market timing

Sound Advice Risk Indicator, Equality to GDP, Inverted Interest Curve and Death Cross make up the lazy man's market timing. Google for the current values of the four. If you cannot get the last one, calculate it from Finviz.com.
Using VIX as a timing model

When I overlapped VIX and the S&P500 index, I found a consistent pattern. However, it has not been conclusive to me. Try to enter VIX in any chart system such as Yahoo!Finance with the S&P500 overlaid. In the summer of 2008, VIX jumped about 500% from about 15 to 89.

\# VIX
http://en.wikipedia.org/wiki/VIX
\# VIX from Yahoo!Finance.
http://finance.yahoo.com/echarts?s=^VIX+Interactive#
\# There are several articles on the topic.
http://seekingalpha.com/instablog/434935-south-gent/3373095-vix-asset-allocation-model.
\# Ted Talk: 1
http://www.ted.com/talks/didier_sornette_how_we_can_predict_the_next_financial_crisis

Fear and Greed

This index from cnnFn.com is a similar contrary index. Leave the market when Greed is high and vice versa.

Many high-flying internet stocks lost more than 95% of their peak values. As in any bubble, the last ones to get into the bubble suffer most. The investors make out pretty nicely if they use the strategies below:

- Use a stop loss to protect your profits. Periodically adjust the order when the stock appreciates.
- Use SMA-20% (from Finviz.com). When the stock falls below the Simple Moving Average for the last 20 sessions, sell it. Use SMA-50 instead if you have a higher risk tolerance.

Other related hints on value

The oil and industrial commodities (copper, steel...) are within 20% of their record highs. From my memory, it is the first time that oil is in sync with the market due to the dumping of stocks by the oil-producing countries today.

The total market cap is higher than the GDP. As of Nov., 2013, "Market Cap / GDP" is about 110% (fair value at 85%) and hence it is over-valued. Daily ratios can be obtained from GuruFocus.com, a paid subscription service. It does not work in the current cycle from 2008. It may be today due to most large companies are multi-national. However, today most large companies are global companies, so it loses some luster in using this ratio.

Dow **Theory** and many similar market timing strategies may become less effective as every market is different. Many ignore the service industries such as selling music and games via downloading.

From my observation, the higher the interest rates is, the higher the chance that a market plunge will be. The companies will have less earnings due to the higher borrowing costs especially in businesses that require a lot of borrowing and/or most of their customers' purchases are via financing. The stocks are more expensive to buy using margin accounts. Hence, the market will not fare well when the Fed hikes the interest rate.

Q including intangible assets is with P/E in evaluating the value of the market. It is harder to calculate.

Shiller P/E (same as CAPE or PE10)

It can be used to detect the valuation of the market. The P is the S&P500 (or use SPY) and E is the average earnings of the last 10 years. It can also be used on sector ETFs and stocks. Use it as one of the hints. The major flaw is 10 years is too long of a time.

To simplify, most likely the market valuation is low (good to buy) when the P/E is below 15. The market valuation is high when it is above 20. As of 2014, it is far above 20 (17 in 2/2016). CAPE (cyclically adjusted price/earnings ratio) is available from the web by searching "CAPE P/E" to get the current reading.

Shiller's P/E   http://www.gurufocus.com/shiller-PE.php

From the above links, CAPE has been pretty decent. The reason why it does not work in 2014 is the excessive money printing that makes the market not act rationally. Treat it as a secondary yardstick at best. Here is a good article on P/E and PE10.
https://www.advisorperspectives.com/dshort/updates/2016/11/01/is-the-stock-market-cheap

My experiences

I did not time the market seriously until 2008.

- 2000 Exit. I moved most of my sector funds (most in tech) to traditional sectors after reading articles on how over-priced the internet stocks were. It would be more profitable if I moved them to cash. They did not have contra ETFs then. I could not short in my retirement accounts and I did not have experience in options.

- 2003 Return. I bet the market would return in two years. I bought many stocks which could survive in two years with the cash they had. I was lucky that the market returned in the same year. One stock was acquired by IBM with a huge gain.

- 2008 Exit. I did have the chart but I did not follow it. My big wins in energy stocks in 2007 gave me false security. When the market crashed, the energy stocks crashed too. I sold some stocks during the crash. I should have bought contra ETFs.

- 2009 Return. My chart told me to return in mid-March, 2009. I started buying in Feb., 2009. With the accumulated short-term capital losses, I traded stocks. I used my home equity loan that has far lower interest rates than my margin account – not recommended. I used the margin account only to fill up the gaps between trades. Most of the time, the margin and the loan were zero. It could be my best year with making about 80% profit in my largest taxable account.

Other technical indicators

- Head and Shoulder would predict a market plunge as evidenced in 2007. The reverse pattern would predict a market surge as indicated in 2009.
- Double Top is a bearish signal and double bottom is a bullish signal.
- Death Cross is used to detect large plunges and it does not require charting via Finviz.com. Golden Cross detects when to return.
- MACD (Moving Average Convergence Divergence). When the indicator is below the zero line, it is bearish and vice versa. Use it as a secondary indicator to detect the market direction.
- When RSI (14) is over 65%, the market is most likely overbought (i.e. over-valued).

- Use the following SMA-20 as a secondary indicator as an alternative to the SMA-350. When the stock price is below SMA-20 (Single Moving Average for the last 20 sessions) for three consecutive days, it indicates a possible market plunge. In theory, the institutional investors dump the stock on the first day and then the retail investors follow on the second day. If it continues on the third day, most likely it is not the trick of the institutional investors to take advantage of the retail investors.

Buffett's Equity to GDP

It measures the value of the market. It has been quite successful. Google for the current value. Advisor Perspectives may have this value and many insights on the current market. It will not detect the peaks and bottoms as no one can consistently. About a third of the earnings of the S&P 500 companies come from abroad. Hence it boosts market cap but doesn't include those countries' GDP. It is a major fault.

Fidelity

From Fidelity.com, click on "News & Research" and then "Stock Market & Sector Performance" for Equity Market Commentary.

False alarm

From 2000 to 2010, there is only one false alarm. From 2011 to 2016, there are more false alarms. We can change the parameter from SMA-350 to SMA-400 to reduce the number of false alarms at the expense of detecting the plunge a little late. The market before 2000 is quite different from the market today. Hence, I do not use the data before 2000.

4   *Spotting big market plunges*

The first chapter is easy to use and understand. This chapter is lengthy, complicated in some concepts and requiring you to try it yourself. However, the result is far better. Make your market decision by combining all the hints described in this article.

No one can consistently predict the correct stages of the market cycle. This chapter is intended for educational purpose only. However, if we have more rights than wrongs with our calculated and educated guesses, we should do well. As in everything in life, there is no guarantee.

There are my 11 hints to identify a market plunge. The average loss of market plunges from top to bottom for the last two crashes is about 45%. It could wipe out most gains for the entire market cycle. We target to avoid half of the loss.

Do not buy stocks during market plunge that could last for more than a year, which is defined by me from the market peak to the market bottom. It is a million dollar decision for many including myself. This low-cost book serves as a reference and past performances do not guarantee future performances.

From 2000 to 2008, we only have one false signal for our SMA-350 out of 3 signals. Since then, we have more false signals. To adjust to this volatility, do not move everything to cash on an exit signal. Adjust the amount of cash according to your own risk tolerance. Usually we do not lose much (sometimes we gain some) as another signal tells us to return to the market shortly. They only have tax consequences in taxable accounts.

Eleven hints of a market plunge

1. Technical analysis (TA).

   The following chart is created by Yahoo!Finance. If it does not display well on a small screen, copy the following link to your browser to display it on your PC.
   http://ebmyth.blogspot.com/2013/05/ta-graph-for-spotting-plunges-chapter.html

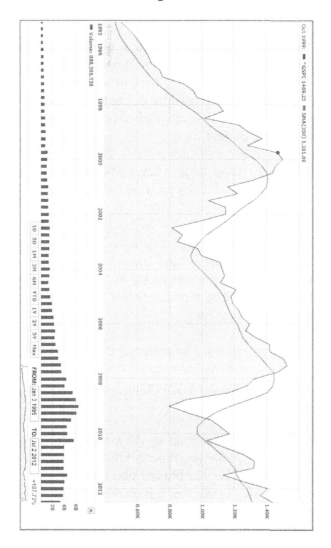

350 days simple moving average (SMA). Yahoo!Finance

The red line is the 350-day SMA, Simple Moving Average. If the stock price is below the moving average, it has detected a market plunge by this chart. Return to the market when the price is above the moving average line described as Early Recovery later. "350 days" are trading sessions. I have tried different "days" and 350 is the best fit for the last two market plunges, but it does not mean it would be the best fit the next market plunge.

We have two cycles described in the chart. From the above, we should leave the market in the first quarter of 2000 and return to the market on the first quarter of 2003.

On the second cycle, the chart tells us to get out in Dec. 2008 and come back in July 2009 approximately. Enlarge the chart by selecting 5 years instead of the maximum or use a larger monitor for a more detailed chart. The chart sometimes gives false signals to tell us to exit but tell us to reenter briefly. In most cases, we do not lose much except the tax consequences for selling. No technical indicators are perfect.

I started to come back on Feb. 2009. It was perfect timing but most likely or partly it was due to good luck. I was partially influenced by several articles I read.

Technical Analysis is based on the past data, so you cannot avoid the initial losses but it could reduce further and larger losses. From the above, the chart detected the two big plunges nicely allowing enough time to take actions. Will the next plunge be detected? It will I guess. However, it may not allow enough time as the last two.

Sometimes, we time it wrongly or prematurely and miss some gains by leaving the market too early. We need to treat it as buying insurance; it only pays big when the worst happens. When the "reward / risk" is too low, it is better to stay in cash. One's opinion.

Return to equity when the price is above the moving average (the red line). You should profit more by following the chart than 'Buy and Hold' or keeping your money under the pillow. For the last two market cycles, I returned to equities in Early Recovery (a stage of the market cycle defined by me) and profited. Can I be 100% sure for the next market plunge and come back in a timely order? Certainly not.

If most of your stocks are in tech, use QQQ instead of SPY. In addition QQQ is more volatile than SPY and the tech sector usually leads the market.

It can be created by following the steps; you need to create one yourself to detect the next plunge with current data.
- From Yahoo!Finance or any chart systems, enter SPY (or the S&P 500 index) or an ETF that represents the total market.
- Select Interactive Chart.
- Click Technical Indicators.
- Select SMA (simple moving average).

- Enter 350 days (actually it is trade sessions). Many chart systems use 'month' as unit, enter 12 or 11.67 if decimals is allowed (=350/12) instead of 350.
- Enter 1-3-2000 on "FROM:" or any "from date" that fits your screen.
- Select Draw.

Note. I switch to Fidelity for charting now as I cannot produce the same info from Yahoo!Finance. It could be my fault or a bug that should be fixed. If you cannot use Fidelity, try StockCharts.com.

---

2. Do the opposite of the flow of the dumb money.

When everyone is buying recklessly, making money and proclaiming that they are geniuses, sell. In 1999, my friend told me that he should quit his job and concentrate on investing as he was making many times in the stock market over his regular salary by spending half an hour a day. I would call myself a genius by making $1,000 an hour. When AAII's bullish sentiment (a contrary indicator to me) is over 70%, watch out.

On the same year, there were so many successful IPOs with '.com' names and these companies did not know how to make profits but blindly captured their market shares at all expenses.

They gave me $20 for just registering in their site. The poor quality of their ads showing their products during the Super Bowl reflected the quality of their management. The so-called 'MBA's business model' of capturing a potential market of one million potential sales by spending five millions is not Business 101 but Fool 101.

The inverse flow of money market funds is a good indicator too. The more money flowing into the equity funds by retail investors, the riskier is the market. Greed is a human nature. It is hard to resist buying stocks when your friends are all making good money in the market and you feel you do not want to miss the boat. I tried unsuccessfully to convince lottery winners not buying lottery and they showed me they had made another thousands yesterday.

3. Duration.

Cycles usually occur every four or five years. This is a very rough estimate as cycles often vary from 1 to 8 or even more years. After the market plunge on 2007-2008, we are having (as of 12/2018) one of the longest bull market.

The longer it stays at the peak, the higher the chance the market will plunge and the further it will sink. I call it Newton's Law of Gravity or 'What goes up must come down'. When we follow the charts (technical indicators), we still stay in the market most of the time.

4.   Valuation.

The average historical P/E of the S&P 500 is about 15 (or 16.5 depending on when you start the data). When it is over the average, be careful. Obtain the P/E of SPY (an ETF for the S&P 500) from Yahoo!Finance and confirm it in many other sources. When the average P/E of a sector is over 35, most likely there will be a fierce correction for that sector. When it is over 40, the market most likely has peaked. When you find fewer value stocks than before, it means the market is more risky now.

The P/E of the S&P 500 index was 28 in 2000. It was 18 in 2007 and 16 in 2015. Both are over 15, the average value for the last five years.

The value of the average P/E has to be adjusted as the market conditions are not the same 10 or so years ago. Today (2016) part of the earning (the E in P/E) is due to the low cost in borrowing and less wage cost due to hiring overseas. Most global corporations can offshore jobs to reduce expenses. The global economies are inter-connected far better than before. When the global economies fall, we will fall too.

5.   Triggers to burst a bubble.
In 2000, the trigger was the tech bubble. In 2007 it was the housing (or financing) bubble. It was easy to spot a massive tech bubble in 2000. I moved most of my tech sector funds to traditional sectors (cash for 20-20 hindsight) in the beginning of April, 2000, which was too close for comfort to this market plunge.

Most investors including myself did not understand the workings of the derivatives of the mortgage loans and could not recognize the bubble. I made good money in the oil sector in 2007. However, in 2008 most of my investments were losers including the investment in the oil sector. If I followed the hints described in this chapter, I would have avoided heavy losses.

6. Rising interest rates.

It is more expensive for investors using margin to buy stocks, for companies to borrow money and for consumers to buy high ticket items and houses.

A related hint is rising margin debt (the debt used to buy stocks backed up by the current stock holdings). When we have a record margin debt as in 2016, the chance of a market plunge is high when the Fed hikes the interest rates.

When the Fed discount rate is 5% or above, be careful. This is also the time to buy long-term bonds. When it is 1% or less, most likely the market starts to recover. This is also the time NOT to buy long-term bonds. This strategy was proven in market cycles in 2000 and 2008.

7. Yield Curve.

When the short-term (say 3 month) interest rates is higher than the long term (say 30 years), it is abnormal and a bearish signal. Click here to check the yield curve.

Many use two-year Treasury and ten-year Treasury. As of Oct. 15, 2018, they were 2.82% and 3.09% and it was very close to be equal and gave us some warning on a potential recession. You may want to move some of your risky investments such as stocks to safer investments such as CDs and short-term bonds. As of 2018, only two false warnings from the last seven recessions when an inverted yields occurred. Again, your action depends on your risk tolerance.

http://www.treasury.gov/resource-center/data-chart-center/interest-rates/Pages/TextView.aspx?data=yield
http://blogs.marketwatch.com/thetell/2014/05/13/bear-market-wont-come-until-the-yield-curve-says-so-kleintop/

8. Rising oil price.

It is the same as the above as rising oil price will cause everything more expensive. However, today (2015-2016) is an exception. The falling oil price correlates with the market. It is due to falling too much and the oil-producing countries have to dump the stocks to rescue their economies. If I have to put a number, I would say the market is risky when the oil price is below $30 or above $120.

9. Market experts.

There are always two camps predicting the market trend. Check out those that make sense and ignore those who try to sell you books or their services. The media try to scare you to improve the circulation. The reason I exited the market in April, 2000 is the result of reading an article that said the entire company of an internet company could fit into a conference room of a company with the same market cap. Good seeds fall in fertile soil will prosper. The opposite is true when bad seeds fall in any kind of soil.

10. Politics.
The long market rise from 2009 to 2016 is due to the low interest rates even the economy is not doing well. The interest rates is controlled by the Federal Reserve Bank, which is an agent of the government. After WW2, the market has never been down in a year right before election. As of 2016, the low-interest saves the market at the expense of our national debt which is at the recent peak. Trump's proposed 45% tariff could bring global recession starting in the US and China.

11. Miscellaneous.
In 2000, I exited the market after reading an article describing how the entire corporation fitting into a big conference of a large corporation. In 2008, we had a "Double Top" technical indicator that correctly told us a market plunge.

Be conservative
As in any new strategy, test it out and try it out gradually with real money. Most of you paid less than $25 for this book and most likely you do not want to risk all your money based on a $25 advice, so consult your financial advisors. You should not lose money by exiting the market too early, but miss the opportunity to make more money. If the market does not crash, treat it as insurance. No one can predict market directions consistently and correctly. This article gives you better hints to time the market and all markets are different.

The chart worked fine for the last two crashes, but as in life there is no guarantee to detect the next market crash for the following reasons:

- It may not give us ample of time to react as the last two. The current market is high and is caused by excessive money supply. When the money supply is reduced (or no more QEn), the market will react negatively.

- When too many folks buy my books and use the same chart, it will lose its effectiveness. It is most likely not, but there is always a chance.
- Past performances do not guarantee future performance.
- The market is not always rational.
- There are more noises (crossing the red line and backing again briefly) since 2011. The chart is not the only indicator I follow. Adjust it according to your risk tolerance.

Since 2011, there are several exits/entries as the market is not rational. However, if you follow it, you're still faring well as they tell you reentry very quickly. You do not lose or gain a lot by doing so. Even if you lose a little, it could be the best insurance you bought.

The noises would be increased if we use 200 days in SMA in the chart instead of 350. For the same reason, they will be decreased if I use 400 days but the signal will be later delayed.

As in life, there is nothing guaranteed, the chart is far better than market timing without charts and/or no market timing at all since 2000. As of 6/2015, I started looking at my charts more frequently months as we've been living dangerously on borrowed time for a long while.

Conclusion

This article provides my basic tools and my views on market timing. Market is not always rational otherwise there are no poor folks as stated before. When the market is about to plunge, run the chart more frequently and read more articles written by market experts.

Market timing is not an exact science but it is based on educated guesses. The better guesses should have more rights than wrongs in the long term. Your actions depend on your risk tolerance. Initially you should be careful on using any strategy that you do not have full understanding and enough proven record.

Technical analysis (SMA-350) is more important than fundamentals as an over-valued market could linger for years as in 2009 to 2017. Also recommend to read articles on experts on the current market. There are always two camps.

5 Market timing example

The market is making new highs. There are always two camps of market timers. One camp predicts a crash is coming while the other predicts it will continue making new highs. This article includes both arguments and suggests how and what actions you need to take to protect your investments.

Management summary

The market is fundamentally unsound evidenced by fundamental metrics but technically sound evidenced by technical metrics that both will be described in this article. The data were obtained on 09/22/2018. The market has not changed a lot as of 01/2020.

Suggested actions
No one predicts the market correctly and consistently. Otherwise there are no poor folks. Moving the risky investments such as most stocks to cash too early would miss the potential profits. Moving it too late would risk the loss of your stocks.

Your actions depend on your risk tolerance. If you are conservative such as a retiree, you may want to have a larger portion of your investments in lower risk such as CDs and bonds. You can take one of the following three actions or combine all of the three actions.

1. When the market turns to technically unsound, it is time to move your stocks to cash. The market timing indicators may give false signals. In this case, the indicator would tell you to move back to stocks. Most likely you do not lose much except dealing with the consequences of taxes in non-retirement accounts.
2. Move a portion of your risky investments into cash, laddered CDs and/or short-term bonds. Again, the size of the portion depends on your risk tolerance.
3. Use stops. The sell orders would be changed to market orders when the stocks dip below prices specified by you. I prefer to use SPY or other ETF to determine the market direction. Some sectors and some stocks move faster than others. In one crash, my energy stocks were still profitable while the market was tanking. Eventually these energy stocks caught up and fell fast. Today's highly profitable stocks are FAANG stocks as a group.

I propose and prefer 'manual stop orders' to prevent market manipulation. However, usually large ETFs cannot be manipulated easily. Manipulators try to profit from your stop orders. Set a stop order price in your `mind. When the stock falls to that specified price, sell it via a market order.

My friend confirmed my "manual stop order":

"High-frequency trading via Algo Trading Strategy can see exactly where pre-set trailing stops are and sweep across them (play them) like strings on a violin. Pre-set a trailing stop and it is bound to be triggered because Algo hunt them down. Then watch the market rip higher."

Analysis: Fundamentals and Technical
It consists of Fundamental Analysis and Technical Analysis. The former measures how expensive the current market is and the latter measures the trend of the market.

Many metrics were obtained from Finviz.com as of 9/22/2018 while others are obtained from other websites. With the exception of Fidelity.com, all websites described here are free and readily available. It also serves as a guide on how you can do your own market timing especially after a few months.

The following chart uses SPY to represent the market of the top 500 stocks. It is market cap weighted. It means the higher the market cap the stock, the higher percent of the stock is represented in the index. It turns out most are riskier FAANG stocks.

Enter Finviz.com in your browser and enter SPY. I am not responsible for any errors.

Indicator	Pass	Current Value	Indicating
• Technical			
Death Cross[1]		SMA-50 = 2.3% & SMA-200 = 6.3%	Pass
Technical Analysis: 350 SMA%[2]	>0	Price above the SMA-350.	Pass
RSI(14)	<70	61	Pass
Duration (yr.)	<5	10	Fail
		Overall	**Pass**
• Fundamental			
Valuation			
P/E[3]	<15.7	25.4	High by 62%. Fail.

Shiller P/E[3]	<16.6	33.5	High by 102%. Fail
P/B[3]	<2.78	3.52	High by 27%. Fail.
P/S[3]	<1.50	2.33	High by 55%. Fail.
Oil price	30-100	70.71	Pass
Interest rate[6] T-Bill 1 months[7]	<5	2.05	Pass
T-Bill 3 months[7]	Yield	2.18	
T-Bill 30 years[7]	Curve	3.20	Pass
Flow to Equity[4]		-3.371M	Fail
Flow to bond[4]		7.206M	
Corporate debt/GDP[8]	<40	45%	High by 13%. Fail.
USD[5]		Strong	Fail
Gold		High	Fail
Bubble		Several	Fail
Market experts		Fear long term	Neutral
Politics		Trump	Fail
Misc.		Trade war	Fail
		Overall	**Fail**

[1] This is the market timing technique without using a chart.

[2] I tried to use SMA-400% to reduce false signals without success.

[3] Get it from http://www.multpl.com/ Same as CAPE.

[4] Get it from https://www.ici.org/research/stats. It is based on 09-12-18. "Flow to Equity" is based on domestic ETF estimate. Treat it as two phases in moving to equity. First phase of moving excessively to equity indicates the market is peaking. The second phase indicates the market is plunging when flow of equity is excessively negative.

[5] Global corporations will suffer in profits converted back to USD and hard to sell to foreign countries. [4] Get it from the above link.

[6] Rising interest is bad for corporations and high-ticket products, but good for lenders.

[7] Get it from https://www.treasury.gov/resource-center/data-chart-center/interest-rates/Pages/TextView.aspx?data=yield based on 09/21/18

[8] With the low interest rate, it may not be that critical. Corporations take advantage of the low interest rate.

Overall
Overall, technical is fine as the market is making new highs. Many aggressive investors exit the market on technical indicators only as the over-valued market could linger on for a long term such as from 2009 to 2017 so far.

Overall, fundamental is not sound. The increasing market price also is decreasing the fundamental metrics such as P/E, P/B and P/S. It is bad unless there is reason to support such as the fast earnings growth in 2009.

Many metrics are deteriorating

RSI(14) is getting closer to 65 (a passing grade specified by me).

Inverse yield curve (1.5 vs. 2.33) is about 61% apart from my interpretation and calculation. It is not a warning now but we should keep an eye on it. Most market crashes have occurred when it is 0% or negative. The theory is that in a normal case the short-term interest rates should be lower than the long-term interest rate.

Another source calculates it is 1.1% and that is very close to inversion since the last recession. From MarketWatch, the 30-year fixed interest rates is 4.66% and 1-year rate is 3.96% giving an inverse yield curve 18% apart, which is quite alarming.

Mathematically incorrect, today's full employment is at 4%. Most recessions are closely preceded by troughs in unemployment and the reverse for economy recovery.

GDP growth has been predicted from 1.8% to 3%. The 3% is from the White House for their obvious purpose. I predict it will pop up due to meeting the tariff deadlines, tax cuts and spending increases. It will then be declining to 2%. A healthy US economy should maintain 3% without special factors such as excessive immigration.

We have record debts: investors' margin, corporate debt and Federal debt. These are bubbles going to burst. Federal debt / GDP is about 95% (https://fred.stlouisfed.org/series/gfdegdq188S) today. It does not predict the market performance as this ratio was 53% and 55% before the last two market crashes. It will affect the long-term performance of the economy when we have to service the huge national debt.

We do have 10 years of stock growth at the expense of record Federal deficit. Thanks to President Obama from investors and no thanks from next generations who have to pay back our national debt. It is overdue for a correction. Hopefully it is not a crash which has an average loss of about 45%.

We did have two recent corrections losing more than 10%: 2011-12 EU debt crisis and 2014-16 oil crash. The oil price has been rising from $30 per barrel to today's $70. It is still a long way from my warning of $120.

Potential triggers
Trade wars with China, Canada or EU will be the strongest trigger. Our most profitable companies are virtually all international companies. They need fair trade to prosper.

The other trigger is the possible impeachment of President Trump.

Check the validity of our charts
It seems some metrics vary. It could use after hour trading. It could be the "Days" may be "Sessions" – calendar day is different from trading session. I selected 10 years for most of the charts and StockCharts let me select only 5 years.

Here is a list of sites for charts.
https://www.stocktrader.com/2013/12/10/best-free-stock-chart-websites/
These are the three sites I use a lot: Fidelity (customers only), StockCharts and Finviz.com (missing some metrics).

As stated before, SPY may not be the best to represent the market. I prefer an ETF for 1,000 stocks and weigh the stocks evenly (i.e. not according to the market cap). Google "market timing 2020 (or current year)" for more expert info. Here is one.

Mid-year (6/15/2020) update
This is an update to my two articles: "Market timing example" and "Disaster of 2020".

Basically nothing significant has changed recently: The market is fundamentally unsound and technically sound after the recent rally. The only update is our national debt is skyrocketing. Today's "Debt/GDP" is similar to the market height in 2000 and we know what happened afterwards. That's why Buffett has accumulated a lot of cash now.

Even with the unlimited QE (i.e. printing money excessively), the high inflation and market crash predicted by many experts have not been materialized so far. This is my third prediction in "Disaster of 2020". The status of USD as a reserve currency will be shaken; I do not know when, as I do not have a time machine.

Why the market keeps going up while the economy is going down? The Fed has provided a lot of cash and the cash is chasing a fixed number of assets such as gold and stocks. It is the simple, proven theory of demand and supply. It will continue for a while as long as there is unlimited supply of money. At some point, it will pop. At that time, it could lead to a long recession, unless the economy improves as it did in 2009. The smart Fed chairman knows how it will harm the country by excessively printing money. However, he has to obey his boss who is seeking for reelection.

I expect we are in a prolonged period of low interest rates and even negative interest rates. When the rates are negative, our Treasury bonds are no longer marketable. The foreign central banks including China would dump our national debts if it has not been already started. The economy is dressed up nicely in an election year. Giving us free money is the easy way to buy votes, but the long-term effects are very harmful.

Using cheap money to buy back the company's stock would boost the stock price and hence make the management wealthier. It is a false sense of the stock value. When the company cannot pay back the debt obligations, the company would go bankrupted. If the U.S. were a company, she has gone bankrupted already.

As of 6/15/2020, QQQ (representing NASDAQ stocks) has been up 11% YTD and it is far better than DIA (representing DOW stocks) and SPY (representing the 500 large stocks in the S&P Index and losing about 5% YTD). QQQ has a lot of tech stocks while DIA has a lot of losers including Boeing. Most FAANG stocks are making record highs and QQQ is market cap weighed.

Most of the ETFs on chips have been up more than 40% in a year. I bought Amazon and two chip ETFs. I use trailing stops to protect my portfolio. Huawei is buying a lot of U.S. chips in the 120-day relaxed period. In September this year and if there is no extension, I would sell these chip ETFs fast.

I have used the strategy described in my book "Profit from the recovery of the pandemic" to take advantage of this volatile market. I used 5% as the threshold and I had too few trades; now I changed to 3%. Expecting a market crash, I weigh more on contra ETFs. As described in the same book, I bought a lot of contra ETFs, GLD and the stock of a gold miner. It is for insurance. ETFs on oil is my big mistake.

If the U.S.D. loses the status of reserve currency (not likely soon), it would bring prolonged depression and high inflation in the U.S. In this case, it is safer to invest in real estate, precious metals and profitable companies than in CDs and bonds that would lose values due to inflation.

Check out many articles on the status of the current market. Many have opposing views, so you have to make your own decision. In any case, play it safe with stops. Here is one article from MarketWatch.com.

Canary warning?
When I was working on my new book "Best stocks to buy for 2021" on Dec. 10, 2020, I found something really strange. I have never rejected so many stocks that have Fidelity's Equity Summary Score higher than 9. I rejected them as there were a lot of dumping from the insiders. Insiders know their companies better than most of us. Is it the canary telling us the market is over-valued? Initially the following stocks have been screened by my value screens. Buy any one of the following stocks, **only** if you have good reason(s).

Symbol	Fidelity Score	Insider Purchase
BCC	9.9	-24%
GPI	10.0	-17%
HEAR	10.0	-75%
HIBB	9.4	-30%
HVT	9.5	-37%
HZO	9.5	-27%

How can HEAR score a perfect 10 while the Insiders' Transaction is -75% (I treated -2% is normal). The analysts must be wrong this time, or they believe the market will continuously make new heights. Will update the performance results later to see who is wrong.

A correction or a crash
On Dec., 2018, the S&P500 is about 15% down and a crash is about 45% down. If a crash is coming, there should be additional 30% down. If it is a correction (15% average), then we have it already. Should we pick up bargains now? Or, are they bargains? It is a trillion dollar question.
We need a trigger for a market crash like the financial crisis in 2008 and the internet bubble in 2000. Besides the record-high margin debt, the possibility of Trump's impeachment and a trade war, I do not see any.

6   Simplest strategy on market timing

Follow the article "Simplest Market Timing" to time the market. If it tells you the market is going down, buys contra ETFs and/or move stocks to cash depending on your risk tolerance.

Recommended ETFs (3 total)
SEF
PSQ
GLD
Money Market / CD

My reasons

Contra ETFs are betting the sectors represented to go down. During a market downturn, I would bet against bank/financial stocks (SEF, a contra ETF) and tech stocks (PSQ, a contra ETF for NASDAQ which includes a lot of tech stocks).

GLD is an ETF for gold. During a recession, gold should fare better than stocks but could perform less than most of the contra ETFs. If the value of the USD depreciates, gold would fare better. Every portfolio should have 2 to 10% in gold. The allocation depends on your risk tolerance. If you are conservative, move everything to Money Market fund / CD.

We have only one false alarm from 2000 to 2010 and more after 2010. The false alarm tells you to exit the market and then tells you to reenter the market shortly. If you do not buy any contra ETFs, most likely you do not lose anything.

After the crash

When the market timing tells you to return to the market, sell contra ETFs and buy SPY (or any ETF that simulates the market) and value stocks. You need more time to find and evaluate value stocks. Use stops to protect your portfolio.

7   Why the market fluctuates

The following chart uses SPY (simulating the market) with SMA-350 for the year of 2020 using Fidelity's charting function. It will be used to demonstrate how SMA-350 worked for 2020; the dates may be several days off. This article is written on 1/1/2021.

Market Timing

SMA-350 (Simple Moving Average for the last 350 sessions), described in this book, worked fine in 2020. It told us to exit the market on about 3/11/2020 and return on about the beginning of June. There were two false signals (on about 4/28 and 5/8) that told you to exit but return to the market shortly.

The other indicators are RSI(14) and P/E. Fidelity's chart uses 80 for overbought and 30 for under-bought for RSI(14). The market has been over-priced for a long while. In this case, technical analysis (SMA-350 I used in my example) works better than fundamental (P/E as one of the metrics); It has been sold for the entire 2020.

Why there is a big drop in late March and why it comes back

The trigger is the pandemic.

The market came back for many reasons:
- We understood the pandemic better.
- A lot of money in the sideline.
- The government supplies more money by printing it excessively.
- The government lowers the interest rate (almost to zero).

2021 prediction

It is quite hard to predict the market. Here are my thoughts. The market is not rational (fundamentally speaking).

For:

- The government keeps on excessively supplying money.
- With easy credit, the rising housing market leads to many profitable sectors such as furniture.
- Due to easy credit and recovering, many companies buy back their own stocks.
- Low margin interest rate usually boosts the stock market.
- If the vaccines can control this pandemic, many sectors will recover. As I demonstrated before, we have to wait one more year for some sectors such as airlines, restaurants and cruise lines.
- Trade war with China could be reduced under Biden.

Against:
- The pandemic has not been stopped.
- Unemployment is breaking previous record.
- Small businesses continue to go bankrupt.
- Complete decoupling with China.
- The government tools do not work anymore such as lowering interest rate.
- Super inflation is due to ample supply of money chasing a fixed amount of assets (stocks for example). It would also shaken the status of the USD as a reserve currency.

As in any market, there are two camps opposite to each other. Need to watch the market like a hawk and take actions accordingly (talk to your financial advisor first). I expect the plunge would cause the market to lose about 40% if it happens.

Strategy 2: Rotation of 4 Sectors

Rotate sectors via ETFs and/or mutual funds. When the market is risky, move them to cash, short-term bond ETF/mutual fund, money market fund or a combination of the above and reenter when the market is not risky.

1   Rotate four ETFs

We can beat the market by rotating one ETF that represents the market such as SPY and cash (or short-term bond ETF) via market timing.

During a market uptrend, rotating the following four ETFs could be more profitable. Be warned that a short-term capital gain in taxable accounts is not treated as favorably as the long-term capital gain; check current tax laws.

The allocation percentages depend on your individual risk tolerance. You can use indexed mutual funds. Compare their expenses and restrictions. Some mutual funds charge you if you withdraw within a specific time period.

Select the best performer of last month (from Seeking Alpha, cnnFn, or the ETF/mutual fund site). Add a contra ETF such as SH to take advantage of a falling market for more aggressive investors. Add sector ETFs to the four ETFs such as XLY, XLP, XLE, XLF, XLU, IYW, XHB, IYM, OIL and XLU to expand your selection.

ETFs	Money Market	US	International	Bond
Fidelity		Spartan Total Market	Spartan Global Market	Spartan US Bond
Vanguard		Total Stock Market	Total International Market	Total Bond Market
My choice	Fidelity	SPY	Vanguard	Fidelity
Suggest %				
During Market plunge	90%	0%	0%	10%
After plunge	10%	60%	10%	20%

Explanation

- The above are suggestions only. If your broker offers similar ETFs, consider using them.
- Check out any restrictions of the ETFs.
- 4 ETFs (one actually is a money market fund) are enough for most starters. They are diversified, low-cost and you do not need balancing except during a market plunge (refer to the chapter on Detecting Market Plunges).
- The percentages are suggestions only. If you are less risk tolerant, allocate more to a money market fund, CD and/or bond ETF.
- Have at least 10% allocated to the money market fund. When there is a mild market dip, move the money market fund to the US equity fund. Move it back to money market when there is a mild market upsurge. If you do not have time to check the market, allocate this 10% to the bond ETF.
- When the market is risky, reduce stock equities (i.e. increase money market and bond allocations).
- The symbols for Fidelity ETFs are FSTMX, FSGDX and FBIDX.
- The symbols for Vanguard ETFs are VTSMX, VGTSX and VBMFX.

Filler: Chicken feet, lobsters and trade war

Lobsters are literally flown to China for the rich. The trade war changes all these. Chicken feet, a delicacy for Chinese, will be thrown to the ocean. I can finally enjoy a $12 plate of lobster in Boston.

Soybeans and pork are on sale in the US. I may buy a whole bunch, and cross ship them to China via a country that has no tariff from China.

Many farmers have been bankrupted as the banks do not loan them money to buy seeds for next years. Our storage is over-flowed. Soybeans and pork are rotting. Trump's subsidies will not help a lot and he is going to lose all the votes from these farm states.

Strategy 3: Rotation of more sectors

It is similar to the Strategy 2 but includes more basic sectors. Add a contra ETF such as SH to take advantage of a falling market. Add the following sector ETFs to the four sectors described in Strategy 2: XLY, XLP, XLE, XLF, XLU, IYW, XHB, IYM, OIL and XLU. They should cover most of the sectors.

Start keeping the top two sectors to start. The allocation percentages depend on individual risk tolerance. You can use indexed mutual funds. Compare their expenses and restrictions.

Select the best performer of last month. Besides cnnfn.com and finviz.com, the current, favorable sectors can be found in many web sites including SeekingAlpha.com and Fidelity.com (customers only). Following the top performer(s) for the last month is following the short-term trend. In addition to the last month, following the top performer(s) for the last 3 months is following the trend for the intermediate trend.

As of Feb., 2016, the utility index within S&P 500 has been up about 8% year-to-date while S&P 500 was down by about 8%. It is another example that the correct sector rotation is profitable.

The primary sectors are: Basic Materials, Consumer Discretionary, Consumer Staples, Energy, Financial, Health Care, Industrial, Technology and Utilities. Click the links or search from Wikipedia for description of these sectors.

https://www.fidelity.com/sector-investing/overview

We can sub divide a sector into industries. For example, Technology can be divided into Computer and Software. When computer industry is good, it does not mean software industry is also good. Some industries such as banking software can cross more than one sector.

The above links describe sectors pretty good by Fidelity with the exception of Technology, which is divided into several sectors such as Software, Computer and Telecom by Fidelity. Here are my views on the major sectors. Many vendors including IBD provide industry rankings. Here is my additional description to cover the basic sectors and some will be described in the appropriate chapters.

Consumer Staples and Discretionary

Consumer Staples are food, beverages, household products and the products we buy as necessity. They are recession-proof. The US products have demonstrated high quality and safety. With the growing middle class in developing countries such as China and India, we expect they should grow outside the USA. Currently it is not due to tariffs.

Consumer Discretionary are just the opposite.

Besides introducing the sectors and their corresponding mutual funds and ETFs, I introduce how to evaluate sectors fundamentally and technically. For beginners, skip the rest of this section.

Links

A list of sectors.
http://www.investorguide.com/sector-list.php
Check's sector analysis.
http://seekingalpha.com/article/2806655-the-stock-market-2015-a-sector-by-sector-valuation-perspective-part-1-an-overview

1   ETFs / Mutual Funds

What is an ETF

Fidelity: Index ETFs (https://www.fidelity.com/etfs/overview).

Wikipedia on ETF (http://en.wikipedia.org/wiki/Exchange-traded_fund).

List of ETFs
ETF Bloomberg
http://www.bloomberg.com/markets/etfs/
ETF data base
http://etfdb.com/
ETF Trends
http://www.etftrends.com/
A list of ETFs. Seeking Alpha.
(http://etf.stock-encyclopedia.com/category/)

Fidelity's commission-free ETFs. Check current offerings and whether they are still commission-free.
(https://www.fidelity.com/etfs/ishares)

Fidelity Annuity funds with performance data.
http://fundresearch.fidelity.com/annuities/category-performance-annual-total-returns-quarterly/FPRAI?refann=005

A list of contra ETFs (or bear ETFs)
http://www.tradermike.net/inverse-short-etfs-bearish-etf-funds/

Misc.: ETFGuide, ETFReplay (highly recommended).

Other resources
Your broker should have a lot of information on ETFs and many offer commission-free ETFs.

Most subscription services offer research on ETFs. IBD has a strategy dedicated to ETFs and so does AAII to name a couple.

Seeking Alpha has extensive resources for ETF including an ETF screener and investing ideas.

Not all ETFs are created equal
Check their performances and their expenses.

Small but well-performing ETFs

Here is a list.
http://finance.yahoo.com/news/small-etfs-pack-big-punch-195430875.html

Guggenheim Spin-Off ETF (CSD) looks interesting. The ETF tracks corporate spinoffs. It has beaten SPY for a long time; check the current performance. Not a recommendation.

When not to use ETFs

I prefer sector mutual funds in some industries but you need to do extensive research. They are drug industry, banks, miners and insurers.

Half ETF

Taking out half of the stocks that score below the average in an index ETF could beat the same full ETF itself. I call it HETF (half the ETF). You heard it here first.

To illustrate, sort the expected P/E (not including stocks with negative earnings) in ascending order and only include the stocks on the first half. Add more fundamental metrics. It will take a few minutes.

Disadvantages of ETFs

- When you have two stocks in a sector ETF one good one and one bad one, the ETF treats them the same. Stock pickers would buy the one that has a better appreciation potential.
- The return is better than the actual return due to stock rotation. To illustrate this, on August 29, 2012, SHLD was replaced by LYB in a sector fund. SHLD was down by 4% and LYB was up by 4% primarily due to the switch. Unless you sell and buy at the right time (which is impossible), your return would not match the ETF's returns due to the replacement.
- Ensure the performance matches the corresponding index, but will most likely not include dividends.

Advantages of ETFs

- We have demonstrated that you can beat the market by using market timing. Between 2000 and Nov., 2013, you only exit and reenter the market 3 times and the result is astonishing.
- It is easy to rotate a sector vs. buying/selling all of the stocks in this sector. It makes sector rotation the same as trading a stock.
- The risk is spread out and your portfolio is diversified especially for a market ETF or buying three or more ETFs in different sectors.
- Eliminate the time in researching stocks.

Leveraged ETFs

I do not recommend them. Some are 2x, 3x and even higher. They're too risky. However, when you are very sure or your tested strategy has very low drawdown, you may want to use them to improve performance. I recommend skipping all leveraged ETFs.

My basic ETF tables

I use a list of selected ETFs and commission-free (check the details) ETFs from Fidelity for my purpose. I include some mutual funds in Fidelity's annuity. Some of these may be interesting to you. I use ETFs for sector rotation and parking my cash when the market is favorable and I do not have stocks that I want to buy.

ETFs and funds come and go. Some ideas and classifications are my own interpretation. More tables can be found in the Appendix.

Table by sectors:

Sector	ETF	Fidelity ETF	Mutual Funds	Fidelity's Annuity
Banking[1]			FSRBK	
Regional	IAT			
Bio Tech	IBB		FBIOX	
	XBI		Large	
Consumer Dis.	XLY	FDIS	FSCPX	FVHAC
Consumer Staple	XLP	FSTA	FDFAX	FCSAC
Finance	KIE	FNCL	FIDSX	FONNC
	IYF			
Energy	XLE	FENY	FSENX	FJLLC

Energy Service			FSESX	
Gold	GLD		FSAGX	
Gold Miner	GDX		VGPMX	
Health Care	IYH	FHLC	FSPHX	FPDRC
	VHT		VGHCX	
House Builder	ITB		FSHOX	
	ITB		Perform	
Industrial	IYJ	FIDU	FCYIX	FBALC
Material	VAW	FMAT	FSDPX	
	IYM			
Oil	USO			
Oil Service	OIH		FSESX	
Oil Exploration	XOP			
Real Estate	VNQ		FRIFX	FFWLC
REIT	VNQ			
Retail	RTH		FSRPX	
	XRT			
Regional bank	KRE		FSRBX	
Semi Conduct	SMH			
Software	XSW		FSCSX	
	IGV			
Technology	XLK	FTEC	FSPTX	FYENC
	FDN		FBSOX	
			ROGSX	
Telecomm.	VOX	FCOM	FSTCX	FVTAC
Transport	XTN			
	IYT			
Utilities	XLU	FUTY	FSUTX	FKMSC
Wireless			FWRLX	

Footnote. [1] Also check Finance.

2   Quick analysis of ETFs

Evaluate an ETF
ETFs are a basket of stocks according to a specific sector, country or a specific theme.

Yahoo!Finance used to give the P/E of an ETF. Try to get it from ETFdb.com. Enter the symbol of the ETF such as XLU. It displays its historical P/E (last twelve months). If it is below 15 and above zero, it could be a value ETF. Also, if the current price is lower than its NAV, it is sold at a discount (or premium vice versa). Compare its YTD Return to SPY's.

Alternatively, get it from http://www.multpl.com/. In addition, this web site provides the following metrics: Shiller P/E, Price/Sales, and Price/Book.

From Finviz.com, enter the ETF symbol. If SMA-20%, SMA-50% and SMA-200% are all positive, most likely the ETF is in an uptrend. To illustrate, SMA-200 is Simple Moving Average for the last 200 trading sessions (no trading on weekends and specific holidays). The percent is how much the stock price of the ETF is above the SMA. If the percent is negative, it means the stock price is below the SMA.

For example, if your average holding period is about 50 days, SMA-50% is more appropriate to you.

If RSI(14) > 65, it is probably over-sold; if it is < 30, it is probably under-sold (i.e. value).

In addition, ensure the average volume is high (I suggest more than 10,000 shares), also the market cap is more than 200 M, and it has low fees. Most popular ETFs have these characteristics. Avoid the leveraged ETFs for now.

How to determine if the sector has been recovered

It is easier to profit by following the uptrend of an ETF using the above info. It is hard to detect when the bottom of an ETF has been reached. If SMA-20%, SMA-50% and SMA-200% are all positive, most likely the ETF is in an uptrend or it has recovered. It does not always happen as predicted, so use stops to protect your investment.

An example

This example illustrates how to evaluate ETFs. First, determine whether the market is risky. Most beginners should not invest in a risky market. Advanced investors can bet against the market or a specific sector by buying contra ETFs or puts.

Next, you want to limit the number of sector ETFs by selecting those that are either in an uptrend or hitting bottom (bottom is hard to predict). Personally I prefer sectors with long-term uptrends (indicated by cnnfn.com). Seeking Alpha has many current articles on ETFs.

Today's market (as of 2/5/2016) is risky. For illustration purposes only, I select the following ETFs: SPY (simulating the market based on large companies), XLP (consumer staples) and XLY (consumer discretionary). XLP should perform better than XLY during a recession as those products are the necessities.

Technical indicators such as SMA-50 (Simple Moving Average for the last 50 sessions), SMA-200 and RSI(14) are from Finviz.com and the rest are from Yahoo!Finance.com. After you buy the ETF, use a stop loss to protect your investment. Bio tech sector moved up for many months until it crashed later in 2015.

As of 2/5/2016	SPY	XLP (staples)	XLY (discret.)
Price	190	50	71
NAV	192	50	73
• Technical			
SMA-50	-4%	0%	-7%
SMA-200	-6%	2%	-7%
RSI(14)	44	50	36
Other	Double bottom at $186		
• Fundamental			
P/E	17	20	19
Yield	2.1%	2.5%	1.5%
YTD return	-5%	0.5%	-5%
Net asset	174 B	9 B	10 B

Explanation

- The figures may not be identical from the two web sites due to the dates they are using.

- XLY has best discount among the 3 ETFs as most investors believe a recession is coming.
- XLP has less down trend among the 3 ETFs as expected.
- XLY is more undersold among the 3 as expected.
- Double bottom is a technical pattern that indicates the stock would surge upward.
- SPY has a better value according to its P/E.
- XLY's dividend is the least among the 3 as they have more tech companies in the ETF. They have to plow back the profits to research and development.
- XLP has the best YTD return among the 3.
- As long as the asset is above 500 M (200 M for specialized ETFs), it is fine and all three pass this mark.

3   Sectors to be cautious with

There are many reasons to be very cautious when investing in the following sectors. However, Technical Analysis (a.k.a. charting) would give you more hints than the fundamentals for stocks in these sectors.

Loan companies/banks

The financial statements do not show the quality of their loan portfolios. Following this advice, you may be able to skip the banks that melted down in 2007. The peak of Citigroup is $550 and several banks went bankrupt.

Drug (generic is ok)

Understanding the complexities of the drug pipelines, its potential profits for new drugs and the expiration of its current drugs may not be worth the effort for most retail investors. In addition, a serious lawsuit and / or a serious problem with a drug could wipe out a good percentage of the stock price. When a drug shows unpromising sign(s) in any trial phase, the stock could plunge and vice versa.

Miners

It is extremely difficult to estimate how much ore (sometimes a miner owns several different types of ores and/or of different grades in the same or different mines) that the company has. It is further complicated by the complexities to extract and transport them. When the total of these costs is greater than its production price, the company will not be profitable. Understanding the market for ore futures is another discipline.

Many mining companies are in foreign countries such as Canada, Australia and countries in South America. Their financial statements of Canada and Australia are more trustworthy than those from most other emerging countries.

One potential problem of mining companies from many emerging countries is nationalization.

Mining rare earth ore is extremely risky when the profit depends on how China, a major producer of these ores, will price its ores. After China announced the export restrictions on rare earth elements, several non-Chinese companies announced to reopen their mines for rare earths but few have made any profits as of 2013. Developed countries have stricter environmental regulations.

Coal suffers from the rising use of cleaner oil and gas.

Insurance companies

Insurance companies profit by:

1. The difference between the total premiums received and the total claims minus expenses in running the company.

2. How well they invest your premiums; you pay your premiums earlier than you may collect from the claims.

They can protect the profits in #1 by restricting claims by natural disasters such as earthquakes and by re-insuring. However, a bad disaster could wipe out a lot of their profits.

Even if the insurance company shows you its investment portfolio, most of us, the retail investors, do not have the time and expertise to analyze it.

Emerging countries (not a sector)
Their financial statements especially from small companies cannot be trusted and many countries use different accounting standards. Emerging

countries are where the economic growth is. I trade FXI, an ETF, rather than individual Chinese companies. I have lost a lot in small Chinese companies due to fraud. To check out whether the stock is an ADR, try ADR.COM. https://www.adr.com/

Stocks with low volumes (not a sector)
Most likely you pay a high spread to trade these stocks. They can be manipulated easier. I remember when I had a hard time trying to sell a stock of this kind. The majority of this company is owned by one person.

For simplicity, I trade stocks with the average daily trade volume over 6,000 shares (double it if the price is $2 or less). A better way could be in calculating the percent of your trade quantity / average daily trade volume to reduce the effect of penny stocks that have larger volumes due to the low prices. You need special skills to trade these stocks but it could be very profitable.

Good business and bad business

Banking is a good business. My deposit in them makes virtually zero interest, and they loan the same money making 3%. If they are more selective in loaning my money, they should make a good profit.

Restaurant is an easy business to open/run, but it is very hard to make good money. With the rising of minimal wages, it will get even tougher. That could be the reason for so many coupons today. The high-end restaurants are doing better due to the rising stock market. As of 8/2014, the new comers Noodles & Company (NDLS) and Potbelly (PBPB) are not doing very well.

Retailing is a tough business. Look at the top 10 retailers 15 years ago, I can only find two including Macy's that are still surviving. Most are either bankrupt or being acquired. Even Macy's was at one time in financial trouble.

Airlines are a tough business. You can tell by the average increase in fares in the last 10 years. It cannot even beat inflation. They have to charge you for everything. The next frontier charge is the rest room (especially for long-distance flights). Now I understand why they call themselves "Frontier Air". As of 2014, it is quite profitable due to mergers and lower fuel cost.

There are several software companies that produce software such as the virus detecting programs and tax preparation software. The customers faithfully buy new versions every year. That's great business.

Afterthoughts

As of 8/2013, is the emerging market oversold?
http://seekingalpha.com/article/1658252-have-emerging-markets-gotten-oversold
When an index of an emerging market is up by 10% and the currency exchange rate to USD is down by 20%, then it is not profitable.

Links

Nationalization:
http://en.wikipedia.org/wiki/Nationalization
Spread:
http://en.wikipedia.org/wiki/Bid-offer_spread
Insurance:http://seekingalpha.com/article/1239671-property-casualty-insurance-and-reinsurance-what-you-need-to-know

4   TA for sector rotation, reentry & peak

There are 3 uses of TA for sector rotation.

1. Detect sector plunge and when to reenter the market after plunges.
2. Regular use (usually after its recovery from a plunge).
3. Detect market plunges and/or sector plunges.

#3 has been described on the chapter Spotting Market Plunges and it will not be repeated here.

The difference in #1 and #2 is in the number of days in SMA (Single Moving Average). Use 350 for sector plunge and reentry.

Use 30, 60, 90 or 120 for regular use (i.e. after the reentry from a market plunge) depending on how frequently you rotate. If you rotate in 60 days, use 60 for the average of number of days.

Exit / Reenter a sector ETF

To illustrate, the following example uses XHB (an ETF for the housing sector). Use the same chart for other sector ETFs such as VGK for Europe.

Produce the following chart by using Yahoo!Finance. Enter XHB and select Interactive Chart. Select SMA and then 350 days. Select Max for 'From'.

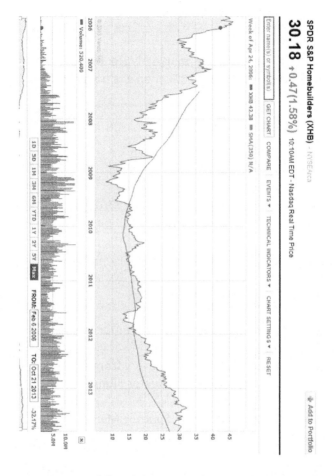

Source: Yahoo!Finance. XHB on 350 SMA.

- Exit when the price falls below the red, single-moving average (the SMA) and enter when it is over the SMA. All the dates and prices are approximate and for illustration only.

- I use Max for the period. Let's assume the chart instructed us to exit at $45 around 2006 and reenter on August, 2009 missing a loss of about $30 per share. Not too bad!

- There are brief exits and reentries before 2012. I call it noises. The gains and losses are negligible. However, make sure you exit and also reenter. If you use 60 days instead of 350 days in this example, you have more noises. If you trade the ETF more often, then you use 60 or 90 days. It depends on your risk tolerance and your time to trade. Sometimes the performance makes a difference in selecting shorter days, but not all the time.

- From the end of 2012 to today (10-2013), it gains more than 40% compared to -32% for the period for buy-and-hold. A difference of 62%! Even a difference of 10% would be great.

- The chart works at least for this period. It is every one's guess whether it will still work in the future. I bet it will but as in life nothing is guaranteed.

- When a housing stock, the housing sector (XHB) and the general stock market all above their respective SMAs, the stock most likely will appreciate (again nothing is guaranteed).

- From my other chapters, the offending sector (housing and finance for 2007 market plunge) takes about two years to recover from the bottom.

  I interpreted the bottom was 10-2007, so the recovery would start in 10-2009. If you bought XHB in 10-2009, you would have gained about 100% today (10-22-2013).

- Some sectors never recover such as the internet and some high tech companies in 2000.

Now, it is your turn to try out the chart. This time, use 60 for the number of days in SMA.

Afterthoughts

- We have discussed how to use TA to spot market crashes and individual stocks. TA can help us to determine a sector. For my purpose, I usually use 90-day moving average on an ETF for that industry, but 350-day moving average for detecting sector plunges / reentries.

- The big boys (hedge fund managers) moved their money into GOOG and AMZN solely to make a ton of cash when AAPL reached $700 and they will move their investment out of AMZN (too high value as of 1-2013) or GOOG back into AAPL.

Instead of fighting the big movers, join them by using the tool of TA. Make good money by winning the second place of a horse race.

- A stock will always go up and down for more than several days in a row. Take advantage of the trend and make some quick money if you are a short-term trader.

- If all the following are above the single moving average (SMA) line, most likely (most and not all) the stock price will rise in next month:

    1. 350-day SMA of SPY (representing the market).
    2. 60-day (or 90-day) SMA of the sector ETF that represents the sector the stock is in.
    3. 30-day SMA (or 20 for some folks) of the stock and it passes our (or your) scoring system.

Most technicians use 20, 50 and 200 days for moving averages for stocks. To save you time, use finviz.com to obtain the % of the stock deviates from its moving averages. When it is positive, it is usually a buy.

- Norman:
With cyclical dividend paying stocks, entry and exit points can be equivalent to yield. For example buy CAT at 3% yield and sell it at 1% yield.

- A book mentioned to me on TA: Stan Weinstein's book, "Secrets for Profiting in Bull & Bear Markets".

- If you are a customer of Fidelity, try the option to include all indicators in charting a stock. To illustrate of using index S&P500, use .SPX (^GSPC in Yahoo!Finance).

- Sectors can also be divided by market cap. Use the same charts to find the trend of small cap for example.

- When TA tells you to sell a stock, try to find the reasons by using google, SeekingAlpha, Yahoo!Finance board, calling the company, etc.

- More related articles.

Based on performance.
http://stockcharts.com/help/doku.php?id=chart_school:trading_strategies:sector_rotation_roc

Fidelity.
https://www.fidelity.com/learning-center/trading-investing/markets-sectors/sector-rotation-introduction

A subscription service.
http://www.sectortimingreport.com/articles/sector-rotation.html

Fillers:

Rocket stocks

As of 3/2014, TSLA, AMAZ, NFLX are all over-priced by most fundamental metrics. However, they are the darlings of institutional investors. My advice is not to short them as you cannot fight the city hall. If you're the lucky owners, use trailing stops to protect your profit. They will plunge when they are no longer the darlings of the institutional investors – they do rotate as they did to Apple.

Fillers:

My doctor asked me to try an experimental drug to cure my psoriasis. The drug is so strong that it would kill me. However, in either case, my psoriasis will be cured.

Strategy 4: Sectors in a market cycle

Here are the favorable sectors in different phases of a market cycle. Here is my suggestion:

Market Phase	Favorable	Unfavorable
Early Recovery	Financial, Technology, Industrial	Energy, Telecom, Utilities
Up	Technology, Industrial, Housing	
Peak	Mineral, Health Care, Energy, Long-Term Bond, Consumer Discretionary	
Bottom	Consumer Staples, Utilities	Consumer Discretionary, Technology, Industrial, Long-Term & high-yield Bond

The sectors that cause the recession usually take longer time to recover. In 2000, the technology sector was not favorable in the Early Recovery phase, contrary to the above table. In 2007, the financial sector was not favorable in the Early Recovery phase. These are the "offending" sectors that cause the plunges.

In a recession, we usually cannot cut down on consumer staples and utilities, but we can cut down buying consumer gadgets. Companies usually postpone investing in equipment and systems during a recession and expand when the economy is humming.

All the description in Section I and III apply here. The next chapter describes the market cycle and how I define he phases of a market cycle.

1   Market cycle

"Bull markets are born on pessimism, grow on skepticism, mature on optimism, and die on euphoria" - Sir John Templeton

The stock market has cycles as our practical interpretation of the above. It is about five years apart, but it fluctuates widely. I divide it into four stages: Bottom, Early Recovery, Up and Peak.

My defined four stages of a market cycle

We need to apply the right investing strategies to each of the four stages of the cycle.

- **Bottom**

  I would not invest for at least the first six months (or even a year) after the big plunge starts, which could lose over 25% in a few months. The exceptions are investing in contra ETFs and selling short for aggressive investors.

  I estimate it will take a year from the start of the plunge to the bottom, so I will normally sell stocks early in the plunge and do not buy stocks that are in the sector (sometimes sectors) that causes the bubble for about two years after the plunge.

  At the bottom, the high-yield corporate bonds (i.e. junk bonds) would prosper when the interest rates is decreasing to stimulate the economy.

  From mid-2007 to mid-2008, bonds suffered as the investors thought the sky was falling down - it was to those who lost the jobs and/or their houses. After that, some bonds especially the long-term bonds appreciated about 50% for the following year.

  The government lowered the interest rates and these bond prices with high interest rates surged. Correct timing in buying bonds could be very profitable.

  Long-term bonds have more impact by the interest rate: The lower the interest rate, the higher the bond prices of higher-yield bonds. The older bonds with higher interest rates are more valuable to the newer bonds with lower interest rates.

I define this period of the bottom from the start of the plunge to the start of Early Recovery.

- **Early Recovery**

It usually starts after one year from the plunge; no one can pin point the exact time consistently. By this time preferably earlier, we should have closed out all positions in contra ETFs and shorts.

Roughly speaking, October, 2007 (some use 2008) is the start of the market plunge. March, 2009 is the end of the bottom stage and the start of the early recovery stage of the 2007 cycle. However, every market cycle is different in where it starts and ends.

The one-year gain from the bottom is most profitable. It usually gains over 25% in a year from the market bottom. I, a conservative investor, had huge gains using some leverage in my largest taxable account in 2009. From my memory, I had a similar return in 2003 but I had not saved the statement as in 2009.

In this phase, value is a better parameter than growth in searching for stocks. If your investment subscription provides a composite value score and a composite timing score, the sort parameter of your screened stocks could be "Composite Value / Composite Timing" in descending order. Select the top stocks in this order. You still have to analyze the top-screened stocks.

Forward (same as Expected) P/E is a good metric. However, most companies may be losing money at this stage. Those companies that can last for more than one year with its cash reserve are potential good buys. The best appreciated stocks are beaten companies that have precious technologies and good customer bases. They could be candidates to be acquired if they are small enough.

- **Up**

Usually the growth metrics such as PEG could be better than the value metrics such as expected P/E during this phase. Most stocks are winners except contra ETFs and shorting stocks. When the growth stocks are making headlines and the defensive stocks are being dumped, this is the hint that we're well into the Up phase of the market cycle.

Locate stocks with growth metrics such as favorable PEG and high SMA-200% (from Finviz.com). Do not be scared on how much they have already appreciated. The strategy "Buy High and Sell Higher" works in this phase. Protect your profits with stops.

Ensure that they have value too. Skip the stocks with expected P/Es higher than 35 unless there are good reasons. Most stocks will gain due to the tide of the market. However, when they're overbought (RSI(14) over 60), be careful. When institutional investors sell these stocks, they will crash.

- **Peak**

When everyone makes easy money and the interest rates is high, watch out. Stop loss and/or stop limit should be used to protect your investment. Check out whether there is any bubble that would be burst like the internet in 2000 and the finance (and housing) in 2007.

Internet crisis is easy to spot, but not the financial crisis. In 2007 we had a cycle longer than the average which is about 5 years. The plunge is very fast and very steep – thanks to the institutional investors who drive the market down.

Run the technical analysis chart described in the Chapter on Spotting Big Market Plunges at least monthly (weekly if you have time). Protect your investment. Do not fall in love with any stock (you can buy it back later at a deep discount). Making the last buck is a fool's game.

Accumulate cash according to your risk tolerance. A retiree or a conservative investor would accumulate from 25% to 50% and should be ready to move to all cash when the plunge starts.

We can lower the cash percent if we use enough stop loss protection. Be psychologically prepared because the stock market may still rise for a while. There is no perfect market timing.

The 2007 Cycle

The market plunged starting in 10-2007 and ending in 3-2009 (bottom), started to recover in 3-2009 (early recover), and trended up from 2010 to 1-2013 (the up phase of the market cycle). As of 3/2016, it is the peak phase defined by me.

As of 1/2013, we have recovered all the market losses since 2007. However, as of 7/2014, the economy has not fully recovered compared to the economy before the plunge. The employment judging by the medium salary has not fully recovered and the economy is not expanding. It is uncommon that the economy does not follow the market. It is due to the excessive supply of money by the government and partly due to globalization to allow companies to hire overseas.

Although a W-shaped recession seldom happens, we have a chance today. We hope we do not have a depression and/or the similar lost decades that Japan has been experiencing. Some may conclude we are close to completing a market cycle from 2007 to 2016. As of 2016, the economy is recovering slowly and we're better than most other global economies.

Again, market timing is not an exact science as it involves irrational human beings and government interventions. The timing using market cycle described here is a guideline as it is hard to time it exactly.

The average market cycle is about 5 years, but they fluctuate. If we consider 2007 as the plunge, we have about 8 years of this cycle as of 2015.

In a typical cycle (few are typical), we have about one year in each of the 4 phases I defined (plunge, early recovery, up and peak).

Events/Triggers

There are financial events and triggers that cause the transition of one phase of the market cycle to another. They usually do not change the sequence of the phases (say not from Peak to Early Recovery), but they may change the duration of the phase. Examples are:

- The government announcing change of the interest rate,
- Change of employment, and
- Change of GNP.

Sectors in a market cycle (my suggestion)

Market Phase	Favorable		Unfavorable
Early Recovery	Financial, Technology, Industrial		Energy, Telecom, Utilities
Up	Technology, Industrial, Housing		
Peak	Mineral, Health Care, Energy, Long-Term Bond, Consumer Discretionary		
Bottom	Consumer Staples, Utilities		Consumer Discretionary, Technology, Industrial, Long-Term & high-yield Bond

The sectors that cause the recession usually take a longer time to recover. In 2000, the technology sector was not favorable in the Early Recovery phase, contrary to the above table. In 2007, the financial sector was not favorable in the Early Recovery phase. These are the "offending" sectors that cause the plunges.

In a recession, we usually cannot cut down on consumer staples and utilities, but we can cut down on buying consumer gadgets. Companies usually postpone investing in equipment and systems during a recession and expand when the economy is humming. The government usually lowers the interest rates right after the plunge to stimulate the economy.

Conclusion

When the market is about to plunge or change from one stage to another, run the described chart more frequently and read more articles written by the experts.

Again, market timing is not an exact science but it is based on educated guesses. The better guesses should have more rights than wrongs in the long term. Our actions depend on our risk tolerance. Be careful on using any new strategy that has not been fully understood and proven. Since 2000, market timing is very important to your financial health with two market plunges with an average of about 45% loss.

Afterthoughts

- The Dow Theory has a lot of followers in detecting market directions. In a nutshell, the market heading upwards is confirmed by the Industrial Index and the Transportation Index (less important in today's market especially with internet sales such as songs and movies), and vice versa. As of 4/2014, the two indexes are not in uniform.
  http://finance.yahoo.com/blogs/talking-numbers/this-is-a-130-year-old-warning-sign-for-stocks-231901097.html

  - The bear market has the following three phases.

  1. The market is over-valued.
  2. Corporations are not doing well with decreasing earnings and sales.
  3. Investors are selling due to fears.

  It is the reverse for a bull market: 1.The market is under-valued. 2. The market increases due to increasing corporate profits/sales and 3. Investors are buying due to greed.

- Investopedia has several articles on this topic.
  http://www.investopedia.com/terms/b/businesscycle.asp

- The yield curve could predict the interest rates change and hence the economy. There are three main types of yield curve shapes: normal, flat and inverted.

  A normal yield curve is one in which longer maturity bonds have a higher yield. Similarly the long-term CD should have a higher interest rates than the short-term CD.

  When the shorter-term yields are higher than the longer-term yields, it indicates an upcoming recession. A flat yield curve indicates the economy is transiting. Now, you've read the essence of a book on this topic costing about $50 to buy.

  However especially today, it does not mean anything as the government supplies too much money to stimulate the economy unsuccessfully. My simple chart described using SMA-350 (Simple Moving Average for 350 trading sessions) which depends on the stock price works better.

Click here for "The dynamic yield curve" (http://stockcharts.com/freecharts/yieldcurve.php).

The interest rates plays a role too. The easy money encourages folks to borrow money to buy stocks and companies to acquire other companies.

- As of Feb., 2013, I believe we're in the Up stage of the market cycle. I checked the performances of my top screens from each stage (a.k.a. phase) of the market cycle for the last 60 days. The best performance as a group belongs to the screens for the Up stage. Controversial! Always use the screens (same as searches) that perform well recently.

  In addition, the market has recovered 120% of the loss of 2007-2008. Hence the duration for an average Up stage of the market is quite close.

- Total Market Cap / GNP ratio is hotly debated on the market value. Different from the traditional 100%, I would suggest that the boundary ratio should be 130%. If it is over 130%, the market is over-valued and vice versa.
  http://www.investopedia.com/terms/m/marketcapgdp.asp

2 Sectors according to the business cycle

Market Cycle is usually ahead of the Business (economic) cycle by 6 months as a rough prediction. In the 2008 market cycle, it is not due to the excessive printing of money.

During a recession some sectors such as Consumer Staples and Health Care work better than other sectors such as Technology. They will be opposite from above during the go-go era when consumers have more money to buy non-essential goods and companies have money to invest.

Some industries could be peaking due to over production and/or diminishing demand of their products. It happens frequently in electronic chips. In my town, at one time we did not have enough super markets. Suddenly they built three new ones at the same year. After a few years, one was closed.

Some sectors are more volatile than others. Some sectors such as Health Care would be benefited by the growing or aging global population. The favorable sectors for the down phase lose their values less than the unfavorable sectors when the market plunges.

Sectors	Major Industries	Favorable
Basic Materials	Metals, Mining, Chemicals	High inflation / Growing economy
Consumer Discretionary	Auto, Building, High-end Retail	Low interest rate
Consumer Staples	Food	Recession
Energy	Oil, Gas, Exploration	Growing economy
Industrial	Machines	Economic recovery
Health Care	Delivery, Drugs, Biotech	Recession for Delivery
Financial	Bank, Insurance	High interest, Growing economy
Technology	Computer, software	Growing economy
Utilities	Electricity, Gas	Recession

The following is from Fidelity. As of 4/2019, Fidelity identifies the current business cycle is in the Late phase.

Sector Performance by Business Cycle Phase

The table below shows how sectors have tended to perform in each stage of the business cycle. For more information on sector performance patterns, read The Business Cycle Approach to Sector Investing (PDF).

Sector ▲	Early	Mid	Late	Recession
Comm	--			++
Consumer Discretionary	++		--	
Consumer Staples	-		+	++
Energy	--		++	
Financials	+			
Health Care	-		++	++
Industrials	++	+		--
Info Technology	++	+	--	--
Materials		--	++	-
Real Estate*	++			--
Utilities	--	-	+	++

++ Consistently Overperform	-- Consistently Underperform	No Clear Pattern
+ Overperform	- Underperform	

#Filler: Accidental genius

In the recent rise, I moved 80% of my annuity to cash. After that day, the market was still climbing. I looked like a fool. Now an accidental genius! :). The moral of the story: The market fluctuates and do not let it influence your mood.

3   Actions for different stages of a market cycle

There are different strategies for the different stages of the market cycle.

Strategies during market plunges

The market plunge is defined as the period between the market peak and the market bottom. It usually lasts for one year or two.

When you spot the potential plunge, consider the following actions. It depends on your risk tolerance and your investment style.

1. Contrary to popular belief, parking cash is a strategy too. Cash is needed later to move back to equities.

2. Be conservative: Buy stocks based on value and not based on momentum. Reduce your new purchases and take profits especially on momentum stocks. I buy one stock for every two or three stocks I sold during this stage.

3. Protect your portfolio with stop orders. It is one of the few times I recommend stop orders. If you watch the market every day, just place market orders when your stock falls to a specific price.

4. Buy contra ETFs for aggressive investors.

5. Sell cover calls. I prefer to sell the stocks I own.

6. Older folks may not want to sell the stocks with huge gains (due to tax consideration) or stocks that give them income stream of dividends. They can use options to protect potential losses for the stocks they own.

What to do after the plunge

In the first year after the start of the plunge, do not start to buy unless they are very good values. Aggressive investors should start closing their short positions/put options and selling contra ETFs.

When the market plunges, it usually takes at least one year to recover as investors believe they have to sell to protect their remaining nest eggs. Those sectors that cause the bubble will take even longer to recover.

After the plunge, watch out for the interest rate. If it is still high, it is the best time to buy high-yield bonds (i.e. junk bonds). Ensure that the corporation issuing the bonds would not bankrupt; the bonds from the old GM in 2007 lost most of their values. They will appreciate when the interest rates drops that the government would routinely do to stimulate the economy. 2008 is not a good year to invest in stocks and bonds except the contra ETFs and selling shorts, but 2009 definitely is (it is my Early Recovery phase of the market cycle).

Personally I prefer not to buy any stocks until the chart tells us to reenter the market. It is the fear that investors do not want to reenter the market. The market will always recover as in the past history.

Even before the recovery, some sectors (called consumer staple) are doing better such as health care, foodstuffs, utilities and pharmaceuticals that are always in demand. Interest-sensitive sectors such as housing and auto will suffer disproportionately. They are also called cyclical stocks. Consumer Discretionary are sectors that suffer a lot in a recession such as high tech products.

What to do in early recovery and after

When the market is starting to recovery (2003 and 2009 in the last two market cycles), the potential profit is the highest. Buy deeply-valued stocks on companies that have been beaten down. They will recover with the highest appreciation potential. I call it the bottom fishing strategy.

Larger companies are fishing too to acquire smaller companies that fit into their corporate synergy or small companies with the technology and/or the customer base they need.

Valued stocks could be defined a little differently in this phase. Many times P/E is not a good metric as most companies are losing money. 2003 is such a year. If you expect the recession will end in 2 years and the company has enough cash to survive in two years based on its annual burn rate, then it would be a buy candidate.

In both 2003 and 2009, I spotted at least one company that was acquired by a larger company. From my memory, one company in 2003 was acquired by

IBM giving me more than 2 times return. In 2009, at least three companies were acquired giving me an average annualized return of over 200%.

Momentum strategy rewards us best from the end of the early recovery phase to the peak phase. The up phase started in 2004 for 2000 market cycle and 2010 in the 2007 market cycle.

Note. The parameters of SMA-200, SMA-350, SMA-90, etc. and RSI are different for market exit/reentry, correction exit and individual stocks. These are the guidelines only. Stocks are more volatile than the market and are very different among them. Hence, define the 'days' according to the historical pattern of the individual stock and how often you trade them.

Filler: My translation from my Chinese friend's poem

When you understand "everything is changing", you won't be boosting your achievements. Today's splendid life could be a mess tomorrow.

When you understand "everything is changing", you won't be sad. Today's gloom could turn into sunshine tomorrow.

When you understand "everything is changing", you know today's gain could be tomorrow's loss and vice versa.

When you understand "everything is changing", there is no need to react to today's loss, gain, happiness and sadness.3   Actions for different stages of a market cycle

There are different strategies for the different stages of the market cycle.

Strategies during market plunges

The market plunge is defined as the period between the market peak and the market bottom. It usually lasts for one year or two.

When you spot the potential plunge, consider the following actions. It depends on your risk tolerance and your investment style.

7.   Contrary to popular belief, parking cash is a strategy too. Cash is needed later to move back to equities.

8. Be conservative: Buy stocks based on value and not based on momentum. Reduce your new purchases and take profits especially on momentum stocks. I buy one stock for every two or three stocks I sold during this stage.

9. Protect your portfolio with stop orders. It is one of the few times I recommend stop orders. If you watch the market every day, just place market orders when your stock falls to a specific price.

10. Buy contra ETFs for aggressive investors.

11. Sell cover calls. I prefer to sell the stocks I own.

12. Older folks may not want to sell the stocks with huge gains (due to tax consideration) or stocks that give them income stream of dividends. They can use options to protect potential losses for the stocks they own.

What to do after the plunge

In the first year after the start of the plunge, do not start to buy unless they are very good values. Aggressive investors should start closing their short positions/put options and selling contra ETFs.

When the market plunges, it usually takes at least one year to recover as investors believe they have to sell to protect their remaining nest eggs. Those sectors that cause the bubble will take even longer to recover.

After the plunge, watch out for the interest rate. If it is still high, it is the best time to buy high-yield bonds (i.e. junk bonds). Ensure that the corporation issuing the bonds would not bankrupt; the bonds from the old GM in 2007 lost most of their values. They will appreciate when the interest rates drops that the government would routinely do to stimulate the economy. 2008 is not a good year to invest in stocks and bonds except the contra ETFs and selling shorts, but 2009 definitely is (it is my Early Recovery phase of the market cycle).

Personally I prefer not to buy any stocks until the chart tells us to reenter the market. It is the fear that investors do not want to reenter the market. The market will always recover as in the past history.

Even before the recovery, some sectors (called consumer staple) are doing better such as health care, foodstuffs, utilities and pharmaceuticals that are always in demand. Interest-sensitive sectors such as housing and auto will suffer disproportionately. They are also called cyclical stocks. Consumer Discretionary are sectors that suffer a lot in a recession such as high tech products.

What to do in early recovery and after

When the market is starting to recovery (2003 and 2009 in the last two market cycles), the potential profit is the highest. Buy deeply-valued stocks on companies that have been beaten down. They will recover with the highest appreciation potential. I call it the bottom fishing strategy.

Larger companies are fishing too to acquire smaller companies that fit into their corporate synergy or small companies with the technology and/or the customer base they need.

Valued stocks could be defined a little differently in this phase. Many times P/E is not a good metric as most companies are losing money. 2003 is such a year. If you expect the recession will end in 2 years and the company has enough cash to survive in two years based on its annual burn rate, then it would be a buy candidate.

In both 2003 and 2009, I spotted at least one company that was acquired by a larger company. From my memory, one company in 2003 was acquired by IBM giving me more than 2 times return. In 2009, at least three companies were acquired giving me an average annualized return of over 200%.

Momentum strategy rewards us best from the end of the early recovery phase to the peak phase. The up phase started in 2004 for 2000 market cycle and 2010 in the 2007 market cycle.

Note. The parameters of SMA-200, SMA-350, SMA-90, etc. and RSI are different for market exit/reentry, correction exit and individual stocks. These are the guidelines only. Stocks are more volatile than the market and are very different among them. Hence, define the 'days' according to the historical pattern of the individual stock and how often you trade them.

Filler: My translation from my Chinese friend's poem

When you understand "everything is changing", you won't be boosting your achievements. Today's splendid life could be a mess tomorrow.

When you understand "everything is changing", you won't be sad. Today's gloom could turn into sunshine tomorrow.

When you understand "everything is changing", you know today's gain could be tomorrow's loss and vice versa.

When you understand "everything is changing", there is no need to react to today's loss, gain, happiness and sadness.

29   Market timing by asset class

Two major trading strategies are:
1. Buy high and sell higher.
    It is a kind of momentum play. You may keep these stocks for less time (say, less than three months). The momentum could change very fast. In my momentum portfolio, I keep most of my stocks less than a month.
2. Buy low and sell high.
    When the asset class is totally out-of-favor and it has high value, buy it. It is a value play. You are swimming against the tide. You need to hold these stocks longer (say, longer than 6 months) for the market to realize its value.

It is not possible to predict correctly the peaks and bottoms of any asset class consistently. However, #1 usually starts first and followed by #2. The holding period is just a suggestion.

Your success will be improved by using technical analysis correctly. Try the 50-day moving average (actually the last 50 trade sessions) to start with. Buy when it is above the moving average and sell when it is below. Next, try the 20-day moving average and many other technical analysis indicators such as exponential moving average and different days for the moving averages. The moving averages are available from Finviz.com without charting.

Basically there is a tradeoff on switching too frequently and reacting too late. Some stocks are more volatile than others.

Try out different asset classes such as gold and oil. To illustrate, no one can predict that a gold price at $1800 is the peak. If you buy gold coins at $1000 and ride the gold wagon to $1600, you're doing quite well. In this case, trade GLD, the ETF fund for gold for technical analysis. The way to protect your profit and let the profit rise is using stops. Adjust the stop when the asset appreciates.

My experience in gold

I had gold coins bought at about $400 each many years ago. Gold did not appreciate much for over 20 years. When its price rose to $800, I sold some. I made 100% return, but it may not even beat inflation. If I invested in stocks instead of gold coins, I would be far better off in total return (appreciation plus dividends). When gold rose to $1000, I sold more. Our rational thinking (part of human nature) would not allow us to hold these coins until $1,800. The moral is no one can predict the peak value of an asset and act accordingly.

Trading coins in your local shops would cost you a lot (commission and the spread) but it is safer. The coin shops do report your sales to the IRS if the sell is below a certain amount. Check the current rule.

4   Profitable Early Recovery

I had an 80% return in 2009 in my largest taxable account. I did not include it in my other books before as I just found the statement. Early Recovery, a phase of the market cycle defined by me, is the best time to make a profit. My chart told me to start to move to equity in September, 2009. I did in March, 2009 with other reasons. It could be luck, technique or both.

I did dip into the credit line of my equity loan (not recommended to most) due to lower interest rates than a margin interest. I paid back the loan right after I sold some stocks. The turnaround was high until I exhausted my short-term losses (tax loss harvest). The strategy is bottom fishing. Some sectors described are better in this stage of the market cycle.

I had similar success in 2003. I did not have a defined bottom fishing technique at that time. I expected the market to be fully recovered in two years. From Value Line, I selected stocks with high "Projected 3-5 year returns" and the short-term assets can last for two more years (judged by the burnt rates).

As the stocks are recovering earnings (E), the trailing P/E may not be a good indicator, but the Forward P/E may be. Most sites on evaluating stocks such as Blue Chip Growth have a value grade. Also look for candidates for acquisition. From the last recoveries, I spotted at least one such candidate. They are usually small companies (50 to 300M market cap) and have valuable assets such as customer base, technologies...

Strategy 5: Country sectors

The current events as of 5/2014, Russia (Ukraine incident) and S.E. Asia (the Vietnam riots) are not good countries to invest at least for the next two or three years. However, Vietnam with low wages could be the next China. As of 2016, the US is still a good place to invest. Again Section I and Section III apply here also. For example, use the P/E to evaluate an ETF corresponding to this country.

1   My Coconut Theory

Coconut Theory

In a tropical island, every one sleeps under a coconut tree assigned to him. He wakes up only when a coconut falls on his head once in a while. He eats the coconut and goes back to sleep. He is lazy due to the nice weather (no need to find shelter) and the nice resource (the coconut tree). He is happy and rich by his own standard. However, he is lazy, fat, and stupid due to the lack of any need to work, exercise, and think out of his 'perfect' environment.

The worst that happens to the natives is borrowing coconuts from other natives with the coconut tree as collateral or cut down the coconut tree to make a canoe without plans to replenish coconuts in the future.

This is a simple theory. It can be used to explain how and why many countries are rich, poor, and continue to be so. Let's check how this theory stacks up with countries.

It also explains why people migrate to places with lots of coconuts. It is demonstrated by Chinese during war time to South East Asia and the Irish moving to the US during potato famine.

U.S.A.

The U.S. is one of the richest countries due to its development, highly educated citizens, hard-working immigrants and the huge natural resources per capita (i.e. having a lot of coconuts in my theory). The U.S. is declining as we spend more time enjoying our wealth (borrowing coconuts so he can eat more) rather than creating more wealth (i.e. not planting new coconut trees in my theory).

The wealth is equivalent to the bountiful of coconut trees that were available originally and the many that were planted by our ancestors. There were fewer natives to consume the total number of coconuts, so there was a surplus of coconuts grown, eventually to be given away (as welfare and entitlements). Many of our citizens have no incentive to plant more coconut trees (work) when they have unlimited coconuts to them (generous welfare).

Because of WW2, most coconut trees in the world were destroyed while ours were isolated from the war. We were rich to ship our better coconuts to the rest of the world.

God gave us plenty of natural resources, good soil and climatic wealth (coconuts hidden under the land) and hopefully we continue to be wealthy. Unfortunately, we're now consumers (of coconuts) instead of producers (planting new coconut trees).

Why the U.S. is falling? We cut down a lot of coconut trees and make spears. We use the spears to threaten our neighbors to give us coconuts. In some cases, we borrow coconuts.

Norway

Norway is the richest to its population group (3 millions) while Brunei is richest in its own population group. Norway is rich due to its rich resources and its intelligently governed wealth. I hate to compare any country to Norway as most likely we are comparing Apples to Melons.

From its long coast line Norway has rich off-shore oil fields and abundant fish exports which is second in the world-- only 6% of its export, after China but far, far #1 per capita wise. Because of the world's oil addiction and food dependence secures its income flow.

Peru has a long coast line, but it is not wealthy. My theory does not apply fully here, as there are always exceptions. It could be Norway's educated citizens, close location to its trade partners and buying assets around the world (planting more coconut trees). The dividend payments allow Norway to prosper for decades. They have about 600 billion sovereign fund to be shared by 3 million citizens. Simple math!

Norway will be rich for centuries to come as they plant the coconut trees all over the world.

Iceland

Some smart guys suggested cutting down all the coconut trees (their financial asset) make canoes (more global banks) so they can earn a rich life by fishing (lending). The world blindly loans them with coconuts. When the fishing (no global market esp. after 2008) fails, their land is lost with no coconuts and no coconut trees left. Do not bet all the coconuts in one venture and always have an exit strategy.

Singapore and SE Asia

Singapore is rich due to its important location for the sea route for trade and commerce, as well as being the cultural intersection between the east and the west and its industrious citizens (most are Chinese). When the hard-working folks land on a land of coconuts (i.e. resources), they naturally become rich.

Mekong River is a good resource providing fishing, irrigation, transportation, and fertile land in the delta for SE Asia. Hence, SE Asia should be rich, and at the same time attracts hard-working immigrants from India and China to enhance their wealth. However, the river is being polluted by industries and the future is cloudy.

Japan

Japan has few natural resources. Its only resource is the educated and hard-working citizens. With a decreasing population and the policy not welcoming immigrants, Japan will face problems.

Haiti

Haiti used to have enough coconuts for its small population. French imported African slaves to the sugar cane plantation and changed the allocation of natural resources per capita. Coupled with frequent natural disasters and bad governance, Haiti becomes the poorest country in the world.

Haiti and many countries have their coconut trees destroyed by hurricanes from time to time. That's why they're always poor. So are some states in the US that suffer from periodic flooding and hurricanes.

UAE

When the west helped UAE to explore its oil resources (the hidden coconuts under the sand) about 50 years ago, UAE becomes one of the richest countries. She expands in different areas and it could be over-expanded. When the oil dries up in 100 or so years and/or the shale energy competes better, they could be in big trouble. [Update: the problem appears as of 1/2015.]

Russia

Russia is a country full of resources (coconuts). Its citizens become lazy having a good time under the 'coconut' tree. Chinese are just the opposite. That's why the Russians hire the hard-working Chinese to tender farm in the border while they enjoy life with plenty of Vodka.

The primary reason why USSR fell was the temporary low prices of their resources oil and timber (coconuts). Trying to be #1 was another reason.

China

China has roughly 20% of the world population, but it has far less than 20% of the world resources (coconuts). For example, it has only 6% of the world land area. The situation was worsened in the last 300 years during the Opium Wars, and then semi colonization by the eight countries (led by Brits, the opium pushers). It bankrupted China by their colonial masters. It caused massive migration to escape from the land without coconuts. It was followed by WW2, war lord era and then the bad governance. Their bitter lessons ensure this generation and the next generation to work hard and be smart. When they do not have 'coconut trees' (the colonial masters cut most of them down), you have to work hard or die.

China ranks #2 in the economy. It is only important to its trading partners. Its own citizens care about their living standard which is about the middle in the rank of all countries.

Greece

Greece has its natural resources: tourism (coconut). Euro gives them unlimited borrowing. Olympics boosted their dumb ego. The result is bankruptcy.

Caribbean islands

Literally a lot of their coconuts are destroyed from the hurricanes every year. It makes them poor even they have a lot of coconuts (ample sunshine and beaches for tourists). Many set up tax shelters for rich folks and corporations. It is similar to earthquake prone countries.

Hong Kong & Singapore

Both have good governance learned from Britain and are supported by hard-working Chinese. Hong Kong is rich due to its proximity to China and Singapore due to the sea port location between the East and the West. Coconuts are in many forms.

Ancient civilizations too

Greece, Iran, India, China and Italy are among the oldest civilizations. Most do not do well in today's economy and many of their citizens have immigrated to other countries. My theory suggests that they have exhausted their coconuts (farm land and metals) throughout the long history. Hence, they have to migrate to lands with more coconuts. To illustrate this, there is a huge discrepancy in natural resources (oil, metal and farm land) between China and the U.S., which has a relatively short history.

Corporations too

Microsoft was a tougher company with more innovations fifteen years ago than today. However, they are enjoying easy profitability of upgrades of Windows and Office (coconuts planted by their ancestors). For a long time, she only has one successful new product, the Xbox. Her managers are counting their bonuses instead of taking risk. The Coconut Theory works again.

Rich families too

It is very rare to have rich families that last over three generations. The first generation grows the wealth (planting coconuts), the second generation enjoys the wealth, and the third or fourth generation usually becomes poor due to the easy life.

Conclusion

So far, no one tells me that this theory has been 'discovered' by others. Shamelessly I claim it is mine. To me, it is just common sense.

Afterthoughts

- I did not have a coconut tree (i.e. financial aid or money from my dad), and that is why I worked two jobs in my first summer while attending college here. The first one was a bus boy job from 5 pm to 10 pm. The other one was cleaning slot machines from 4 am to noon for 5 and usually 7 days a week. Lack of coconut makes you desire to work hard or you vanish. With an average IQ, I can make it by working hard in a land of coconuts.

  My children have too many coconuts and they live in a more lavish life style than the old man. They ask me why I work that hard during my retirement or why I still go to Burger King with a coupon even they do not treat me like a king.

- According to my friend Norman, the problem with a small place filled with coconuts is someone would likely to colonize you and steal your coconuts as happened to Norway during WWII. Similar to China about 250 years ago. Once a while, need to cut down one among many coconut trees to make spears to protect the rest of the coconuts.

2   Aging global population

The aging of the global population is due to the proliferation of baby boomers after WW2.

- India will suffer from the population explosion despite the abundance of younger citizens.

  They will eat up all the limited food and consume most of its limited natural resources. They will run out of water in 100 years which is also controlled by China as more water will be directed to the north of Tibet. There are too many problems that cannot be resolved easily. There is no bright future for India. I wish I were wrong as a poor India would affect the rest of the world.

http://en.wikipedia.org/wiki/South-North_Water_Diversion_Project

They classify themselves literate if they can write their name in any language compared to 1,500 Chinese characters for China. Chinese have nine years of compulsory education. These statistics are just being manipulated.

Source: Ted Talk.
http://www.ted.com/talks/yasheng_huang.html

The brain drain is alarming as the most privileged / educated do not want to wait for India's infrastructure, its economy and its governance to be fixed.

I hope rich countries like the U.S. will not take too many doctors / nurses from poor countries such as India as we're doing now. This is the worst disservice to a poor country. We deprive thousands from medical care for each doctor we import. Why do we send our doctors to help the poor while we take their doctors? It just does not make sense. There should be more foreign aid allocated to medical training to poor countries.

Just compare the sub way system and the number of high-rises in India to any Tier 3 city in China. The top Indian city just built its sub way recently in 2011 while Hong Kong has developed into a modern metropolitan with a modern and extensive sub way system many years ago. As of 2012, more than half of India's population live in less than $2.50 a day (the UN definition of poverty is $2.50 / day).

India has to understand its problems first before they can fix them. It has to fight inefficiency, corruption (partly due to inefficiency) and protectionism (to improve quality and encourage foreign investment). Copying China's model is a good idea. China's model is to create specific economic zones close to a port with the essential infrastructure for that area. You need to build infrastructure like highway, electricity...

for that area first. It should target its products first to the foreign market and then include the home market.

The 2011 Indian Kolkata airport has limited road access while the 1980 Hong Kong airport is supported by extensive suspension bridges. Without the road access support, any airport would not be world-class as demonstrated by all major airports in the world. Documentaries on both projects are available from Netflix.

Some told me it could be old, wealthy families controls India's economy and they do not want changes. I argue the opposite is true. Expensive projects usually allow the corrupt rich and the local governments to steal money from public projects.

- China still has plenty of cheap labor.
  Cheap labor will be minor but education will be important as they need to move up to the next level of industrialization with higher-value products. China is already there in many areas.

  China has its own problems, and plenty of them, but demographics are not the major one. Gender imbalance, pollution and corruption are many among others.

  Click this link http://bit.ly/ybAnoW to compare India and China.

- Russia and Brazil still thrive on commodities and oil as long as global economy grows.
  Russians fit my Coconut Theory. They become lazier (and more intoxicated with Vodka☺) as the economy continually grows from its wealth of natural resources including oil. As long as the global economy is humming, there are demands for these resources, and vice versa.

- Africa and some S. American countries.
  The explosive population will bring miseries to their worlds. There will be more wars for food and life expectancies are already lowered. The citizens will migrate legally and illegally to richer countries like the U.S. for a better living. If the farming technology to produce more food with less farm land did not improve drastically over the last 50 years, the world's supply of food now would not meet the demand. As 2012 closes, there are higher food prices due to the floods and droughts all over the

world. It will continually be rougher for the poor countries that cannot afford to pay for it especially when China and India have more cash from their exports.

- The U.S.
  In 2023, the U.S. may look like Japan is today as most developed countries whose populations shrunk to below zero growth. However, the U.S.'s black and Hispanics have a higher fertility rate and the U.S. has more immigrants than all other countries combined. The U.S. will have its different problems / advantages as below.

The U.S. welcomes immigrants (as opposed to Japan). Most qualified Indians are welcome and so are Chinese (who come for economic reasons, to escape from pollution, or because of corruption prosecutions).

In the U.S., today's minorities will become the majority. If you look at their high school dropout rate, social welfare recipient percent, prisoner percent, etc., we do not have a bright future. There will be more political leaders from these groups as we usually vote for politicians that belong to the same race as ours. These are facts and it might be offensive to you if you're a minority.

When we do not have jobs for everyone, a large population is a big burden. We have recent college graduates begging for any job for years, lines for unemployment and welfare offices are getting busier. Why we encourage illegal aliens to come here for jobs and welfare is beyond my comprehension.

The brightest future for us is agriculture and its demand from many countries grows by leaps and bounds. The other is American culture, like movies and music since English is, and will be, the most popular language. The recent discoveries in shale gas and oil are very promising. It could lead us to be a major energy exporter in the next 50 years. Military weapons are a big seller that I do not think it is good for the rest of the world.

Starting in 2012, the baby boomers are retiring (those who were born after the WW2). Hence, we will have about 20 years of increased entitlements such as Social Security considering the average life expectancy of about 82 years. Now we should have a boom in health care delivery.

- Japan.
  Japan does not have a lot of natural resources, and the educated citizen is their most important resource. Japan will suffer the most due to aging population. However, most of us will still drive a car from a Japanese company, play video game on Wii or PlayStation... Its competitors (now Korea and later China) will share their market. Japan will continue its lost decades to another decade. Japan seems turning around in 2013 but it could be just "the dead cat bounces". Only time can tell. Depreciating its currency further stimulates its export at least in the short term.

Conclusion

Investors should look at the sectors that will be benefitted from the aging population for the next 20 years. They are health care delivery, medical equipment, drugs, elderly housing and all sectors that cater to this growing age group.

Links

Water re-directed.
http://en.wikipedia.org/wiki/South-North_Water_Diversion_Project

Ted Talk.
http://www.ted.com/talks/yasheng_huang.html

3   The states of the United States

Contrary to popular belief, we DO make and build something especially per capita wise. We're still the largest economy on earth and are number one in most disciplines in science and technology. We have a stable government with an enviable constitution, workable regulations, highly-educated citizens and the strongest defense (or offense to me).

Our government and the private citizens (Gates and Buffett for example) donate funds and assistance to poor countries more than the other five richest countries combined. We provide food to the world. We export our culture via movies and music. We accept foreign students to enrich our culture, fund our colleges, and provide us with skilled workers when they graduate.

We have a lot of innovations such as Facebook. Most of our products have high profit margins such as airplanes, heavy equipment, high tech products including Apple's consumer products and medical equipment. Nobody can deny that.

Our success leads to higher living standard. Naturally the higher labor cost and more regulations to protect us and our environment follow. Too many regulations would restrict businesses in taking risks (such as developing new drugs and nuclear reactor technologies) and add costs to product developments.

We have to leave the low-end products to low-wage countries such as China. It is called free trade and globalization, which would benefit all participants if they play the game fairly. China's 1.35 billion citizens would not be able to buy our expensive products if they do not have the cash from selling their products to the world.

We have to protect those products that we have an edge. It is not an easy job just by comparing the quality of our high school education to the rest of the world. Japan and S. Korea have passed us in auto and consumer electronic industries. China is at the gate with bigger impact in the future. China is catching up with us. In addition, it has a large internal market, plenty of qualified engineers / scientists, low-wage workers and incentives / guidance from the government. The most important is their desire and spirit to succeed after three centuries of humiliation.

God still blesses us with the new discoveries of shale energy that could extend our prosperity to another 50 years. It gives us more time to fix our problems, but time is running out. The benefits of the shale energy will be clearer by 2015. It could turn out to be a pure fantasy or even a sham. We are still a net natural gas importer (most from Canada) and our gas industry is currently sitting on heavy losses.

Compared to China, we have far, far more farm land and natural resources especially per capita wise.

Our welfare system is too generous due to our previous economic booms. If the able welfare recipients lose the free medical care for taking a job, do they work? They're lazy but not stupid. With the long dependence on this welfare system, they cannot break the viscous cycle of poverty. Multi generation of teenage mothers is one among many examples.

The new immigration bill could be a disaster. If it is passed, how many new legal residents will collect welfare (they can't today as they're illegal) and how many illegals are encouraged to cross the defenseless border. I hope the new immigrants will contribute more than burden our society. Only time can tell. However, protecting the border is easy by severely punishing the employers. When there are no jobs, they will not come. The USA is still the best country for immigrates.

There are many frauds and fats that the government can trim. The government employees are assigned to tiny work load and they are overly compensated. Should we assign them to chase after the frauds in Medicare, food stamp and cheatings in disability entitlements that are so common?

The two wars are bankrupting this country and we need to prevent starting future wars and end the current wars. As of 2013, our military budget is larger than the total of the next top five countries combined.

From this article, you know the government can fix a lot of our problems. Printing money is not the solution, but the problem by itself.

We need to encourage productivity and discourage consumption. Buying a car is consumption and building a bridge is improving productivity. Welfare to the able poor is consumption and teaching work skills to the poor is improving productivity that leads to production increase.

What worries me most is: We're declining while many developing countries (China in particular) are surging up.

The future will be decided by our high school system which is falling apart. Our society is too permissive from gun controls to legalizing drugs, which may bring infant defects. Our lawyers sue every one for profit no matter how ridiculous the cases are.

Solutions are quite simple

To summarize, we should cut most expenses and balance the budget. It is hard to implement as most do not want to bite the bullet. We're a nation of free loaders with over 40% not working.

1. No illegals to legal. When they become legal, they will collect welfare legally and bring their families in for the same reason.

2. Train and encourage the able welfare recipients to work. Cutting their benefits in taking a job will not encourage them to work. Clinton's Initiative has more holes than Swiss cheese.

3. Cut down our generous welfare. That's why we have three generations of teen age mothers. Laziness is a human nature.

4. End the endless wars. If they do not want to fight for their own freedom, why should we (suckers in their eyes)?

5. We cannot borrow forever and pass our debts to next generations. USD will not be a reserve currency in 10 years. Printing money excessively is a short-term solution but a problem long-term problem.

6. Invest in our infrastructure.

7. Cut down foreign aids. A big brother is only in the mind of our leaders.

8. We need a small and efficient government. Guard changing when another party takes over is expensive.

4   Issues that could change the US economy

With expensive parking fees, it is quite cost effective to commute to the city on Saturdays. On our way back at about 4 pm, the bus was full of Spanish-speaking workers. I bet most if not all are illegals working in the suburb such as our Mall, the hospital and many restaurants. Why illegals? I bet most legal citizens would get welfare instead of working in that shift. If you work, they will take out the freebies such as health care in Mass. They are lazy but not stupid. The illegals do not have this option.

What will happen if the politicians turn the illegals to be legal? There will be nobody doing these jobs. No one in the right mind wants these jobs as it is far better to collect welfare. Why politicians would make this stupidest decision? They want to buy Hispanic votes.

In addition, more politicians side with the welfare recipients. Since 40% of the population do not pay Federal taxes, they have to satisfy their needs in order to buy votes. Representation without taxation is worse than taxation without representation.

That's why our taxes are so high and the good jobs are outsourced as we're no longer competitive. That's why we have a high exodus of the top 1% as they do not care about the entitlements but their taxes. Also, that's why we have the highest exodus of corporate headquarters recently so they can lower or in many cases do not pay their taxes.

When one is allowed in, they can bring their entire family in. The US will become a welfare state. On their first day in the US, they will ask for the direction to the welfare office. If you have an elderly, you can collect a nice salary for taking care of him/her. What a country! Great for the immigrants, bad for most workers and incentive for the rich to give up citizenship.

The middle class who cannot go away is squeezed from both ends.

5   Losers in a trade war with China

The following are based on my predictions on a full-fledged trade war with China. I would buy the winners and short the losers. When the trade war is settled, reverse the losers and winners. Losers are:

- American farmers and their suppliers such as fertilizers and farm equipment will be the chief losers. The government subsidies cannot last forever. Many have already lost their farms while their products have filled up storage spaces. Currently Brazil and Argentina are filling in the gaps to supply these products to China. It could change as China has to satisfy the trade talks plus their flood and pig flu problem.
- After the cutoff date, many chip suppliers to China will lose a lot of sales as China is the chief importer. It will take at least a year for countries to take up the slack. In 10 or so years, China will develop their own chip products. Hence, they will be back to normal in 2 years, and they will face China's competition in 10 or so years. I bet Huawei will have all chips made in China in 2030.
- Many U.S. companies are still profiting in China. These days are numbered with the trade war. Apple and many U.S. fast food joints will suffer.
- China in the future will reduce their number of buying new planes from Boeing and/or switch the orders to Airbus. Today China still needs a lot of new planes and hence the effect may not be immediate. China is the largest market for airplanes. If the U.S. bans selling GE's jet engines to China, China will buy them from EU and/or Russia.
- Australia siding with the U.S. will be a serious loser. Australia supplies China with iron ores and agriculture products. Ironically, some of Australia's farm products were replaced by the U.S. It will be a big blow to Australia's economy. The losses of Chinese tourists and students add to the suffering. The current government may be reelected. Actually the national security would be better if they sided with China.
- Many Chinese companies especially Huawei will suffer a lot even with the help from the Chinese government. Huawei could lose their popular mobile phone sales outside China. Korea and Japan have been supplied Huawei a lot of components.
- The markets in both the U.S. and China will fail. It could lead to a global recession.
- China would withdraw Treasury. Together with trading energy not using USD, it could shake our reserve currency status of our USD. In 2008, U.S. asked China to buy Treasuries, and China did but not this time.
- China would limit their export of rare earth elements and active ingredients to our drugs to us.

The phase one of the trade war as of 1/16/2020 is a win for Trump. However, it is not sustainable in the long run. For example, China cannot consume the amount of the farm import. When China is ready to say No, they will not honor this unfair treaty and the phase two would have more problems. At that time, Iran and Russia will side with China for the oil / gas. EU will too or they are losing a lot of orders such as Airbus from China. Our EU allies Germany, Italy and Spain most likely will side with China. It would force EU countries to seek side.

Link: China & US

https://www.youtube.com/watch?v=XepCi0I_g6I

6 Winners in a trade war with China

Winners are:

- Vietnam is the obvious the largest beneficiary from this trade war. Many factories have been moved from China to Vietnam. Many are owned by Chinese. China has helped Vietnam to improve their infrastructure. It has already gained about 8% of its GDP from the new business and is experiencing an influx of foreign direct investments.
- India could be a beneficiary too. They have a lot of problems to be fixed internally. They should copy the model of China by opening a special economic zone.
- Malaysia is a winner too. China will eventually cut the rare earth elements to the U.S. Many countries including U.S. and Australia produce these ores. They do not refine them due to the damage to the environment. Most will be refined in Malaysia instead of in China.
- Countries may replace the U.S. as the chip and product suppliers to China. Japan, S. Korea, Taiwan and many EU countries are obvious beneficiaries. Some of them do not want to do business with China at the fear of being punished by the U.S.
- Russia will replace the U.S. as the supplier of energy such as LNG to China. They will have a closer tie than their history has shown.
- The South East Asia countries and some South American countries such as Brazil and Argentina would benefit and replace American agricultural products for China.
- Ericsson and Nokia will be the primary supplier of a 5G network to countries that ban Huawei's products. However, Ericsson's initial implementation is very poor compared to Huawei's. Taiwan could be the biggest winner when many consumer electronic products would be switched here from China. Rural areas in the U.S. will suffer without Huawei's network.
- Many companies such as Samsung and Apple will capture Huawei's mobile phone market in Europe.
- More tourists and Chinese students will come to Europe particularly the EU countries.

7   EU's mess

We follow the similar procedure in finding the reentry points and use VGK, an ETF for European countries.

There are two sectors that bring down the financial crisis in 2007 (or 2008 for some). We should reenter the European market via technical analysis (TA) and via fundamental analysis.

Technical Analysis

There are two ways to find the reenter points after 2007.

1. Use the same chart in described in TA chapter as follows. Bring up Yahoo! And then Finance from the browser. Enter VGK, an ETF for Europe. Select Chart, then SMA (single moving average), and enter 350 days for reenter points (different from our usual 30, 60, 90 or 120 days).

    Loosely we have two major reenter/exit sets: 08/31/09 to 08/01/11 and 08/20/2012 to 01/13/14. Without considering compounding, we calculate the averages of these two sets of data.

2. From the Market Timing chapter, reenter the market 2 years after the initial plunge for offending sectors. They are not the offending sector but the sovereign debt is partly the culprit. Hence we use 18 months instead of 1 year for the general market or 2 years for the offending sector.

    Assuming 01/14/2008 the market starting plunging, the reenter date is 07/14/2009.

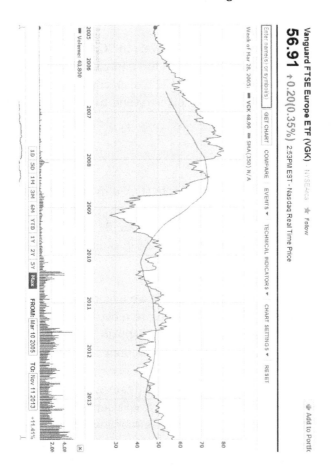

Source: Yahoo!Finance (http://ebmyth.blogspot.com/2013/11/screen-vgk-350-day-sma.html)

The 350-day Single Moving Average could be a good guide to trade VGK, an ETF for European countries. Buy when it is above the moving average line and sell when it is below.

The following table summarizes the returns based on reenter points to 01/13/2014.

	Reenter Date	Return	Annualized Return	Beat SPY
Chart	08/10/09	-9%	-5%	-185%
	08/20/12	29%	21%	0%
Average		10%	8%	-93%
18 months	07/14/09	59%	13%	-42%

If you have a time machine, you may not want to invest in VGK at all as SPY beats both strategies by a wide margin. However, the annualized return is 8% and 13%, not too far away from XHB's 21% and 21% respectively. It seems Europe had more ups and downs during the recovery and the recovery is slower than the US market.

Fundamental analysis

Here are my personal thoughts as of 2009. I prefer to stick with the technical analysis and fundamental analysis is used to further analyze the housing market such as the cities that may have better recoveries. By the time you read this article, the information may be obsolete. Use it as a reference for future guidance.

As of 1/1/2012, my predication about EU's mess that we talked about more than two years ago (my blog mentioned it long before most media). Even today (9/2013), there are not a lot of changes and EU is still on its early stage to recovery. Here are my random remarks.

- EU will be dissolved or will at least kick out the cheaters, free loaders and parasites such as Greece. In any case, Euro will depreciate a lot compared to gold [Update as of 2013: It has]. Germany wants to keep Greece in the union despite of all the problems and little to gain. Germany have to compromise to the opposition from her own citizens in not giving up their own money.

- After that, a default is not a bad option.

- There will be conflicts in the citizens in Greece between those who have (still a lot collecting over $40,000 USD pension) and those (especially the young generation) who have to suffer due to passing the debts / miseries to them.

- Greece will recover faster if it has its own currency and it can default its debts. At that time, it would be profitable to invest in Greece.

  Their government will be halved and the salaries / pension obligations will also be halved. To conclude, it will run the country about ¼ of the original cost. Tax revenues will come back with tourists looking for bargains. When the other industries such as shipping (when global trade improves) and processing olive return, the investment will have a good chance to gain 100% in a year. Timing is everything.

- The days living off from the treasures / commodities they stole from their colonies have been long, long gone. Most European countries need to live within their means.

- The lesson of having a good life without working hard (short work week and long vacation) is learned again and again. First it is Ireland, Iceland, then Greece, then Spain/Italy and now the USA.

- When they learn so many bitter lessons, they will not repeat them for a long while. The USA should learn the same lessons as we seem to be heading to the same direction unless the shale energy rescues us.

- EU will be a problem for years to come. When the country has that high debt with regard to GDP, they will not be competitive especially the drain of their best citizens to other countries.

- Decoupling is the solution. The U.S. and China will not be stupid or big enough to rescue a sinking ship.

Afterthoughts

- Update on Greece as of 1/2013.

Greece should be bottom out in a year. Investing in Greek stocks at that time would double your investment for the following reasons.

1. Greece is small, so it may not be a big deal to recover as Iceland did. It is better than Iceland with its nice climate and many attractions for tourists.
2. Besides attractions for tourists, Greece has beautiful beaches. They need to cut down protests before the tourists would return.
3. The government could be mean and small with about 1/4 of the previous expenses to run it.
4. The olive industry and the shipping industry will return big time after the global recession.

Strategy 6: Asset class

It includes house, oil, commodities and precious metals.

1   Market timing by asset class

Two major trading strategies are:
3. Buy high and sell higher.
    It is a kind of momentum play. You may keep these stocks for less time
    (say, less than three months). The momentum could change very fast. In
    my momentum portfolio, I keep most of my stocks less than a month.
4. Buy low and sell high.
    When the asset class is totally out-of-favor and it has high value, buy it.
    It is a value play. You are swimming against the tide. You need to hold
    these stocks longer (say, longer than 6 months) for the market to realize
    its value.

It is not possible to predict correctly the peaks and bottoms of any asset class
consistently. However, #1 usually starts first and followed by #2. The holding
period is just a suggestion.

Your success will be improved by using technical analysis correctly. Try the
50-day moving average (actually the last 50 trade sessions) to start with. Buy
when it is above the moving average and sell when it is below. Next, try the
20-day moving average and many other technical analysis indicators such as
exponential moving average and different days for the moving averages. The
moving averages are available from Finviz.com without charting.

Basically there is a tradeoff on switching too frequently and reacting too
late. Some stocks are more volatile than others.

Try out different asset classes such as gold and oil. To illustrate, no one can
predict that a gold price at $1800 is the peak. If you buy gold coins at $1000
and ride the gold wagon to $1600, you're doing quite well. In this case,
trade GLD, the ETF fund for gold for technical analysis. The way to protect
your profit and let the profit rise is using stops. Adjust the stop when the
asset appreciates.

2   Commodities: bottom or mirage?

Most authors reveal a statement first and then illustrate with examples to substantiate that statement. Hence, such writers are always right. I am doing something just the opposite in this article. In analyzing what coal stocks to buy (the example) and you help me to verify the bottom for coal stocks (the statement).

This process has its risks, as I try to emphasize that investing is a prediction, which will not be 100% certainty. However, the better educated the guesses are, the better chances the predictions will be materialized. Even if that prediction is wrong, there is nothing wrong with the logic here.

Actually the recommended stocks should be bought in the future as it may not be the bottom today (7/4/13). Confusing? Read on.

Several articles convince me that commodity especially coal should be close to the bottom. Here are the links to these articles. That's the reason why you want to read economic news to take advantage of any new opportunity.

1. The coming rebound of coal and coal stocks.
    http://seekingalpha.com/article/1530202-the-coming-rebound-in-commodities-coal-and-coal-stocks

2. A credit analysis of coal mining companies.
    http://seekingalpha.com/article/1509622-a-credit-analysis-for-coal-mining-companies

Is the bottom near for commodities?

For the last three years, the bottoms of coals stocks have been predicted several times. Nevertheless the coal stocks went up temporarily and then continued its bearish trend. Many coal companies could go bankrupt. I bet most of them will not and offer one of the best appreciation potential, but I do not go that far to proclaim it is one of the best deals in our generation.

Many experts believe natural gas would replace coal to generate electricity. The impact of natural gas will be even clearer by 2016. That may be true in the USA, but not in China and many countries. Even with all the nuclear generators on-line in ten years (2023), China will still depend on coal to generate more than 60% of its electricity.

The following tables may not look good on small screens. You can enter the link below to display it on a larger screen of your PC.

(http://ebmyth.blogspot.com/2013/07/screens-on-commodity-chapter.html)

The stocks

I include 15 stocks and one ETF for analysis. After the initial analysis, I classify them into the following groups.

	Coal	Gold miner ETF	General Mining	Steel	Petroleum w Nat Gas
No.	11	1	1	1	2
Stock	ACI,ANR,ARLP, BTU,CLD,CNX, JRCC,NRP, WLB,WLT, YZC	GDX	RIO	SID	CHK,DVN

Value

These stocks have very high potential for appreciation. However, they are risky. Nothing risked, nothing gained. Most have high debts (the average debt/equity is 133% in this group) and their survival depends on many factors such as the prices of the commodities. The following table concentrates on their values.

Stock	Price (7/4/13)	Forward Yield	Cash Flow	P/B	Debt/ Equity	P-Score
ACI	3.69	-35%	Worst	.3	184%	-4
ANR	5.33	-75%	Worst	.2	70%	-6
ARLP	71.06	10%	Average	3.6	109%	8
BTU	14.86	3%	Worst	.8	126%	-2
CHK	20.92	5%	Worst	1.1	106%	1
CLD	16.19	5%	Worst	1.0	83%	-2
CNX	27.12	10%	Worst	1.6	81%	-1
DVN	53.05	5%	Worst	1.1	82%	-2
JRCC	1.82	-80%	Worst	.3	255%	-5
NRP	20.48	10%	Average	3.4	172%	3
RIO	40.69	10%	Average	1.6	57%	0
SID	2.61	15%	Worst	5.6	329%	2

WLB	11.4	5%	Best			-1
WLT	10.79	-35%	Worst	.5	276%	-2
YZC	7.03	15%	Best	.5	90%	4

BTU has coal mines in Australia, which is closer to its primary customer, China. RIO has mines of different ores all over the world. ARLP and NRP are partnerships.

If you do not want to deal with extra effort in filing the tax returns, do not buy partnerships. I have not checked out the requirements for filing tax returns for ARLP and NRP.

GDX, an ETF for gold miners, is not included in the above table. It has a huge non-correlation between GLD, the ETF for gold, so I believe there is good value in gold miners. GDXJ (not included in this article) is a similar one for junior miners, which is too risky for me.

Most data are obtained from Finviz.com. Forward yield is my estimate and it is defined as forward E/P. Cash Flow is based on the free site Blue Chip Growth. Cash Flow and Debt / Equity measure whether the company will survive. The table does not include all the metrics. P-Score is based on my book Scoring Stocks and 3 is the passing grade.

I have two scoring systems. One is described in my book Scoring Stocks and the other one uses information from several subscription services. In general, the two systems are quite compatible. When the commodities are in the market bottom, the scores for these stocks would not be good. Actually most of them do not pass (the passing grade is 3).

YZC scores the highest and it has the high dividend yield.

ACI and ANR though risky have the most upside potential and both prices are less than 30% of their book values.

Risk levels
The following table summarizes how safe are the stocks.

	Safer	Middle	Risky
No.	3	6	7
Stocks	ARLP, NRP, YZC	CHK, BTU, GDX, RIO, SID, WLB	ACI, ANR, CLD, CNX, DVN, JRCC, WLT

My contradiction

I contradict myself in the following statements.

1. I do not trust the financial sheet of emerging countries including China. However, when many miners are foreign companies, I do not have a good option.

2. Mining is a sector I try to avoid.
   It is extremely difficult to estimate how much ores (sometimes a miner owns several different ores of different grades in same or different mines) the company has; complicated by the complexities to extract and transport them. When those costs are greater its production price, the company will not be profitable. Understanding the market for ore futures is another discipline.

   One potential problem of mining companies from many emerging countries is nationalization.

Timing

Besides ARLP, NRP and YZC as of 7/4/2013, I would select the following to purchase after another analysis in Nov. 1, 2013: CHK, BTU, GDX, RIO, SID and WLB. I would skip the worst scored stocks, which are too risky for me but they may have the highest appreciation. ACI and ANR are very tempting though.

Why November? Most of these stocks have been down for the year and there is more pressure to sell them for window dressing for fund managers in Nov. (even earlier) and for tax write-offs for retail investors in Dec.

Technical analysis will not detect the bottom, but the trend. When the trend is up, the risk is less but the opportunity to buy at the bottom is gone. Today, the trends of most of these stocks are down. I will explore whether there is a correlation of the bottom with the percentage from the last peak.

Timing is a suggestion and you buy the stocks at your own risk and risk tolerance.

My plunge into commodities

I could not resist and bought two stocks from the above list. As of 8/9/13, the performances are quite good.

Stocks	Buy Date	Return	Annualized return
BTU	06/24/13	18%	140%
GDX	07/15/13	14%	150%
FCX	07/31/13	21%	850%
DBC	08/08/13	2%	Too early
NGD	09/12/13	14%	Too early

FCX is too good a price to pass and the insiders bought many shares. Annualized returns usually have no meaning when the holding period is less than 30 days. The annualized return is calculated by the formula: Return * 365 / (days between the buy date and today's date). For example, the annualized return for FCX = 21% * 365 (8-9-13 minus 7-31-13). The 850% return is not sustainable.

The return of DBC, an ETF for commodities, is tracked today 8/12/13. The above are actual and verifiable trades from my largest account. NGD, a gold miner, is added most recently and the return is calculated on 9/18/2013.

Filler: Roots of EU's problem.

1. Euro is initially a good idea especially for tourists. However, it forces the rich countries to pay for the free loaders.

2. Laziness is a human nature. When you work 30 hours (even less if you consider the long vacation) a week, you cannot compete with folks who work 50 hours a week.

3. The loots from the days being colonial masters were long gone except the displays in museums.

4. Socialism encourages folks to be parasites until the host dies.

3   Housing recovery?

There are two sectors (housing finance) that caused the financial crisis in 2007 (or 2008 for some). We should reenter the housing market via technical analysis (TA) and via fundamental analysis.

Technical Analysis

There are two ways to find the reenter points after 2007.

1. Use the same chart in described in TA chapter as follows. Bring up Yahoo! And then Finance from the browser. Enter XLB, an ETF for housing construction. Select Chart, then SMA (single moving average), and enter 350 days for reenter points (different from our usual 30, 60, 90 or 120 days).

    There are 2 or 3 exit points and followed by brief reenter points. They are noises and they do not change the final performance.

2. From the Market Timing chapter, reenter the market 2 years after the initial plunge for offending sectors (they are Finance and Construction for 2007). Assuming 10/12/07 the market starting plunging, the reenter date is 10/12/09.

The following table summarizes the returns based on reenter points to 01/13/2014.

	Reenter Date	Return	Annualized Return	Beat SPY
Chart	08/10/09	-9%	-5%	-185%
	08/20/12	29%	21%	0%
Average		10%	8%	-93%
18 months	07/14/09	59%	13%	-42%

The Chart method makes more money but the annualized return is the same. However, the '2-Year' strategy beats SPY 100% better than the Chart strategy.

Fundamental analysis

Here are my personal thoughts as of 2009. I prefer to stick with the technical analysis and fundamental analysis is used to further analyze the housing market such as the cities that may have better recoveries. By the time you read this article, the information may be obsolete. Use it as a reference for future guidance.

- Location.
  NYC does not lose a lot in housing values. Las Vegas, many cities in Florida and sunny area does. Cities that are going to bankrupt such as Detroit and a few cities in California are great bargain but too risky.

  A well-maintained house in a good neighborhood at 2002 price is a good bargain when you compare to build the same house with both increased material cost and eventually labor cost. You may get a newer and modern house, but the location is usually better and is less pricy.

- Inventory still high.
  We do not have a lot of building since 2008. The inventory is very low now but some banks are still holding a lot of foreclosed properties and properties that should be foreclosed. Some properties are in very bad shape and they should be demolished.

- What drives the housing market.
  If we have a W-shaped recession and/or a lost decade similar to Japan's, the housing recovery will take longer than two years. The builders will be profitable if they can manage their resources and projects on smaller houses for today's smaller and / or less affluent families and more elderly housing for the aging population.

  One of the major forces that trigger the housing boom is the college graduates. When they have children, it is time to buy a house. It does not look good today as most are under-employed or unemployed with large college loans. The U.S. economy may recover without job recovering. Many jobs have been outsourced and most lost jobs will not return. The rosiest sector is energy. We may have 2.5 million new jobs in this sector in 3 years. The house prices in these selected cities skyrocket.

Are today's houses affordable? You can afford a house costing 2 ½ of your yearly income. I would use 3 times today especially with the low interest rates and today's rent alternative. As of 5/2013, the basic housing is on the cheap side for potential buyers especially for those who are still employed and it will remain so as long as the interest rates remains low.

Interest rates.
The housing market depends on interest rates more than most other industries. Low interest rates would make housing more affordable. That's what happened in June, 2013 when the interest rates moved up from the bottom and the housing recovery came to a halt.

I bet the interest rates would be less a factor when the economy is fully recovered.

- Foreigner purchase is the key.
  On the bright side, there are foreigners (a lot from China and some with money from questionable sources) want to buy them in cash. Finally we encourage rich immigrants who invest in the US. It also helps a lot of corrupt officials to escape prosecution by buying residency in the US. Some initial purchases have lost more than 25% of their investment, but some later ones have experienced more than 100% return. Timing is everything!

Compared to Hong Kong and most big cities in China, the US houses are bargains. Many cost about half a million to buy a 500 square feet apartment in a desirable area compared to some 3000-square feet mansions (relative to 500 square feet) in Southern states.

The quality in life is far better here in terms of air quality, water quality, food quality, education (ease to go to colleges) and opportunities.

Most Chinese and many Asians do not buy a house with street number 4 (pronounced 'dead' in Chinese) and bad Feng Shui that many sellers in Vancouver and Toronto have found out. Cities with better culture and well-known colleges such as Boston attract rich foreigners sending their children there. When I was in NYC, I (and 1.3 billion Chinese) would tell you Pam Am Building had bad Feng Shui as the road was running through the building. There are some locations where businesses fell one after. I can explain most are due to very bad Feng Shui. I am not superstitious, but good Feng Shui provides a relaxing living place.

Afterthoughts

- Is the recent (1/2013) rise in housing stocks justified? There are two camps of opposing arguments. Only time can tell which one is right.

  For the low housing inventory and the slowly improving economy, it could be time to buy on construction stocks and REITs (especially the hospital REITs but not the REITs on mortgages). The recent recovery could be temporary due to lower inventory and the interest rates is climbing.

- If you believe the housing will be recovered soon and you do not want to buy specific construction stocks, try the ETF XHB.

- The housing market is irrational. 'Buy Low and Sell High' applies here. From an economist as of 5/2013: Comparing to rents and incomes, the overall housing market is still under-valued by Rabout 7% from the bottom of 15%. It was over-valued by about 40% in 2006.

- Before the takeover of Hong Kong by China, Vancouver properties doubled in values very fast. It is happening in some cities in the US by Chinese buyers this time. However, we do not see this effect here as Vancouver is small compared to the entire USA. It is a double-edged sword. The sellers are happy and the potential local buyers are not as they have to compete with foreigners who pay more and in cash.

- The average house has been increased excessively since 2000. As many times in this book, excessive valuation will bring down to the average value. Compare to Hong Kong and most big cities in China, our houses are still underpriced.

  Depending on which yardstick you're using, you get different conclusions. The better one should be: The average house price should not be more than three times the average annual income.

- I remember Uncle Ben told us not to worry and four months later the housing market crashed. Cheat me twice, shame on me.

-

Strategy 7: Market correction

We have about 1 to 2 corrections every year – the frequency fluctuates. It provides a good time to enter. It is a great strategy in a side way market: Buy at dip and sell at temporary surge.

1   Correction

Market timing has been judged wrongly by many. Just check out how the two major plunges can be detected easily by my simple chart.

Corrections are harder to detect. So far, I have more rights than wrongs in detecting corrections.

Everyone has its own definition of a correction and mine is as follows. A correction is a 10% or more down from the peak of the last 180 days or more than 5% down in a month. Sometimes, corrections continue to 20% loss. My definition of a market plunge is the loss of 40% or more from the recent peak to the bottom. There is a gray area between a 20% to 40% loss.

From my definition, there is no correction in 2013 and that is quite rare. On the average it happens at least once every year since 2000 depending on my interpretation. I also estimate two minor corrections of 5% every year if we do not have a 10% correction.

Corrections provide us opportunities to enter the market. Temporary peaks provide us opportunities to sell. They happen about one to two times a year on the average but their frequencies fluctuate widely. I usually start selling at the expected peaks, and buying at the expected bottoms. Your cash position depends on your risk tolerance. 'Buy-and-hold' investors can just ignore corrections and this chapter.

Some hints (not always reliable) predict the temporary market peak:

- Up more than 10% of the expected gain. To illustrate, you predicted this year's total return is 12% in the beginning of the year. In March, the market has already gained 12%, there is a good chance it is close to the yearly peak and you should act accordingly. Review the stocks you own and sell those with less appreciation potential first.
- The market exceeds a good percent over the last peak. Define this percent based on your risk tolerance.

- Compare the annualized market P/E (SPY or any market index ETF) to its 5-year average (10-year average is fine too).
- Foreign markets are down and ours are up by a good margin.
- The interest rate. When it rises, the market will be down.
- It happens more than three consecutive days that there are more stocks advancing than retreating.
- It happens more than three consecutive days that the number of new highs is more than the number of new lows.
- From Finviz.com, SPY's SMA200 exceeds 10% (= (Price − SMA)/SMA). SMA-200 is Single Moving Average for the last 200 sessions. It indicates it may be temporarily peaking. Use it for reference only as it is not always reliable.
- From Finviz.com, SPY's RSI(14), the relative strength index based on the last 14 days, exceeds 55%. It indicates that it may be overbought. This is for reference only as it is not always reliable.
- There are always reasons for corrections such as the market is overvalued, rising interest rates, degrading corporation earnings and trade wars.

Conclusion

Corrections are harder to detect in comparing to the market plunges which we have excellent results so far from 2000.

Do not bet the entire farm on corrections especially when the market is risky. Keep less than 25% of your portfolio in cash on the expected peaks.

When the market corrects, it is a buying opportunity. However, when the market starts to plunge, we should exit the market as the losses could be high. If all the conditions in the following table are exceeded, most likely the market is peaking. One's opinion.

SMA-50%	SMA-200%	SMA-350%	Avg. of the 3 the SMA%	RSI(14)
4%	6%	11%	9%	65%

2   Six signs of a correction

The following is an article titled "Six signs of a correction" I wrote for Seeking Alpha on June 29, 2014.

http://seekingalpha.com/article/2291605-6-signs-of-a-correction?v=1404308839

The best protection is playing defense now. The chance of a correction (10% or more) is high.

Six signs of a correction

1. All my technical indicators show the market is peaking and overbought. SPY is an ETF simulating the market of the S&P 500 stocks. As of 6/29/2014, the RSI(14) is at 67% and the SMA-200% is at 8.35%. SMA-200% measures how far away the stock price is from its simple moving average of the last 200 trade sessions.

    You may argue that you do not believe in technical analysis. However, many institutional fund managers learn technical analysis and they will act accordingly. It is one of the many tools that hedge fund managers use to 'hedge'. Most mutual fund managers cannot practice market timing bound by the rules and regulations.

2. Newton's Law of Gravity has never been proven wrong (some humor to get your attention). What goes up must come down. The market has been up even after inflation. However, it takes a breather from time to time. A small one is called a correction and a big one is called a market plunge.

3. We did not have one such correction of 10% in 2013, so the time is ripe. The average is about one correction of 10% or more and about 1.5 corrections for 5% in a year. Many experts predicted wrongly on a correction in 2013. I do not bet against them to be wrong two times in a row.

4. There are more articles predicting a correction than articles arguing against it. It could be a self-fulfilling prophesy. It is the herd psychology. One's opinion.

5. The market has low volumes and narrow ranges for many days may indicate that the market is changing direction. The sea is calmest before a storm.

6. I am not convinced that I can make a lot of profit even if there is no correction. To me, the market is fully valued. It is my reward / risk ratio. I prefer not to make the last buck and have a good sleep.

How to protect yourself

It depends on your risk tolerance.

1. Accumulate cash from 0% to 50%. I recommend 15% for most. 0% is for those who ignore the signs. It was a great selection for 2013. I select 50% as I'm more conservative than most.

2. Place stop orders. Adjust them when they appreciate. Some stocks are more volatile than others. I prefer to use stop orders in market plunges rather than corrections, as corrections are too brief to be effective.

3. Short the market. I do not recommend shorting in most cases. Buying a contra ETF may help. In any case, do not risk money you cannot afford to lose.

4. Use options to protect your portfolio.

5. Prepare a list of stocks to buy when there is a correction, and wait for better time to invest.

Do not treat my (or all others') predictions as gospel. Predictions are just predictions. It is like buying insurance that we do not expect to collect from.

I have to admit market timing is not an exact science. Hopefully we are more right than wrong.

Summary of comments on the article

There are two camps: one who believe and one who do not believe. It is as expected. I will not take credit if there will be a correction within a month, or take the blame if there will be none in the next 3 months. From my record, I have more right than wrong predictions, but it may have nothing to do with future market predictions. Here is my summary:

1. I did think of other signs as mentioned by some of my readers: interest rate, oil price, current events... I expect interest rates will start rising by the end of the year. The recent rise in oil price is due to the turmoil in

the Middle East. The current events including Ukraine and the Middle East seem not to be a factor as our leader does not want to participate in this.

2. I do not expect a market plunge (over 30% down) as I do not see any bubbles (those bubble stocks are too few). My prediction: These bubble stocks will be half the peaks achieved in 2013 and 2014 by the end of 2014. To me, all stock trades are predictions. Some materialize and some do not.

3. Corrections are harder to detect than market plunges. After I detect a plunge, I will spend most of my time in protecting my portfolio.

##Fillers:

Where common sense is not common sense

Excessive printing of money is not a long-term solution. Servicing the huge debt weakens our competitiveness. The politicians just want to buy votes today and finance their campaigns. Our next generations will have to pay for these huge debts.

I have never taken any business classes unless required for my engineering degrees and yet I can understand it via common sense. I wonder why our highly-educated (at least by their Ph.D. certificates), smartly-looking (looks could be deceiving), high salaried (many times higher than mine) decision makers do not understand and act on it.

On Shooting and any violence. "Forgive" is the most powerful word in any language in any culture. "Pray for the victims" do not do any good, but take actions to prevent similar shootings from happening. PLEASE.

Why fillers? A blank page space is too much to waste. Most if not all of the fillers are created by me.

Consumption vs. Investing. We consume more than we produce (causing deficits) and investing much less (causing our downfall).

3   Anticipating a correction

'Buy-and-hold' investors can ignore this chapter. This chapter enhances the last one.

You should try to sell as many stocks as you own before the correction comes and buy them back during and after the expected correction. It does not always work. However, it is good to churn your portfolio to ensure it has better appreciation potential at the expense of capital gain taxes in non-retirement accounts.

Signs of a market top (same as correction is coming)

- The market has been up for over 4 months from the last dip.
- The market has gained more than the predicted share.
- If most of your stocks are at the peak, take some profits.
- Use Technical Analysis (via use of charts) as below.

  Here is one of the charts that could predict temporary market dips and surges. Buy when the price is above the SMA (simple moving average) and sell when it is below. This example uses 50 days for SMA for 2012. SMA-50% is also available from Finviz.com.

  Vary the number of days and/or use other indicators to reduce noise or improve the trading frequency to fit your individual needs.

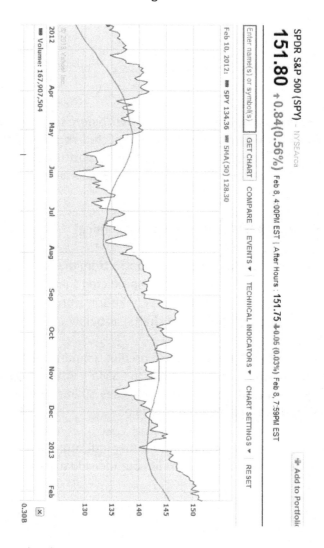

Source: Yahoo!Finance.

If you are reading this book on small screen and cannot see the chart, type the following into your browser.
http://ebmyth.blogspot.com/2013/09/correction-example.html

There are too many trades in the above chart especially in the month of April. The period from July 1 to Oct. 15 is a good capture of the upward trend. It is useful but not perfect. Try to use SMA-100 instead of the above SMA-50.

Example of a market top

The following is from my blog written on May 19, 2011 and it turned out to be quite accurate. Check why I expected a correction would be coming. Hopefully we can spot the next one with similar reasoning. However, there is no guarantee for future performance and predictions.

Click here on the actual blog and the summary follows.
http://www.tonyp4idea.blogspot.com/2011/05/anticipating-correction.html

As of May 19, 2011, the market had been up by about 9% YTD. The experts were divided whether the market would take a correction with convincing arguments for and against.

I had been selling stocks several weeks before and moved most of my Annuity positions to a money market fund. My total cash was 25% and I was still selling. I tried to sell most of my stocks at 5 to 10% higher than the market prices. Hence, even if there were no correction, I was still selling far better than my current prices and it was a reasonable insurance policy. I predicted that the market was risky at that time; you have to trust your prediction and act accordingly as it did.

After I had accumulated more than 30% in cash, I played the 'Buy one and Sell two' strategy betting I could spot stocks better than others. I tried to sell the stocks I bought right away for a small profit as I still expected a correction.

* Arguments for no correction:

- QE3 would be materialized (even it will not amount to a lot of cash due to the debt ceiling).
- Corporate profits are still rising.
- The economy is improving.

* Arguments for correction:

- QE3 will not be materialized and no money will be used to stimulate the economy.
- The market is taking a breather after 9% YTD (I expect 5% rise in mid-year).

- Slim chance for the rule 'Stay away in May' as it had not been working for the two consecutive years except in today's extended bull market.
- There are financial problems from China, EU, Japan and N. Africa.
- With tightening margin requirements on commodities, oil..., speculative trades will be reduced (good for the long term).

The above is a summary of what the experts said. I did not do any research (as it is already available from the web). I summarized their opinions, selected what made sense to me, and acted accordingly.

I chose the middle road by not taking extreme actions such as selling all my holdings and heavily investing in contra ETFs.

Afterthoughts

- My Elastic Band Theory.
  The more you stretch an elastic band, the more it will rebound. When a stock's timing score is 10 (the best), it has no way to go but down. That is similar to the general market.

  The risk/award ratio is too high as of 4/2013. Unless you have a time machine, you may not want to make the last buck.
- A related article from SA.
  (http://seekingalpha.com/article/1344071-5-reasons-why-i-am-shorting-the-market)

Links
Original blog:
http://www.tonyp4idea.blogspot.com/2011/05/anticipating-correction.html
An article on preparing for a correction.
http://www.forbes.com/sites/investor/2014/05/19/five-things-to-do-in-a-stock-market-correction/

#Filler: Teach the able welfare recipients how to fish instead of giving them fish for the rest of their lives. They will not work if you take out their welfare benefits for working.

4   Market correction in August, 2015

I have 50% in cash before the August correction. I should have 100% if I followed my chart. However, we are just human beings blinded by our greed / fears and emotional attachment.

Stocks	Buy Price	Buy Date	Return	Sold date
Apple (AAPL)	107.20	08/26/15	12%	10/19/15
Gilead Sciences (GILD)	105.94	08/26/15	-4%	
General Motors (GM)	27.69	08/26/15	12%	09/17/15
Genwealth Financial (GNW)	4.54	08/26/15	10%	08/27/15

#Filler: Emotionally detached

My friend's father died of worrying too much about his losses in the stock market. When the market returned, he should have recovered most of his losses but not himself.

#Filler: Do you care

When you have a life-threatening disease, do you are care the drug is from China or not?

Listen to the song from the following YouTube link, do you care whether she is from China or not?
https://www.youtube.com/watch?v=_2EEVhRsdVk

#Filler: Vietnamese

In less than a generation, the Vietnamese become productive and educated citizens. All the welfare cheating from the FOB are forgotten.

Strategy 8: Calendar

There is no need to time the market from 1970 to 2000. From 2000 to 2014, the market crashed two times with an average loss of about 45%.

The apples you picked are sour but some other times are tasty from the same tree. You pick them the bad ones in the wrong time or the right ones in the right time.

Market timing is about educated guesses unless you have a time machine. Hopefully we will have more rights than wrongs when we follow general guidelines. It would reduce risk and could benefit us financially in the long run.

I divide the market timing in three categories by durations as follows. All time durations are estimates.

1. Secular Cycle.   Duration: 20 years.
2. Market Cycle.   Duration: 5 years.
3. Correction.   Duration: 1 year for 10% correction.
                       Duration: ½ year for 5% correction.

1   Market timing by calendar

The following predictions are based on historical data. You may have slightly different findings depending on when you start and when you end your testing.

You can load the historical data of SPY via Yahoo!Finance and check out how close you are or different from my own predictions. They are my predictions based on historical data. Use it as a reference only.

- Presidential cycle.
  Usually the market performs worse in the first two years after the election than the next two. During the 3rd year the president has to make the economy look rosy in order to buy votes. Statistically it is the best year for the market and is followed by a good year (the election year). The government may stimulate the economy, the stock market and employment by printing more money, lowering interest rates and lowering taxes.

Democratic presidents have better market performance statistically than Republican presidents. This is not too logical as though Republicans are more pro-business traditionally.

- Olympics.
  It has been proven that the host country has a better chance that its stock market appreciates the year after the Olympics. It could be due to the exposure from the Olympics and / or the huge expenses in preparing for the Olympics.

  The last two Olympics follow this pattern as of 12/23/2013:

Olympics Country / Year	ETF	Period	Return
United Kingdom / 2012	EWU	Jan. 3, 2013 - Dec. 23,2013	11%
China / 2008	FXI	Jan. 3, 2009 - Dec. 31, 2009	43%

Greece could be an exception. It is too small a country to host this world-class event and it has wasted too many resources by building too many white elephants that the country can never justify. Brazil depends on its export of natural resources to China, so I do not count on the Olympics effect there.

Winning a lot of Olympic medals has no prediction for the stock markets. Both the Russian Empire and E. Germany were winners but disappeared in their original forms afterwards.

- Seasonal.
  Best profitable investment period is: Nov. 1 to April 30 of the following year. It is similar to the saying 'Sell in May and Go away'. It did not work since 2009 as it was an Early Recovery (defined by me) in the market cycle.

The market does not always happen as predicted. However, when more folks follow this, it becomes a self-fulfilling prophecy. I prefer "Sell on April 15 and come back on Oct. 15" to act before the herd. The more practical strategy is to start selling in April 1 and become more aggressive (selling at closer to the market prices) when it is close to May 1. For the last five years, I did not find this prediction reliable.

The explanation of the 'summer doldrums' could be that the investors cash their stocks for vacations and college tuition in the fall. Buying quality companies at the dips could be profitable.

- The worst month: September.
  The next worst month is October. However, if there is no serious market crash during October (and this month has more than its shares of crashes), it could be the best month to buy stocks.

- The best month for the bull: November.
  However, several market bottoms occurred in October and November. The next strong month is December.

- Best 30 days: Dec. 15 to Jan. 15, next year.
  It was correct for the period of 2012-2013.

- Window dressing.
  Institutional investors sell their losers and buy winners around Nov. 1. From my rough estimate and on the average, the winners have a 2% percentage point gain better than the market and the losers have 1% worse than the market.

  I recommend that you evaluate the top 10 winners from the last 10 months or YTD in Oct. 15 and sell them at 3% gain or two months later.

  I recommend that you buy in Dec. and sell them 3 months later. Include the stocks with more than 30% loss for the last 11 months or YTD, sort them by Earning Yield in descending order and evaluate the top 10 stocks.

  In both cases, do not buy foreign stocks and stocks with return of capital. Ignore stocks not in the three major exchanges, with low volumes and stock prices less than $2. Do not buy in losing years such as 2007 and 2008. I have my tests with my own assumptions and I use tools not available to most readers.

This is a guideline only. Do not buy any stocks during market plunges. Current events should be considered first such as a potential war and the hiking of interest rates.

2 Summary

I made the following charts so it is easier to time the market by the calendar.

All dates are inclusive.

No.	Metric		Score
1	Seasonal	Nov. - April, Score = 1	
2	Best Month	Nov., Score = 1	
		Sep., Score = -1	
3	Best Days	Dec. 15 – Jan.15 Score = 1	
4	Presidential Cycle	Election Year, Score = 1	
		1st Year in Office, Score = -1	
		2nd year, Score = -1	
		3rd year, Score = 2	
5	Presidential[3]	Democratic = 1 Republican = -1	
6	Market Cycle	Early Recovery, Score = 3	
		Up, Score = 2	
		Peak, Score = 1	
7	SPY (Finviz.com)	SMA200% > 8%[2] Score = -1	
		SMA200% < 0 Score = -1	
		RSI(14) > 65% Score = -1	
		Grand Score	

Footnote.
[1]   Refer to Market Cycle chapter on how I define phases of a cycle.
[2]   For simplicity, use Finviz.com. Enter SPY and you will find SMA200% and RSI(14) to predict whether the market is peaking and overbought.
[3]   I'm political neutral. The selection is based on historical statistics.

Add up all the scores. The passing grade is 0. According to my table which is based on my personal selections/preferences, the market is favorable when the grand score is 1 or higher. I bet it is the first time you see such a scoring system for market timing.

Sectors for market cycle

Market Phase[1]	Favorable		Unfavorable
Early Recovery	Financial, Technology, Industrial		Energy, Telecom, Utilities
Up	Technology, Industrial		
Peak	Mineral, Health Care, Energy		
Bottom	Consumer Staples, Utilities		Consumer Discretionary, Technology, Industrial
Seasonal	Favorable		Unfavorable
Winter	Energy, Utilities		
End of year	QQQ, EWG		
Olympics	ETF for host country[2]		

Footnote.

[1] Refer to Market Cycle chapter on how I define phases of a cycle.

[2] Buy it next year after the Olympics. It could be due to higher GDP or the publicity. However, be selective. Greece is too small a country to host an Olympics.

3 Year-end strategies

I have two: 1. Buy the current year winners (YEW) and 2. Buy the current year losers (YEL).

The first strategy is riding the institutional investors' window dressing to include the winners in their funds to make them look better. It did not work well in 2018, so I skip it in 2019.

The second strategy takes advantage of selling losers for tax purposes. We need to find value stocks, but not stocks that are heading into bankruptcy. I had amazing returns in 2018 and will continue this strategy in 2019.

The following describes how to create your own testing if you have a historical database. It would be a frame for testing other strategies.

- Define the starting date. For the first strategy, I would use 9/1, 10/1 and 11/1 for two sets of test data. For the second strategy, I would use 12/1 and 12/15. Check to see which starting date is better for the specific strategy.
- Define the durations, the number of months before you sell the purchased stocks. I use 1 months, 2 months, 3 months and 6 months for my designated durations.
- Define the number of tests. I would start from the year 2000, one or two years older if your historical database allows for that. Actually I started in last 3 years or so to save time. However, do not use dates older than 1995 as the market was quite different then.
- Compare your results to SPY (or the S&P 500 index).
- Ignore dividends for simplicity.
- Use annualized rates for a better comparison.
- If the date has no data such as during holidays and weekends, use the date after it for consistency.
- Take out stocks that would not be the stocks you usually would buy, such as penny stocks (that likely boost the performance due to survivorship bias), small foreign companies and/or stocks giving huge dividends or giving a return of capital.

- Use different metrics to sort, such as Expected Earning Yield (E/P) or a composite grade. Use the top 5 (or 2) stocks to calculate performances.
- Include the maximum drawdown (the maximum loss from recent height) from many selected time frames (i.e. durations described). My maximum loss is -52% from 12/1/2007 to one year later in my Year-End Loss strategy, but followed by 256% gain in the next year.
- Negative percent numbers could give you wrong calculations when comparing to an index. Check them out manually if your formula has not taken care of the negative numbers.
- A year-end winner strategy should include large companies (traded by fund managers) and stocks that have increased in values year-to-date.
- From my limited testing, my small-cap stocks better than other stocks and they have to be profitable.
- Here are my best results for the two strategies. Again, my results will not be the same as yours due to different selection criteria. Past performance may not have anything to do with future performances.

The year-end loser strategy in 2015 does not work that well as I screened many stocks that were scored very low. I found out many screened stocks were from foreign countries. Many emerging countries have had problems and I do not trust most of their financial info. Besides that, many were energy companies which I already had too many of.

Many have Expected Earning Yields over 35%. However, most have very high debts such as Debt/Equity is over 1 (i.e. 100%). If I bought them, I would unload them within 3 months fearing a market crash in 2016 [Update. As of 2019, we do not have one]. Historically, it is profitable, but I may skip most YEL stocks this year as most were deserved losers. The lesson is: Adjust to the current market conditions.

Strategy	Starting Date	Duration	Avg. Annual. %	Max. Drawn Down
YE Winners	10/1	4 months	40%	-36%
YE Losers	12/1	6 months	42%	-28%

My experience

When trying to make good money, you need to find a strategy that matches the current market. Here are my recent strategies I actually tried with real money in 2018.

* You usually see window dressing from institutional investors from Nov. 1 to Dec. 1 (some use dates earlier than Nov. 1). Buy the current winners and sell the current losers of stocks with a large market cap.

The market was risky so I did not buy winners but shorted some losers.

* Buy year-end losers from Nov. 1 to Dec. 31 (some use dates earlier than Nov.1). The companies have to be profitable (>15%), big losers (most having over 50% yearly loss) and small companies (preferred).

Incorporate the strategy with today's volatile market (i.e. buy when they plunge and sell when they rise). You need to determine what is a "plunge" and a "rise". For me, it is short-term and the percent is 5% from a recent high or low.

There is a selling part of these strategies I have not included here. Most of my strategies are based on exhaustive tests from historical data with a lot of work.

Every market is different. We need to make a lot of adjustments. From my experiences, the best research may not make you money all the time. In the long run, the more educated you become, the better chance for you to make money.

Year-End 2018

This was one of my best monthly returns. The average purchase date is 12/27/2018 and the current prices were based on 1/28/2019. The return is 53% or 648% annualized. Most likely the performance will not be repeated. However, it serves as a procedure for coming years.

I change the quantity Q to 1. Several stocks have been purchased more than once. I sold 3 stocks already indicated by the Status = 'Sold'.

Account	Screen	Year-end loser		Start	12/21/19	End		1/8/2019 Today		1/28/19	
Stock	Q	Buy	Sell	Buy $	Sell $	Buy Date	Sell Date	# Days	Profit $	Profit %	Ann %	Status
401KC												
CHK	1	2.13	2.99	2	3	01/03/19	01/18/19	15	1	40%	982%	Sold
MNK	1	16.41	21.45	16	21	01/03/19	01/25/19	22	5	31%	510%	Sold
MNK	1	16.43	21.45	16	21	01/03/19	01/25/19	22	5	31%	507%	Sold
NNBR	1	5.68	8.58	6	9	12/26/18	01/28/19	33	3	51%	565%	
NNBR	1	5.72	8.58	6	9	12/26/18	01/28/19	33	3	66%	727%	
ESTE	1	4.35	6.45	4	6	12/26/18	01/18/19	23	2	48%	766%	Sold
JT												
LCI	1	4.61	8.29	5	8	12/21/18	01/28/19	38	4	80%	767%	
MDR	1	8.01	9.13	8	9	01/08/19	01/28/19	20	1	14%	255%	
YRCW	1	3.29	5.78	3	6	12/21/18	01/28/19	38	2	76%	727%	
YRCW	1	3.26	5.78	3	6	12/21/18	01/28/19	38	3	77%	742%	
401K												
ASRT	1	3.56	4.18	4	4	12/26/18	01/28/19	33	1	17%	193%	
UTCC	1	7.13	11.00	7	11	12/26/18	01/28/19	33	4	54%	600%	
YRCW	1	2.92	5.78	3	6	12/26/18	01/28/19	33	3	98%	1083%	
Tot/avg				84	119	12/27/18		29	36	53%	648%	

I sold my YRCW (not shown above) on the earnings date that can be found in Finviz.com. When the earnings are positive, it will be sold for my asking price plus a little more but less than the surge. If it is negative, it will not be sold. I recommend to cancel any trade order before the earnings date.

As of 09/07/2019, LCI is up by 185% and YRCW is down by 27% (I sold one position in my retirement account for about 100% gain).

How long should we hold these screened stocks?

Except those in my taxable account, I sold all of them in the first two months. The following is the annualized returns for holding 1 month, 2 months, 3 months and 5 months (as of 6/22/2019). From my previous testing, I should have held the stocks for 6 months. However, I have made my objective already and I want to take advantage of this volatile market.

I could not find UTCC in my historical database. I sold it with an annualized return of 572%. It could be acquired or merged. For simplicity, I used 12/27/2018 as the purchase date for all stocks. I consider one position for each stock and hence 3 purchases of YRCW is considered as one purchase here. Again, I do not include dividends, the bid spread and commissions.

	1 Month	2 Months	3 Months	5 Months
Ann. Return	497%	366%	178%	17%
SPY	72%	74%	52%	31%

From the above, I did well in selling most of them. If I held all of them for 5 months, they would not beat the SPY, the market comparison many use.

Filler

- First bought or sold by insiders and their relatives, then followed by programmed computers, institutional investors, technicians and then retail investors.

- Missed a short of PG&E and VALE when their bad news broke. There is more in life than playing the markets.

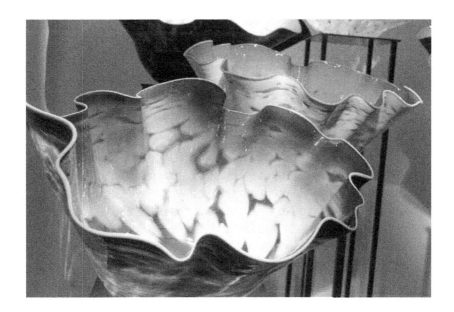

Strategy 9: Interest-sensitive sectors

Buy long-term bond ETFs when the interest rates is high (say > 5%) and short-term bond ETFs when the interest rates is low (say < 2%).

Bank stocks are interest-sensitive: The higher the rates, the more profitable the banks.

As of 2016, high interest stocks and ETFs lose some of its previous luster.

When the market is risky, it is better to invest in safer investments. For more aggressive investors, buy contra ETFs and short stocks.

1   My A.B.C. on bonds

Bonds are classified into several categories and each has its different characteristics. Briefly, they are classified as 30-year Treasury bonds, 20-year Treasury bonds, 10-year Treasury bonds, short-term Treasury bonds, municipal bonds, investment-grade corporate bonds and high-yield (junk) bonds.

As of 5/2013, the long-term Treasury bonds were very risky. The interest rates are so low and it has no way to go but up. It will when the economy is improving. I do not expect we are following Japan's low interest rates for the last decades.

Here are random comments on bonds.

- Japan has had almost virtually zero interest rates for a long while. If you borrow 1 M from them at almost 0% and invest in another country's bond at 8%, you may think you win. However, you need to consider the risk in converting the country's currency back to Japanese Yen, inflation, bond loss, and taxes.

- In 2008, almost all assets lost money. However, some high-yield bonds (or junk bonds) made over 40% in 2009. To illustrate, you bought these bonds yielding about an 8% dividend in the beginning of the year. The government lowered the interest rates to stimulate the economy and hence the average yield was about 1% at the end of the year. The bonds you held yielding 8% were worth far more than the current bonds yielding 1% as most likely they provide better dividends for the years to come.

- As of 4/2012, the interest rates were almost too low to invest in bonds.

  Even the king of bonds made the wrong call. Do not bet against the Fed as they control the interest rates. They will raise the interest rates when they think the economy is ready.

  Conventional wisdom tells us to balance your portfolio with a combination of bonds and stocks in proportion to your risk tolerance, which for some is determined by their age. I prefer the reward/risk ratio and only buy bonds when interest rates is expected to fall which usually occurs after the first six months of a market plunge. The government has to stimulate the economy by lowering the interest rates in almost all recessions. When the USD loses the reserve currency status, most stocks and bonds would be losers.

  Repeating the important prediction, as of 4/2013, the long-term bond crash seemed to be coming. When the economy improves, the interest rates will rise. The interest rates is so low now that it has no way to go but up. It will affect adversely the bonds you're holding especially the ones with low interest rates and long maturity from today forward.

- The government bond prices could collapse when its issuing country is printing too much money and depreciating its currency.

  A bond at 20% yield may not be good if the company/country has more than 25% chance to default on their bonds.

- Those holding the GM bonds before the reorganization (i.e. the first bankruptcy) lost more than 40% of the bond values. Corporate junk bonds (i.e. high yield bonds) have their risk. Buy a bond fund or ETF on corporate bonds.

- I believe the muni bonds are risky. I do not really care about the small tax advantages. Many may default. If you still want to buy them, buy a bond fund to spread out the risk instead of buying individual muni bonds. Detroit bankruptcy is a good example of this. This article was published far earlier than the collapse of several towns in California and now Detroit.

- The long-term bond price moves in the opposite direction of the interest rate. It is about a 1 to 5 ratio by my rough estimate. If the interest rates move 5% up, then the long-term bond price would move 25% down. It is very rough estimate as it also depends on how long until the bond matures.

- Few hold the bond and see when it matures. If you need a steady income, buy government bonds at an acceptable rate (for example, greater than 8%). 2012 was not a good year to buy bonds with low interest rates. Some bonds did default and the owner lost most or even the entire investment. The GM bonds before its first bankruptcy was one of them however it is quite rare.

- China has been a big buyer of our US treasury bonds. China does not want to kill the goose that lays the golden eggs. They need a good economy in the USA in order to sell their stuff, which would create jobs for its citizens.

Afterthoughts

- This article was originally written in 2012. If you followed the advice about not buying long-term bond, you would have saved a lot of money. The traditional allocating between bonds and stocks was wrong. The decision of buying long-term bonds should be based on the current interest rates and the market direction.

- Bond ETFs: TLT (20+ years Treasury Bond).

  Contra Bond ETFs: TBF (Short of TLT). Click here for an article on contra Bond ETFs.
  http://seekingalpha.com/article/1305371-strategies-for-a-rising-rate-environment-inverse-bond-funds?v=1365862967&source=tracking_notify

  Click here for other bond and contra bond ETFs.
  http://seekingalpha.com/article/1305371-strategies-for-a-rising-rate-environment-inverse-bond-funds#comment_update_link

2   Muni bonds

Unlike the Federal government, states and <u>munis</u> do have to balance the budget and we are having more cities going bankrupt than previously predicted. We have to bite the bullet somehow, otherwise we will never service our growing debts. We're running out of suckers like China to lend us money.

If you read this article on 7/2012, you should have saved a lot by selling all of your muni bonds and long-term bonds described in the last chapter.

- States will not go bankrupt, but muni bonds will lose a lot of their values. QEn will be used to rescue the state. Property and state taxes will be raised if they have not already been raised. A lot of foreclosures usually mean less local taxes for the local government.

- State/muni bonds together with Federal bonds will have the junk status, so in the future it is harder to raise money that will be needed for any public project.

- Need to cut down the number of state employees.
  It may be easy to cut about half of the state workers and you may not notice any loss in service (as most of them work short hours and are not motivated under the union's umbrella). I just get sick of the routine 'discoveries' on there are how few hours they have worked as reported by our local newspapers while we've about an 18% real unemployment / under-employment rate.

  However, the firemen, policemen, and teachers should be paid fairly and they should not be cut.

- Cut their pensions and increase retirement age requirements. Most state workers have just a little less than their regular salaries in retirement and they retire at a young age. Most big companies do not have pensions now.

- We could cut the entitlements/benefits that encourage folks not to work such as the generous benefits to teenage mothers. We could cut the free medical care to illegal aliens. All expenditures have to be at a fair percentage of our GDP rather than not how much we can borrow as politicians look at buying votes.

- We do not need large government, but a lean and mean government to provide us efficient services. All those taxes are not good for the economy and businesses (how can you compete with those foreign countries with minimal taxes). Without business expanding (not government expanding), we do not have real jobs.

Afterthoughts

- Our experts told us to stay away from munis. They're wrong in timing – well you do not want to fight the Fed in the short term. However, their arguments are not wrong. Muni government seldom bond default as they cannot issue new bonds in the future if they do.

  The reality is: Some municipals are just dying and they just cannot keep up paying the necessary interest expenses and obligations. There are simply better places to invest.

- As of 8/2012, the defaults on muni bonds are getting to be more. Actually we have more defaults as the defaults in the unrated bonds are not tracked. As the original post was written about a year ago, the advice still holds true. There are better investments than muni bonds in both appreciation potential with less risk.

Filler

Pension is a two-edge sword. Retiring with pensions after 25 year service does not make sense if you are in the real world in a profit-seeking organization. It weakens our competitive edge with other countries. Losing what has been promised was tough to swallow for Detroit city employees.

3 Money Market, CDs & Bonds

I have sold many stocks to prepare for a market crash. I'm a very conservative investor. Do not follow my actions exactly as everyone's situation is different. Adjust your actions according to your risk tolerance.

As of 2019, the market was still making new highs. From my own **predictions**, today may be similar to 2007, the peaking phase of the last market cycle (termed as melt up).

I had too much cash and most of it was in money market funds in my brokers' accounts. Many of many one-year CDs paid about 1.3%. After inflation and taxes, it is a loss, but it is far better than virtually nothing from the money market funds. Our financial system punishes us for not taking risk. However, at the market peaks, we need to play defensively with conservative investments such as CDs.

The holding periods of my CDs depend on when I need the cash to buy contra ETFs such as SH during a predicted market plunge. I don't predict the market will crash in 3 months. Even if it would, I should have enough cash then within a short period of time.

Another consideration is the interest rates hikes. I predict that there would be 0.5% increase in 6 months. Hence, all the new CDs in 6 months will have 0.5% increase in interest with my theory.

We can "ladder" the CDs letting them mature in different months. For example, we can have one CD maturing in 3 months and another one in 12 months. When the first CD matures, we renew it for another 3 months. In this method, we always have cash in 3 months and one CD has a higher interest rate. The more the CDs you have, the better the distribution will be.

Ensure that the FDIC limit of $250,000 is per bank, NOT per account. Some CDs from foreign banks which are also insured by the FDIC offer higher interest rates such as the Bank of China as of this writing.

Some states offer special favorable treatment for taxing interest for CDs from local banks. Being a Mass. resident, I prefer local banks. However, the CDs from my brokers make it easy to trade and select the better rates. In one case, my bank offered a special CD deal of 1.55% for 14 months. It saved me about $200 for 2 trips to go to the bank (vs. doing it on-line).

Do not select CDs that are callable. It means the banks have the right to cancel the deal for their advantage. It is no longer a popular feature – you can cheat folks sometimes, but not all the time. Try to select the CDs having the settlement date closest to today's date. Otherwise, you do not get interest on the extra days.

For the last 5 years, SPY is returning 15% and beats the 1.3% CDs by a good margin. Today buying CDs is an insurance bet. When the market crashes, it usually is fast and deep.

SPY, simulating S&P 500, is market cap weighted. It means Apple has a far larger share than the other 499 stocks. The top five stocks are the rocket stocks to me. It would be less risky if the 500 stocks are evenly weighted.

Other safe investment besides CDs

You may also consider bond funds and/or bond ETFs. They have higher dividends but most likely they are more risky. Today I do not consider long-term bonds. Their performances are inversely proportional to the interest rate. I predict there will be interest hikes. Short-term (less than two years for me) bonds are fine.

Compare the performance of the bond funds. Most make a mistake by comparing the current performance. You should compare their performances during market peaks such as in 2007 and 1999.

The two ETFs I consider are HYG and JNK. Their annualized returns are compounded. SPY is the bench mark I use. Check out their past performances.

In 2008, the market crashed. It was a bad year for bond funds and ETFs. Based on this, I would sell them when the market crashes. However, in 2009 both recovered from the previous losses quite nicely.

	2007	2008	2009
HYG	3%	-18%	29%
JNK	Not avail.	-25%	38%
SPY	5%	-37%	26%

4   Dividend stocks

Basic ratios for dividend stocks

- **Ex-dividend date**

You will be eligible for dividends if you have your stock on the record. You want to buy the stock earlier, or on ex-dividend date in order to receive the dividend.

- Payout Ratio

It is the dividend / profit. Too high a ratio may not be good as the company does not plow back the profit into research / development. Most mature companies have higher payout ratios as they do not need to plow back into research / development when compared to high tech companies.

The other option of using the company's cash is in a stock buyback that would increase the stock values in theory.

Earnings per share = Earnings / Outstanding Shares.

When 'Earnings' is fixed but Outstanding Shares are reduced, the ratio looks good deceptively.

- Dividend Yield.

It is dividend / price.

Why companies pay dividends

Companies can use the profit by plowing back cash into research / development, buying back its stocks, acquiring companies and/or giving dividends to the stock holders. In theory, the company should consider the option most beneficial to the average stock holder. In practice, the management tries to benefit them by choosing the option best to appreciate their stocks and hence they are granted stock options.

My additions to conventional dividend investing

Hopefully my additions would improve the performance of this strategy when it has already been proven to work.

- I add market timing to Dividend Investing. You need to sell most stocks before a market plunge and buy them back as indicated by the chart.

- Diversify your portfolio. Keep 10 stocks for a portfolio of less than a million dollars. Ensure not more than 3 stocks are in the same sector. Keep 20 stocks for portfolio over a million dollars. Holding too many stocks would require more of your time that would be better spent in evaluating individual stocks. Holding too few stocks would impact your portfolio when one stock has a big loss.

  It is just my recommendation. Vary your holding size and holding period according to your time frame, your portfolio size and your expertise in investing.

- Stick with stocks with a stock price over $2, an average daily volume of over 10,000 shares (8,000 for stock prices over $25) and a market cap over 200 million.

  Most big winners usually are in the price range of between $2 and $15 price and a market cap of between 200 million and 800 million. They represent the stocks that big boys are ignoring due to their restrictions. This is just a general guideline. Change them according to your requirements.

  I prefer to skip stocks from most emerging countries, especially the smaller companies as I do not trust their financial statements.

- Ignore the subscription services or books claiming that they make over 30% consistently. Some even have examples of making 5,000%. Most likely they will tell you about the winners but not their losers.

  Check whether their portfolio uses cash or not as they cannot short change in real portfolio. Most likely those portfolios that consistently make over 30% are not real. Ask for the proof of their account from a real stock broker and check the transactions.

  Alternatively they have 10 portfolios and they may only show you the one that makes a good profit. They could use the most favorable trades for the day for their virtual account. For example, the stock rose 20% late in the day and they claimed that they bought it on the open hour. Hence, be careful not to fall for misinformation.

When they back test their strategies, they can cheat on their performances with survivor bias (i.e. those bankrupt stocks are not in the historical database). If their returns are that great, do you think they really will share their secrets with you?

Some made a big fortune and lost it all. So, the turtle investors who make small profits consistently and keep most of the wins fare far better than making millions in a year and losing it all the next year. Market timing and diversifying our portfolios help us win consistently in the long run.

Besides screening dividend stocks yourself, there are many sites providing this information. You can google 'dividend stocks'. The following are some of them.

TopYields
http://www.topyields.nl/Top-dividend-yields-of-Dividend-Aristocrats.php

An ETF on Dividend Aristocrats
http://etfdb.com/index/sp-high-yield-dividend-aristocrats-index/

From Wikipedia on THE S&P Dividend Aristocrats
http://en.wikipedia.org/wiki/THE S&P_500_Dividend_Aristocrats

There are many sites to screen dividend stocks. I select Finviz.com as that should give us the best result and it is free. In addition, we use the same site for market timing.

Screening is only the first step. You need to filter the good stocks from the bad ones. When you have a handful of stocks, evaluate each one.

Filler. DRIP stands for dividend reinvestment plan. It uses the dividend to buy more stock of the company that pays the dividend automatically, and most likely with no commissions and sometimes at 2-3% discount.
I have participated in these plans before. After a long while, the stocks bought from dividends were worth more than the initial stocks. You need to keep track of the cost basis of the purchased stocks when you sell these stocks. Check out whether the company and/or your broker offer such programs. There are many sites that have more info of DRIPs such as Money Paper https://www.directinvesting.com/.

5   Potential problems

When a strategy is over-used, it creates a bubble. There are no exceptions but when one or two have an unusual circumstance (like the gold rush in 2010 due to printing too much money). When the shoe shine boy told a famous Wall Street investor he was buying stocks, the investor unloaded everything. He knew the boy did not do any research and it was the herd mentality.

When Sarah Cohen told the TV reporter she was into dividend stocks, she seemed to be the shoe shine boy except she was prettier and she had a lot of skills except in investing.

When the massive money flows into ETFs specialized in dividend stocks, it is a mild bubble. History tells us that the average retail investor always selects the wrong side of the market. Fidelity's money fund flow has been a good contrary indicator for the market.

Past performance does not guarantee future performance unless the market conditions are the same, but it seldom happens. There are many examples such as the 2000's internet bust. Investing in dividend stocks today (2015) is still a mild bubble by many standards. Dividend stocks perform better than the market but not by a large amount. When the financial companies such as Lehman Brothers, AIG and Bear Sterns are included, dividend stocks do not perform that well.

There were several articles (at least two from WSJ) on how dividend stocks are over-valued. The premium on dividend stocks has been the highest in the last 30 years compared to stocks without dividend on the same fundamentals in theory.

Consider Total Return.

Total Return = Appreciation + Dividend + Covered Call (if used) - Taxes – Inflation

Most likely you and I do not belong to this group who drives the market, but the rich and the institutional investors are. They will consider their total return. Appreciation is usually more favorable than dividend for the tax-wise rich. You can argue that all your dividends are tax-free in retirement accounts and/or your tax rate is not that high. When these retirement accounts except Roth are withdrawn, they will be treated as regular income under the current tax law (2016).

You do not have to realize the gains (for tax purposes) on capital gains in taxable accounts. When you die, the cost basis will be stepped up. In a word, you have more control with capital gains but not with dividends. Check the current low-tax laws. Check the current tax laws. (http://en.wikipedia.org/wiki/Dividend_tax#United_States).

Afterthoughts

- Check the dividend performances and switch when they do not perform. http://seekingalpha.com/data/dividends

- Myths. http://money.usnews.com/money/blogs/the-smarter-mutual-fund-investor/2014/02/04/7-myths-about-dividend-paying-stocks

- SA article in 2016. http://seekingalpha.com/article/3901726-fate-49-dividend-aristocrats-early-1990s-may-give-nightmares

#Filler: Do we need illegal workers?

Without them, no welfare recipients want to work in the farm. Even I was desperate, I could pick oranges for half a day; the experience encouraged me to work hard and not to pick oranges again. I earned enough to have a buffet. I felt sorry for the restaurant owner for piling up the chicken wings and became a soda machine myself (due to drinking too much soda).

6   Dividend growth

As of 2015, this strategy seemed to be working fine for a long time. It is however due to the low interest rates. Retirees cannot depend on the bonds for income, so they switch to stocks that pay good dividends.

In 2015, we have to pay a premium for stocks paying high dividends. When will it end? You can examine the performance of any ETF such as DVY that specializes on high-dividend stocks for the last month and the previous three months. When they performed worse than SPY (an ETF simulating the S&P 500 stocks), most likely this mild bubble has been burst. In 9/2015, they are not doing well as a group.

A list of dividend ETFs. http://www.dividend.com/dividend-etfs/

Filler

Quantitative Easing is supposed to stimulate the economy, create jobs and increase inflation. As of 3-2015, it has not for most countries including the US.

The money has not been passed to the small businesses that generate the most jobs; we should let the SBA assign the loans. Large businesses use most of the cheap money to generate products / services (but not on development) to increase supply and hence deflation is the norm. Stock buybacks do not generate the value as illustrated by my PE (modified from the current P/E).

My PE = (Price − Cash + Debt) / Expected Earnings
        all expressed in per share

It is better but more work for use to use "Net Current Asset" instead of Cash.

The big banks lend money to investors and that explains why the stock market is booming and we have record-high margin debt. It also widens the wealth gap generating inequality conflicts.

Strategy 10: Sector subscription

You can follow a subscription or two that have proven performances.

1   Subscription services on sectors

When your sector portfolio is over a certain threshold (say 100,000), you may want to subscribe a sector service for your primary tool or just a second opinion.

There are many subscription services to advise us to switch between sectors, but you have to pay a fee. Most subscription services such as Zacks.com rank sectors include ranks for sectors.

The following is on sector funds (select funds in Fidelity's terms). It also indicates that Fidelity is the leader in sector funds.

In 2013 most are doing quite good beating SPY by a good margin. Here are some of them.

1. AI Stock Forecast. 39% in 2013.
2. AlphaProfit Sector Investors' Newsletter. 46%.
3. Fidelity Independent Advisor Sector Momentum. 39%.
4. Fidelity Monitor and Insight. 38%.
5. Fidelity Sector Investor. 46%.

It seems their returns are quite compatible to each other. It could be they use the same technique described in this book.

The above info is based on a MarketWatch article on sector rotation.

(http://www.marketwatch.com/story/the-top-5-fidelity-sector-strategies-of-2013-2014-01-15?link=MW_popular)

I have tried a fund that rotates sectors for you. At that time, the performance was not too good.

Additional resources

- **Fidelity Sector Fund**

Without doubt, Fidelity provides a lot of sector funds and some sector ETFs. That's why there are so many investment newsletters on their sector offerings.

From AlphaProfit, the average Fidelity Select (same as sector) fund has outperformed the S&P 500 index by 4.7% annually over the last 20 years. Individual performances would be far, far better if you pick the right select funds.

I recommend picking 3 top select funds and rotating them every 3 months. There would be no need to rotate them if they are still in the top five. Sell all the owned funds if the market is. If you rotate funds in your taxable account, be warned to pay higher taxes if they're profitable – check the current tax laws. This would be the least effort in implementing sector fund rotation using a proven newsletter such as AlphaProfit.

- Finviz.com.

It has the recent sector performance. Vector Vest selects the most timely sectors and industries. So are IBD, cnnfn.com and Zacks.

Links

There are three articles in Seeking Alpha on this topic.
Developing a Rotation Strategy Using Highly Diversified ETFs:
Part I, Part II and Part III.
http://seekingalpha.com/article/2045483-developing-a-rotation-strategy-using-highly-diversified-etfs

Sectors as of 7/2014.
http://seekingalpha.com/article/2322765-sector-rankings-for-etfs-and-mutual-funds
AlphaProfit: http://www.alphaprofit.com/
Strategy: http://etfdb.com/2013/3-sector-rotation-strategies-etf-investors-must-know/

2   Newsletters and subscriptions

Why do you not see too many reviews on investment newsletters and subscriptions from the media? If it is a bad review, most likely they will not advertise in the media. If it is a good review, they may have to face legal actions in the future if the vendor's subscription or newsletter does not perform well.

I've been using investment newsletters / subscriptions for years. Many are priced reasonably and some are even free. While a lot of them are garbage, some are very good.

When you have a lot of money to invest and you're not using a financial adviser and/or not subscribing to any investment service, it could be a big financial mistake. You do not want to be a penny smart but a pound foolish. Very few have the knowledge and the time to make use of the free financial data, including the guidance and articles from the web.

You need a computer, access to the Internet and a spreadsheet in order to use most subscription services effectively.

I'm not going to compare specific services / newsletters at the risk of being sued, but I will include general pointers on how to select them. Yesterday's garbage could be a gold mine today if the subscription improves and/or the market conditions fit what they recommend.

First, you need to find out your requirements and how much time you can afford to use them. If you have $20,000 or less to invest, most likely your investment both in time and money will not pay off. Just buy an ETF and practice market timing described in this book. My pointers are:

- Newsletters giving you specific stocks to buy do not require much of your time. However, if they're successful, there will be too many followers buying the recommended stocks that can drive up the prices at least temporarily. The owner of the subscription service and his insiders will buy the recommended stocks before you unless they're not allowed to do so (who's enforcing this?). I had several of these newsletters, and so far I have not renewed any one of them due to the poor performance.

- If I found the Holy Grail of investing, do you believe I would share it with you for $100 or so? I only will after I invested my money first. My subscribers would push up the prices for me and then I could unload them before my subscribers.

As an experiment, I am publishing a book every month with the title "Best Stocks, As of MM/01/YYYY" recommending a handful of stocks. Due to my relatively small positions and few buyers of the book, it will not have the adverse effects described. If it reaches a wide audience, I will not trade the stocks I recommended in my books. Most of my recommendations should be value stocks for long term hold unless the market is risky such as in 8/2019. My books will not be the Holy Grail as my aim is beating the S&P 500 Index.

- If the volume of the recommended stocks are small, they can be manipulated easily either by the newsletter owners and/or by your peer subscribers. The first ones to sell the recommended stocks win and the last ones to sell them lose.

- I prefer systems that can find a lot of stocks by providing many searches (same as screens). However, it will take a lot of time to learn and test their performance which can be obtained easily with a historical database. Most likely, you need to further research each stock screened. The screens would select a limited number of stocks for further analysis, so it will save you time for sure.

  From my experience, the best performance comes from the stocks that have been screened by more than one search especially for the short term (less than 6 months). My theory is that they've been identified for many folks and hence their prices could be jacked up. It is more profitable to buy them ahead of the herd and sell them before the herd. In any case, research the stock you are interested in.

- I have received promotional mail that indicates their incredible performances such as tripling the money. Just ignore them. If it is that good, most likely they will keep them for themselves. It is the same for seminars that boost some penny stocks. Most likely the recommended stocks would rise initially to lure you and other suckers to move it. Watch out! As of 2016, I do not see these junk mail as often as before; the public is smarter. They must have switched their promotions to YouTube.

- A 'guru' told me that he made a big fortune in silver a month ago. Guess what? He also recommended selling it two months earlier and lost a lot of money in doing so. He is always right but he will not advertise the times he was wrong. We call it a double talk technique.

- There are free trial offers (or deeply discounted) for most subscription services. Take advantage of them. Some services require you to spend a lot of time, so ensure you have the time. Keep track of the performance yourself via paper trading. Do not trust their 'official' performance.

- Subscribe to a newsletter that fits your style of investing. If you're a day trader, newsletters on long-term investing are not good for you. Some subscriptions handle all kinds of investing styles and you need to find the strategies and recommendations to fit your style. A short-term swing trade has different metrics than a long-term investor.

- Newsletters on penny stocks are risky for most of us. They may show you a list of big winners but they do not show you their losers.

  I define penny stocks as less than $2 (officially $5) and a market cap less than 100 M. However, I do buy stocks with prices around $2 or a capital cap less than 100 M. Actually I bought ALU at $1 but ALU's market cap then was about 2 billion at the time. The stocks with prices between $1 and $10 represent the most volatile stocks and a few are real gems. They are routinely ignored by most analysts.

- There are many sectors like drugs, mines, insurance and banks that retail investors cannot evaluate effectively. It is better to seek expert advice from specific newsletters. Check out their past performance and take advantage of the free trial offers.

- Remember there is no free lunch in life. The higher potential return of a stock, the riskier the stock is. To me, all trades are educated guesses. The more educated the guesses are, the higher chance they will perform in the long run. However, noting is 100% sure.

- Some newsletters / subscriptions save us time by summarizing the financial data by providing a value rank and a growth rank. Some provide a timely rank from the momentum of the price. When the market favors growth, you use the growth rank, and vice versa.

- Be careful with the information from radio and TV commercials. Many try to sell to peoples' fear and greed by overstating without necessarily telling the whole story. It is not possible to make 50% in covered calls consistently or making another gold rush from $400 to $1,800. One advertises the market will lose 80% in 2016. It is possible but not likely. [Update: The market was profitable in 2016.] They are tactics to get you subscribe to their services.

- TV financial shows usually exaggerate in order to sell their products. Analyze them before you act on the news.

- As retail investors, most of us cannot afford to do extensive research. Many researches and market opinions are available on the internet free. Start to search for such information from your broker's site and financial sites such as SeekingAlpha.com, MarketWatch.com, CNNfn.com and Yahoo!Finance.com. Analyze the news and some could be obsolete or could be manipulated with a hidden agenda by the time you get it.

- Do not trust the performance of newsletter providers. There are many ways to manipulate their performance.

- Most compare their performances with the S&P 500 index. It is legal for investment newsletters to inflate their performance with dividends while comparing to an index without including dividends.

  To illustrate, the S&P 500 has an average annual return of 1% on appreciation and 1.5% on dividends for a total return of 2.5%. Hence, the performance of a newsletter should compare itself to 2.5% not 1%.

- The performance of the last 10 years (I prefer last 5 years) is more important than that of 25 years. The last 10 years is a better prediction of the newsletter than the last 25 years as the weatherman has found out.

  More than one time, I have found a popular subscription that did not beat S&P 500 in the last 5 years but it did in the last 20 years. It could be that too many folks are using the same strategy.

- When the new major researcher takes over the subscription, s/he may not have the same expertise as the previous researcher.

- Ensure the subscriptions change their strategies according to the current market conditions. For example, 10 years ago ADRs (U.S. listed stocks of foreign countries) performed far better than today. The trend may reverse in the future.

- Few if any use real money for their portfolios, as they cannot cheat with real money. That's why you never achieve the compatible performance by following what the portfolio trades. Some can manipulate by using the best prices of the day. Some omit their losers. Do not trust any performance claims even from reputable monitor services unless the portfolios can be verified with real money.

  Some sample portfolios trade excessively and they may not fit your investment strategy in addition to excessive commissions and taxes.

- When a subscription service has several strategies (say 10 for illustration purposes), they will advertise the strategies with the best returns for a specific time period.

- Today (12/8/2014) TNH was down by 12% by the end of the day. If they used the open price, it would have made a difference of 12%

Contrary to not recommending investment services, I recommend Fidelity or your broker for the stock research. AAII is a low-priced subscription, but Fidelity, Finviz and Yahoo!Finance are free today.

Filler: Golden Gate

Just minutes ago, my mail system asked me to sign in. I did and repeatedly they asked me to sign in again and again. I closed down everything and followed Gates' golden rule: If everything does not work, just power down everything and power it up again. I did this and prayed too. It works. Thanks Gates for fixing my problem.

There is NO one doing BASIC quality control. If it happened in my generation, many guys would be fired. Mediocrity is the new norm?

Strategy 11: Top-down

Basically you pick the best sector and buy the best stocks within the sector. It is the more time-consuming task and the rest of the book is devoted to this strategy.

1   Top-down investing

The nutshell is described here. Only buy stocks when the market is favorable. Find the best industry (a subsector) and then find the best stock(s) within the selected industry. In doing so, our chances of successful investing are substantially increased.

It is so simple and it has been proven by many including myself. I just wonder why it has not been extensively practiced. I offer a simple trade plan as follows:

1. Do not invest when the market is plunging. I have a simple way to detect market plunges without any expensive subscriptions or tools.

2. Select the best industry (most are represented by an ETF or ETFs specific for the industry or sector). For example, Technology is a sector. Computer and Software are industries (subsector under Technology). From time to time I use sectors for simplicity and most free sites do not sub divide the sectors into industries. Check out the best-performing industry or sector from last month in many sites including SeekingAlpha and CNNfn.

   If you're a value investor, you may not want to choose the timeliest sector but the most under-valued sector. Value investors should hold the sectors/stocks longer (such as 6 months or even longer) for the market to recognize their values.

   In addition, you need to detect the sector/stock rotation by the institutional investors who control over 75% of all trades (i.e. smart money). They will rotate sector/stock when they find better profit potential in another sector/stock. Use stops to prevent further losses.

If you do not have time to research on stocks, trade ETFs for sectors and skip the next step.

3. The final step is to select the best stock(s) within the sector via fundamental analysis (including intangible analysis), insider trading analysis, institution trading analysis and technical analysis.

   Do not let these terms scare you. We will start with the simplest approach without any subscription and a lot of effort.

4. The next step is when to reevaluate and sell the stocks when conditions change or they meet your objectives. If the market is plunging, sell all stocks.

Stick with and repeat the entire process.

The easiest retirement planning system

Have a budget and live within your means. Buy good stuff that lasts for a long time. After saving enough cash for emergency and planned expenses such as vacation, new car, college, etc., invest your extra money in a retirement account (Roth IRA if allowable) with 80% in a market ETF and 20% in a short-term bond ETF.

Run the chart described in the market cycle chapters once a month. If the chart tells you to exit the market, move all to cash. Reenter the market when the chart tells you to do so. It beats most if not all of your financial plans from the best experts money can buy.

Afterthoughts

My late friend had a 'buy and hold strategy' that worked pretty well. Most of his stocks were big companies. He died with a house worth more than a million and many millions in stocks. His only mistake was not to transfer more of his stocks to his heirs before his death. He died on the year when the estate exemption returned back to a million. Uncle Sam was the biggest winner and won big without any effort.

Strategy 12: Trade by headlines / Earnings

Buy on good news. Buy expecting good earnings. Sell vice versa.

1   Trading by headlines

On 6/29/2019, Trump and Xi seemed to settle trade war in the G20. The market would likely rise on the coming Monday. Luckily I had closed a short position. Many chip stocks would rise as they can sell their products to Huawei. I have several of these stocks expecting the trade war would be settled. The farmers and their supporting industry would breathe easier.

I bet the shipping companies would be more profitable from the news. Without doing further research, I checked out this shipping sector and found the following stocks had been up more than 4%: DHT, NM, SBLK, STNG, TNK and ASC. It was during the weekend, so your trade account should be able to trade after hours and you need to act right after the news.

I exchanged comments with Andrew McElroy, a sector rotation expert. He does not have the rules set up as in this book but he makes great trades by 'seeing' the market and using technical analysis. The following is from his article.

"The idea is fairly simple. There is more potential for profit (and loss) in individual sectors, especially when the index is trading sideways. I try to buy strong sectors which have pulled back onto support and avoid overbought sectors at resistance. I also use Elliott Wave to identify cycles of buying and selling and stages in trends."

I would like to include headlines such as Trump's election, interest rates hikes and new regulations.

When it rains in Brazil, buy coffee futures

Recently it rained too much in SE Asia, so buy rice futures. I did not trade futures, so I missed out on the opportunity and unfortunately there is no equivalent ETF for rice. In the beginning of 2012, we should know the farming crops especially corn will not be good due to the flooding and drought in different parts of the world. Act accordingly for the profit potentials.

When a war is starting in the Middle East, most likely the oil price will rise. Buy the oil ETF and sell it when the chance of the war is reduced. Many tiny drops of profit could turn into a river of profit.

Trading by headlines is profitable, but it is hard to master and is very time-consuming. Test this strategy on paper for years before you commit real money as in most strategies. Most couch potatoes read the newspaper and watch TV all day long without making a penny. He could be couch potato millionaire if he read this article, paper traded/refined the strategy and acted on it!

However, the media tend to exaggerate headlines in order to sell their ads. Ignore all the recommendations on stocks. Most likely they are outdated information and some may be used to manipulate others. Do your own research as your mother taught you that there is no free lunch.

Rules of the game

1. Do not be too emotional; ignore your past wins and losses except when using them as lessons if they are valid (i.e. educated guesses).

2. Do not trade the entire farm. Consider option, ETFs and/or small trade on stocks, which have too many other factors to be considered.

3. Trade it fast – today's headlines will not be headlines tomorrow. There are very few exceptions.

4. Where there is a winner, there is always a loser. For example, Apple was a winner with the iPhone and BlackBerry was a loser. Same for Best Buy and Circuit City.

5. Ensure you can trade after hours from your broker.

6. Do not forget when to exit for either a small profit or a small loss.

7. Quick evaluation. The headline will be gone if you do not act fast. Skip companies with poor metrics such as high debt and low earnings yield. Prefer to buy an ETF related to the headline.

8. Most likely someone has used the information before you get it. However, some info can be deducted before it occurs. Insider purchases is a good guide.

9. I recommended crude oil at $30 per barrel in Jan. 15, 2016 as the price was at rock bottom. For value sectors, you may have to wait for a long time for the market to realize its value.

10. Sometimes you ignore stock evaluations as the headline news is more important. Learn my 5-minute evaluation process of a stock (a quick way but not recommended if you have time to do thorough research):
    - From Finviz.com, enter the stock or ETF symbol. Look at how many greens in metrics over reds.
    - Check out Forward P/E (E>0 and P/E < 20), Debut / Equity (< 50%) and P/FCF (not in red color).
    - SMA20 (or SMA50 for longer holding period). If SMA20 is > 10%, it is trending up.
    - Scroll down for Insider Trade. It usually is a good buy if insiders are buying recently and heavily with market prices.
    - Be cautious on foreign and low-volume stocks.
    - If most of the above are positive, it is likely a buy. As in life, nothing is 100% certain.

If you have a hard time following the above, most likely this strategy is not for you and it is better to return to your couch. No offense.

Volatile market and headlines
As of 7/2012 (2015 too and historically a positive market in a year right before the election), the market went sideways and was influenced by headlines. 2013 had been volatile with dips and surges influenced by daily news. The trend was up though. The Federal debt problem, EU crisis… had not been resolved. Every time we had good news, the market rose, and vice versa. In this market, buy on dips (3% down from last temporary peak) and sell on temporary surges (3% up from last temporary bottom). Some use 5% instead of 3% depending on one's risk tolerance.

Trend and calendar timing

Usually following the trend is better than ignoring it.

- Many retail investors want to get rid of the losers for year-end tax planning. Buy them at year-end and sell them early next year. In the year end of 2012, it acted the opposite as folks were selling their winners expecting a larger tax bite next year but that turned out to be false.

  This could be the reason for a sell-off of Apple in year-end of 2012 and it gave us a good entry point. To me, Apple's fundamentals were sound though the media said otherwise. In a few months, Apple became a value stock from a growth stock according to the press.

- Investors are not rational and follow the market blindly. The strategy 'Buy low and sell high' works.

- We have so much good news and bad news in the same year. Ensure the bad news will not extend to worse news. Timing is everything. Buy on bad news and sell on good news; it does not work when the market plunges.

- The media influences the market. Analyze their arguments. If they exaggerate them, do the opposite.

- Over-reaction to earnings missed or gained. When the company missed the earnings by 5%, there is a very good chance the stock will be down in a year, and vice versa. However, when it missed by 1% and the stock lost by 10%, it could be a buying opportunity, particularly when it was a temporary condition and the company is fundamentally sound.

- Buy the stock at dip when a solvable problem surfaces. Sell after the problem has been resolved. Ceiling debt is such a solvable problem and it is caused by politics. In the beginning of 2013, I mentioned that the debt problem had not been resolved and we would have this ceiling debt problem periodically until it will be eventually resolved.

Scheduled events

Some events are scheduled such as earnings announcements, unemployment reports, etc. Most likely educated guesses of the outcomes have already been circulated in the web.

The last five events on the Federal debt handling (using fancy names such as sequester and debt ceiling) were scheduled such as the government shutdown. They drove the market down by about an average of 5% each time. Sell before the event and buy back afterward. The Congress has cancelled these debt deadlines as of 1/2014.

Many sectors are impacted by events such as Trump's success in election, hikes of interest rates and trade wars.

Follow the institutional investors

They drive the market. When they see the sector is over-valued or the peak has been reached, they rotate sectors.

Use deduction

In 2014, China has a great harvest on wheat, corn and rice. China's population is #1 in the world and its middle class is growing. The farmers in the US will be hurt as they cannot export these products to their number one customer. Use the same logic to deduct that there will be problems in the companies that supply products and services to the farmers. They are combines, fertilizer companies and seed companies. It further translates into Deere, Potash, Monsanto and AGCO.

Due to increasing wealth in 2017, Chinese demanded more meat. It takes a lot of corn to produce one pound of meat and in turn corn needed fertilizers. Hence, you can expect the companies producing fertilizers will increase their profits.

Geopolitical crisis

Many times no action is the best action. It applies here. I had my experience in selling too many stocks via stops in 911. The market returned in a few days and I did not buy them back.

An analysis from Ned David Research covers 51 events from 1900 to 2014. My interpretation for actions: Trade the affected sector (via sector ETF) in the first few days and reverse the trade 2 months after. Many times it means the oil price and gold price would rise.

I bought SH (a contra ETF to SPY) in August, 2017 as August and September are statistically the worst months in addition to the high risk in the current market. It is expected to be sold on Nov. 1. The North Korea crisis did not do much to the market on the first day but the market (the S&P 500) lost 1.45% and the risky NASDAQ lost 2.13% (see my blog on FAANG) on the second day.

Caveat. Need to understand the crisis. If it would lead to World War 3, most sectors will not recover for a long while. Again, there is no sure thing in investing otherwise there would be no poor folks. However, educated guesses should materialize more often than not.

My experiences
- When the interest rates is expected to rise, plan on investments that are favorable to it and vice versa.
- On the same week, CROX lost almost 40% in one day. I bought some and made about 10% profit in a week. CROX's fundamentals were no good and it did have a history of a roller coaster ride in its stock price. After a year, I found out that I sold it too early as the stock price doubled. Better to buy a stock on its way up than down unless we identify that the bottom has been reached.
- I was on vacation while the second incident of the Boeing Max happened. Should have shorted the stock. In addition, Boeing's suppliers would suffer too similar to Apple's suppliers on Apple.

  https://www.barrons.com/articles/boeing-737-max-jet-production-cut-suppliers-stocks-51554499957?siteid=yhoof2&yptr=yahoo

- I missed applying the same trick to the rise of Apple when Apple announced its new iPod. I should at least buy the stocks of its part suppliers. I hope learn from this lesson and take advantage of future similar circumstances.
  I missed the opportunity to buy uranium stocks. It should be bought after Japan's disaster. When Japan approved the reopening of nuclear reactors today, these stocks including CCJ, DNN, LEU, URRE, UEC, URZ, URG and UUUU surge. When China's new nuclear reactors are on-line, they will surge again.
- Experiences in early 2014.
  Recently and in a short time, I made a good profit on BBY and a tiny profit on TGT. Both were bought due to headlines.

2   Earnings season overreactions

AAII has some screens for stocks with pleasant earnings surprises and bad earnings surprises (Jan., April, July and Oct.). The pleasant surprise screen always beats the other screens from the last time I checked.

Zacks ranks stocks with positive earnings revisions. Their stocks have ranked #1 has an amazing average annual return of 26% according to them. In 2019, the performance of recent tests did not hold up that well.

As with all vendors, we should check their recent performance (say, the last 5 years). If the strategy is proven to be effective, more investors will follow and usually make it less effective.

It usually starts on the first two weeks after the ending of quarters (Dec., March, June and September) as indicated in the following link.
http://www.investopedia.com/ask/answers/08/earnings-season.asp

My experience
Contrary to the conventional wisdom, I enjoy the negative surprises more. If the company has a reason to come back or its problem is only temporary, I buy the stock. Sometimes it takes a few months and sometimes even a year for the stock to come back. The strategy of 'Buying low and selling high' works more often than it does not. However, avoid the stocks that start their long-term plunge.

Missing expected earnings by 1% and causing the stock to drop by 10% is a buy to me. Heading to bankruptcy is a different story though.

My momentum strategy buys stocks with positive earnings revisions. I usually do not keep these stocks for over a month.

As of today (4/6/2016), the quarter earnings season is starting. This year I have worry about the earnings due to the strong USD. It would impact the earnings as about 40% (my rough estimate) of the incomes of global companies are from foreign countries. If we feel there will be more disappointments, we should short the stocks that are expected to have poor earnings.

My lesson
Take advantage of the irrational human reactions. Retail investors and institutional investors are both human beings. Fund managers have more

pressure to sell a loser to keep their jobs. Retail investors usually sell after the big institutional investors. Try to find out whether it is just a sentimental reaction or the stock is going to fall further.

How to hedge your stocks from earning surprises

Stocks might have a wide swing after the earnings announcements. Hedge the unfavorable announcements by the following three methods:

1. Stop loss.
   Usually the swing is steeper than your stop price. When the price reaches or go below a specific price, it will be turned into a market sell order. Institutional investors usually unload the stocks faster than the retail investors, opposite of buying. However, their positions are huge. We can tell they are unloading (or loading) from the unusual high trading volumes of the stocks. Ensure that your trades are allowed after hours.
2. Option.
   It is like buying an insurance to protect your loss. Protect yourself from large losses as insurance is not cheap and smaller losses could be due to volatility.
3. Earnings prediction.
   They are also known as whispers or educated guesses. Zacks has a grading system.

   Also insiders know the earnings before their announcements. However, it is illegal to use this information before its announcement.

Earnings revisions will be available before the announcement and they would provide better guesses to the announcement. With today's dividend chasers, the announcement of dividends or its increase would boost the stock price.

Personally I do not do a lot to protect my stocks from earnings announcements. I have too many stocks. However, when we have evaluated the stocks correctly and monitor them regularly, we should have more pleasant surprises.

Profit from earnings surprises
The stock price usually rises on positive earnings surprises and falls otherwise. Sometimes they are not rational such as 1% miss in earnings that causes 10% loss in the stock price. In some rare cases, the positive earnings

causes the stock to plunge as the investors expected better earnings even better than consensus. Here is the example of looking for finding stocks with positive earnings (you can profit by buying puts or shorting the stocks for stocks with negative earnings).

- Find stocks that have earnings announcements next week or month. Sources are Finviz.com's screener and SeekingAlpha.
- The screened stocks should fit some basic criteria. My criteria are: Market Cap > 200M, stock price > $2, average volume > 10,000 shares...
- If you subscribe to Zacks, check out the earnings grade. Stocks with Grade 1 and Grade 2 deserve our time for further research.
- If there are meaningful insiders' purchases, the chance of positive earnings are high.
- A positive short-term trend (SMA-20% from Finviz.com) is a plus.
- A positive short-term trend for the sector that stock belongs to is a plus. The sector can be represented by an ETF for that sector and use SMA-20%.
- Read articles on the stock for a qualitative analysis. Find these articles from many sources including SeekingAlpha. Today they have fewer articles for free.

Be warned that we do not expect all wins. When we achieve more than 50% wins, we should fare very well financially. When the market is falling or the earnings are expected to be poor, do not buy stocks except those that are fundamentally sound.

Take advantage of others' orders

1. Ensure your account can trade after hours.
2. Use Finviz.com to look for stocks announcing earnings this week. Prefer fundamentally sound stocks with a market cap great than 500 (100 for smaller stocks).
3. Check out earningswhispers.com. They have two estimates: the consensus and the one from this web site. Write down the exact time too.
4. If you subscribe Zacks.com, use its rating too as a reference.
5. Be at least 15 minutes earlier than the announcement date and time.
6. Google the stock and EPS from Google News. Refresh the search every 2 minutes. Check related articles.
7. If it beats the estimates, buy it at least one penny less than the last trade price and sell it within a day or two. The logic is to take advantage of all

those orders that have not considered earnings in a timely fashion. It does not always work.

8. To improve performance, include Revenue with EPS.

Personally I do not do it as it is too time-consuming for me; my beauty sleep is more important than money. Again test it out before committing real money. There are many parameters that can be tuned to adjust to your personal preferences and the current market conditions. This is the essence of an entire book. I read with my own enhancements such as using Finviz.com.

3   Strategies on earnings

Here are two strategies on earnings. It is supposed to make millions for my children but they are not interested in investing. You either hate or love what your old man does.

1. Buy the stocks with earnings announcement soon with Zacks rating 1 (the best) and short those with Zacks rating 5 (the worst). BTW, Zacks rating is free so far for individual stocks.

2. After the earnings announcement, Google the company every second or so. If the earnings are good, buy it fast with market order. If it is bad, short it.

Do not be greedy and set a limit on loss. Do not call me if the trade is good or bad. In addition, check insider transactions and SMA-20%. I use Finviz.com.

I have tried #1 once a long while ago. I have not tried #2 as I have a life too. In the long haul, these strategies should make you some money.

The best complement

My late mother loved Wheel of Fortune. Why it is the best complement you may ask? She did not speak English.

.

Strategy 13: Insider Trading

1   Define Insider Trading

Investopedia defines it as:

"Insider trading can be illegal or legal depending on when the insider makes the trade: it is illegal when the material information is still nonpublic--trading while having special knowledge is unfair to other investors who don't have access to such knowledge. Illegal insider trading therefore includes tipping others when you have any sort of nonpublic information. Directors are not the only ones who have the potential to be convicted of insider trading. People such as brokers and even family members can be guilty.

Insider trading is legal once the material information has been made public, at which time the insider has no direct advantage over other investors. The SEC, however, still requires all insiders to report all their transactions. So, as insiders have an insight into the workings of their company, it may be wise for an investor to look at these reports to see how insiders are legally trading their stock."

If you need more information, click this link from Wikipedia.
http://en.wikipedia.org/wiki/Insider_trading

My additions to conventional insider trading

Hopefully my additions improve the performance of this strategy that has already been proven to work most of the time.

- I add market timing to Insider Trading. You need to sell most stocks except contra ETFs before a market plunge and buy them back as indicated by the chart.

- Diversify your portfolio. Keep 10 stocks for a portfolio less than a million. Ensure that there are not more than 3 stocks in the same sector. Keep 20 stocks for portfolio over a million. Too many stocks would require more of your time that would be better spent in evaluating individual stocks. Too few of stocks would impact your portfolio when one stock has a big loss.

It is just a recommendation. Vary your holding size and holding period according to your time, your portfolio size and your expertise in the sector.

- Stick with stocks over $2, average daily volume over 10,000 shares (8,000 for stock prices over $25) and market cap over 200 million.

  Most big winners usually are in the price range between the $2 and $15 price and market cap between 200 million to 800 million. They represent the stocks that big boys are ignoring due to their restrictions. This is just a general guideline and there are always exceptions. Change them according to your requirements.

  I prefer to skip stocks from most emerging countries, especially the smaller companies as I do not trust their financial statements.

- Ignore the subscription services or books claiming they are making over 30% consistently. Some even have examples of making 5,000%. Most likely they tell you the winners but not their losers. It is easy to pick up winners that fit their strategy but it does not tell you the real performance.

  Check whether their portfolio uses cash or not as it cannot be manipulated such as using the best prices of the day to trade. I bet that those portfolios consistently making over 30% are not real. Alternatively they have 10 portfolios and they only show you the one that makes a good profit.

  When they back test their strategies, they cheat their performances with survivor bias (i.e. those bankrupt stocks are not in the historical database). If their returns are that great, do you think they will share their secrets with you?

  Some made a big fortune and lost it all. So, the turtle investors who make small profits consistently and keep most of the wins fare far better than making millions in a year and losing it all in next year. Market timing and diversifying our portfolio would help us win consistently in the long run.

2   How to profit

My own monitor

The following is one of my performance monitors from the stocks I bought for over a period of 6 months.

All stocks	Stocks with Insiders' Purchases	Beat all stocks
21%	28%	33%

This test was performed on 9/7/2013. They were the actual stocks I screened from the screens that had been proven. Insider Purchase is one of the fundamental metrics I monitored. The total number of stocks is 372 and 77 are identified as having heavy insider purchases. The returns are not annualized (annualized returns are better to compare stocks bought on different dates) and dividends are not added. Most stocks have a holding period longer than 6 months.

The test results are consistent with my previous tests. Beating all stocks by 33% is quite convincing. It does not take a genius to show the strategy of following insiders' purchases works at least in this performance monitor.

I conducted another test using the web site OpenInsider on 11/2013. It listed all the insiders' purchases for more than a year. Selected insider purchases about 1 year ago by the Officer (CEO and CFO) only. I skipped the purchases that do not meet the requirements.

The annualized return is 50%. I only had about 50 stocks and it is not enough evidence to draw a conclusion. Even with 40% return, the strategy proves itself again.

My suggestion

Evaluate the purchased stocks again in 6 months. Sell the ones whose fundamental metrics have deteriorated or the price targets have been met.

Consider market timing. Sell most stocks when the chart indicates that the market is plunging.

Consider the total return. If you can wait for a month or so for less taxes on long-term capital gain, do so. If you expect that your stock does not appreciate a lot in the next few months, consider covered calls (similar to collecting rent with the renter's option to buy the housing unit at a specific price and time).

A recent example

Sometimes all experts are wrong on a stock except the insiders. Today (2/5/2015), GLUU is up by 23% with a good earnings report. It is 31% up since I bought it on 1/28/15, just 8 days ago. The annualized return must be astronomical.

I bought it based on the favorable Insider Purchases and confirmed by a good earnings rating (second best) from Zacks. Pow EY was 7% (passed), short-term score 4 (failed), long-term score 16 (just passed) and Pow Score 2 (just passed). The quarter-to-quarter profits and sales were spectacular at 200%.

The experts were wrong when I evaluated the stock: Safety Margin ridiculously negative, Blue Chip Growth C, Shorter 17%, Fidelity Analyst 4 (1 to 10 with 10 the best), ROE 3%, SMA %(10, 20 and 200 days) all negative (not good), IBD composite grade 33 (far below the average) and its SMD grade D.

Filler: How to fight terrorism?

It is interesting Poland has zero terrorist attacks so far and they refuse refugees. So is Japan.

Most of the countries that have most terrorist attacks are those who welcome Middle East refugees. I like to help them but we have to ensure we do not let terrorists in.

They are called terrorists or freedom fighters. We have bombed their cities so bad that they have no future. They cannot fight us back with their primitive weapons but using terrorism. Every action has a reaction.

Strategy 14: Momentum investing

This strategy provides me with steady income by working an hour or two every week. How long will it last? I do not know. I will describe the concept here, so you can devise your own to fit your risk tolerance and requirements.

As of this writing, this strategy is having amazing returns. Though these returns may not be sustainable, my convictions are so strong that I am boldly increasing my investment. During the risky market such as in 2019, stop using this strategy or do not keep my bought stocks too long.

The concept of a momentum strategy

Each week, I buy about 5 stocks based on the momentum metrics and sell them within a month. I do not use the fundamental metrics as that will not be effective in such a short duration. From my current record, the average holding time is about 20 days.

The details of my strategy will not be disclosed fully. When the strategy is used too often, it will not be effective and would end up churning the same stocks for all its followers. However, let me elaborate on the implementation of this momentum strategy and give you some ideas on how to build one for yourself.

My Theory. When a stock is on the uptrend, most likely it will continue for at least for a week or two. Do not buy stocks when the market is risky. Protect yourself by using stops and / or using technical indicators such as SMA-20.

Subscription services

I spend less than half an hour to find about 6 stocks to buy. My choice is helped by subscription services. Some have earnings revision information (particularly useful during earnings seasons) and most others have provided timing grades. I include the insider purchase information and short-term technical indicators. It worked so far and I constantly monitor the performance.

For starters, use simple screens and procedures to find stocks without getting a subscription service. Paper trade your screens and strategies to include your average holding period and money management before you commit to use real money.

Common parameters

I subscribe to several investment services and select their recommendations. From my recent reviews, I only need a good subscription with historical database plus the free Fidelity, Yahoo!Finance and Finviz. Usually they have provided a timing ranking. The other rank could be for value and you should ignore it while using this strategy.

To illustrate, the composite rank for timing in Blue Chip Growth (not free any more) is the Quantitative Score. It is also known as the buying pressure. Fidelity provides similar rankings.

http://navelliergrowth.investorplace.com/bluechip/password/index.php?pl ocation=%2Fbluechip%2F.

There are several common parameters that on how they rank stocks. These parameters may be obtained from Finviz.com.

- Price momentum. I prefer to use SMA20% (20-day simple moving average). The higher the percentage the better. However, they should not be too high (say greater than 15%). When it is peaking, the stock will fall.

- Change of short %. Favorable if it is over 25% (for short squeezes) and unfavorable if it is moving up (say from 5% to 15%).

- Sales momentum (Sales Q/Q) and earnings momentum (EPS Q/Q or quarter earnings to quarter prior year).

- Earnings revisions. Zacks (free for single stock) has good info based on their estimates and rumors.
- Insider's Purchase. No one knows the company better than its officers.
- Analysts' recommendation. It can be obtained from Finviz.com. However, Fidelity's Equity Summary Score provides a better one and it is based on the past performances of the analysts' predictions.

Reduce Taxes

I use my Roth accounts to minimize my taxes. As of 2016, the gain in the Roth is tax-free from Federal income tax. Its withdrawals are also tax-free from Federal income tax for one's life time. In addition, the Roth is not included in the minimum withdrawal requirement (at 70 ½) during one's personal life time. I converted some of my Roll-over IRA to my Roth as allowed. Consult your tax lawyer or CPS for updated information about your individual situations.

Reduce loss during market downfall

My strategy works best in the up market as I seldom short stocks. However, a major market downfall could wipe out all profits. In 2019, I am shorting stocks more often as the market is risky.

These are two Technical Analysis tools to anticipate a market downfall.

1. Spot market plunges.
2. Spot yearly dips (i.e. correction).

Minimize losses once a downfall of the market has been spotted.

- Do not buy any stock and then cancel any outstanding buy orders you may have.

- Sell any existing positions and/or use stops to reduce further losses.

- Buy contra ETFs such as DOG, SH and PSQ for DOW, the S&P and/or NASDAQ when the market is too risky. It is like buying insurance (hedging your portfolio). Hedging in a rising market such as in 2013 was a loser's game.

- The dip of 2/2013 woke me up. The portfolio for this strategy lost about 1/3 of the total gain of this portfolio since 12/2012, but it returned all the losses this week. It is still very profitable and beats the SPY by a good margin.

  The loss should be much lower. This was the week I just started to increase my position. Poor timing! You need to be emotionally detached and stick with the strategy that has been proven to you.

  In being disciplined, your strategy should be profitable despite its ups and downs. In the long term, I do not believe in luck as a major factor in investing.

- As of 4/2013, the average annualized return of 66 round-trip trades was 127%. It is so far so good, but it will not be sustainable in the longer run.

- I have stopped this strategy for a while due to the risky market and taking a long vacation. I returned trading on 9/4/2013.

Monitor performance

I constantly monitor different but consistent parameters and sources for my stock screening, selection and holdings that affect performance. I am always looking at perfecting better systems and /or adapting to the current market conditions.

- Day of the week.
  Monday is not a good day as most of my available info from my subscription that has not been updated for their ratings and selections by Monday. I try not to buy (shorts ok) on Fridays as I hate to leave unexecuted buy orders the over the weekend.

- Reduce the number of stocks.
  Usually I have an average of eight stocks for further analysis each time and I select the five that have a better chance to appreciate from my expectations. I score the stock using my appropriate parameters. For example, if all the timing grades from different subscription services are high, the appreciation potential of this stock is high in the short term.

- Maximize profit.
  If this strategy proves itself and the market is not risky, I'll increase my position and vice versa.

- Improve performance and reduce risk.
  I have found that about 10% of the gains were due to good timing in the trades so far, so I do not wait for 30 days to sell them. The average holding period is about 20 days and the gain is about 3% (the annualized return is huge due to the short average duration).

  From my limited data so far, holding stocks for 20 days gives them better performance rather than holding them longer than 60 days.

- Calculating the rate of return.

I prefer the annualized rate of return for a better comparison. However, I would skip using those performances of trades with the holding period less than five days. I also compare my return to the return of S&P 500 on the same holding period.

In a way, it is quite hard to calculate the rate of return if I include the cash balances, especially in the beginning of using the strategy since I started with all cash.

A good comparison is to compare the performance of each trade with that of the SPY over the same period.

The better rate to calculate the rate of return is: Total Profit / Total Investment. In the initial year, I would skip the first month as it takes time moving from cash to stocks.

- Money management.
  In a rising market, usually too much idle cash (due to many buy orders are not executed) would decrease the performance of the portfolio and vice versa in a falling market.

  In a falling or risky market, limit your stock holding exposure to market risk. Instead of holding the stocks for a month, try to sell them in a week or two, and increase your cash position.

- If you do not use market orders, try to place the order price as close as the last executed price in the market. I usually submit orders after 10 am; they call the first hour (9:30 am to 10:30 am in NYC) the amateur hour for a good reason.

- My buy prices are about a little less (.2%) than the market prices and sometimes higher if the market is trending downward.

  Hence, my buy orders on stocks heading up will never be executed. I sum up the lost potential profits and the money I saved from the discounts in my buy prices. It turns out they are about the same. In several instances, the stocks just rocket upwards. If I cannot buy the stock after 4 or so hours, I should switch the buy order to market order.

  Alternatively, buy the stock using market order when it is trending up.

- I prefer to beat the market by smaller margin but more consistently.

- Using a trading plan makes it a discipline and avoids emotional influences.

Recent (4/2016) examples

Recently there were two coaster-roller stocks: Fitbits and GPro. Both stock prices surged through the roof and crashed down. Using "Buy High and Sell Higher" strategy should have made you some money. You needed to protect your profit by adjusting your stops.

The momentum is caused by the publicity and the public who follow the trend blindly. If you looked at the fundamentals of both companies (now they're more reasonable), they did not justify the prices. It is like buying a hot dog cart in NYC for a million dollar. Of course, you will sell a lot of hot dogs as long as you do not have another hot dog cart next to your cart. However, your investment may never be recouped. In addition, both are single-product companies; it would be very risky when there is competition. Apple is one for Fitbits and I bet many Chinese companies are making products similar to GPro's. GPro's products could be a fad, or may fall into a limited, specialized market.

Ignore fundamentals for momentum stocks. Ride on the wagon and jump off when the trend reverses.

Links
There are several SA articles on similar topic, click here, here and here.

http://seekingalpha.com/article/1336291-does-momentum-investing-actually-work?v=1365785958&source=tracking_notify
http://seekingalpha.com/article/865091-how-price-momentum-and-bull-markets-go-together?source=kizur

http://seekingalpha.com/article/1350651-seeking-alpha-momentum-investing-with-etfs

#Filler: Percentage wise, my momentum investing has been most profitable so far. I classify this strategy into 3 sub strategies depending on the average durations.

1   Four strategies for momentum

We have 3 strategies according to the different holding periods and the screening is a little different from each other. The screening parameters (i.e. selection criteria) are briefly described here. Adjust them to fit your risk tolerance and requirements. Monitor them from time to time as the market always changes.

Metric	Strategy #1	Strategy #2	Strategy #3
Avg. holding period	< 30 days	60 days	90 days
General			
Market Cap	300 M – 2 B	300 M – 2B	2B – 10B
Avg. volume	>100K	>200K	> 300 K
Analyst Rec	Buy or better	Buy or better	Buy or better
Country	USA	USA	USA
Price	>$5	>$10	>$10
Fundamental			
P/E	>0	>0	>0
Forward P/E	>0	>0	>0
Return on Equity		>10%	>10%
EPS Growth next year		>15%	>10%
Technical			
Performance	Week up	Week up	Week up
SMA-20%	> 10%		
SMA-50%		>0%	
SMA-200%	>0%	>0%	>0%

In addition, they should be in one of the 3 major exchanges: NYSEX, NASDQA and AMEX (Finviz.com allows you to select one exchange at a time).

In general, Strategy #1 does not care about fundamental. Strategy #2 is a typical sector rotation candidate. Strategy #3 cares more about fundamentals.

I recommend to paper trade your strategy using different selection criteria. When you are comfortable, commit a small amount of cash and increase your portfolio size gradually.

Vendors

Most charge a fee for using their services. Most have a score (or rank) for timing. Usually they are based on the momentum of the price. If the price jumps very fast and high, this score is high. Use mental stops to protect your profits and reduce your losses. When the price is below a set price (such as 10% from your purchase price), use a market order to sell it. This would reduce the potential loss of a flash crash. When the timing score is the highest, be very, very cautious as it cannot go any higher.

Example

Here is an example of how to find the momentum stocks for your portfolio.

Bring up Finviz.com. Select Screener. Select 20-Day Simple Moving Average above 20%. Sort the screened stocks with this parameter. Today I have about 100 stocks.

Limit your selection to fit your requirements and preferences. Here are some sample criteria: U.S. companies only, capital cap over 100 M, price over $2, relative volume over 1 and no leveraged ETFs.

Check whether the screened stocks are peaking (say they have appreciated over 200%). Check the reasons for recent surges and evaluate whether the momentum would continue or not. Check out any insider purchases at prices close to market prices.

Strategy #4

This is a variation of the described three strategies. I explain it with a step-by-step approach in implementing it using Finviz.com. Bring it up by typing Finviz.com in your browser.

1. Only buy momentum stocks when the market is not risky. When the tide is up, all ships will flow. Check out my market timing technique. In the simplest way, enter SPY (or any ETF that simulates the market) in Finviz.com. If SMA-20%, SMA-50% and SMA-200% are all positive, most likely the market is not risky.
2. Select Screen. The following are my preferred metrics and you can change them to suite your requirements and risk tolerance.

3. From Descriptive tab, Select Small (300M to 2B) for Market Cap, Over 100K for Average Volume, Over 2 for Relative Volume, USA for Country and Over $5 for Price. Repeat it for other ranges such as 100M to 4B in the Market Cap and over $1 for Price.
4. From Fundamental tab, select Positive in Insider Transaction.

5. From Technical tab, select 10% above SMA-50 in SMA-20 (Simple Moving Average for the last 20 days) and 20% above 200-SMA in SMA-50. Change the selection if they are not desirable for you and/or the current market conditions.

    As of 11/07/2016, I have the following 4 stocks: AAOI, BOOT, LC and NILE. They already had good price increases.
6. Click on the selected stocks one by one such as AAOI. From most other metrics, it is not a value stock. The Forward P/E is 16. Hence, it has some value despite the high P/E of 80. All SMA%s are positive which indicate it is trending up.
7. Qualitative Analysis. After you bought the stock, use stop loss to limit any losses especially in this risky market. Conservative investors should stay away from risky markets. I would set a 15% stop loss (i.e. sell it via a market order when it loses 15%).
8. Most likely you will not or cannot buy it via discount prices when the stock is trending up.
9. Save the screen with a name such as Momentum, so you do not have to reenter the metrics again.

10. This free site does not provide a historical database. You can run the test every week (or month) and write down the results. Only invest with real money when you're comfortable with your tests. Enter the position with money you can afford to lose. Making 55% profitable trades could be very profitable.

11. There are many variations to this strategy. Some are described here. Select Overbought (20) in RSI(14), Double Bottom in Pattern and New High in 52-Week High/Low.
12. If it is moving up, review it every month (preferable every week) and set up a trailing stop. To illustrate, when it is up by 20%, set the stop at the current price (not the price you paid for the stock).

Filler: Definitions of 'ism'
Capitalism is: You do not work, you die.
Communism is: Everyone is paid the same, so there is no need to work harder.
Socialism: As Margaret said, when we have nothing more to give, we all go hungry like the USA is going to.
Idealism: There is no such word in reality. It only exists in our dreams. However, many treat this as it is a reality as they're still dreaming.
Feudalism. Like the Tibetan monks in the 50s. Only they can learn and the rest are slaves.

Strategy 15: Politics

The year before election year has been profitable since WW2. The trade war with China could bring a global recession. Asking for damages of this pandemic could lead to decoupling, a cold war, and even a military war. Our defense industry wants us to find an enemy and China is one now.

1   Politics and investing

You may ask why politics is discussed in this investing book. Politics have been proven to affect the market. For example, the market had reacted to the different stages of Quantitative Easing whose dates had been preset. The following is a more recent example.

As of September, 2015, I predicted 2015 and 2019 would be profitable years even during the fierce correction in August. Why was I so sure? Very **seldom is the market down in a year before an election** including 2007. The last occurrence was 1939, the year when WW2 started. Investing is a multi-disciplined venture including statistics and politics. It may not always happen, but the probability is high for these years.

How to profit

2015 was a sideways market. The market reacted to good news and bad news. The strategy for a sideways market is: Buy at a temporary down and sell at a temporary peak. Define 'temporary' according to your risk tolerance.

For the 'temporary market down', personally I used 5% down from the last market peak. To me the 'temporary market peak' is 10% up from the last market down. The percentages can apply to the percentage changes in the stocks within your watch list. In other words, I buy the stock when the market is 5% down from the last peak and sell it when it gains 10%, or the market gains 10%. Be reminded that this strategy is opposite from market plunges, where you should exit the market totally - again depending on your risk tolerance.

The following are my purchases on 08/26/2015. I should have bought more stocks one day earlier if I were not blinded by fears (a human nature) during this correction. Below you will see my actual purchase orders. The four stocks were described as value stocks in an SA article and I did a simple evaluation. As of 12/31/2015, I sold all of the four stocks except Gilead Sciences. The annualized returns are more impressive such as GNW's 10% gain in one day.

Stocks	Buy Price	Buy Date	Return	Sold date
AAPL	107.20	08/26/15	12%	10/19/15
GILD	105.94	08/26/15	-4%	
GM	27.69	08/26/15	12%	09/17/15
GNW	4.54	08/26/15	10%	08/27/15

There were similar examples in 2013 and 2014.

2016: Politics and the market

No one including all the Federal Reserve chairmen / chairwomen and all the Nobel-Prize winners in economics can predict market plunges. One chairman predicted a smooth market and a few months later the housing market crashed! Many predicted correctly market crashes by pure luck. One even received a Nobel Prize and became famous. However, you would have been glad to ignore his later market predictions.

There were at least two best sellers asking us to exit the market in 2009. If you followed them, you would have missed all the big gains from 2009 to 2014. They did have a point though. However, you cannot fight the Fed. The market had been saved by the excessive printing of money and hence created a non-correlation between the market and the economy. I bet these authors (famous economists and gurus) may have not made a buck in the stock market except selling their books or teaching where his students should request refunds. It is a classic case of the blind leading the blind, or diversion of theory and reality.

From their articles, they do not know the basic technical indicators. You only want to react to the market when the market is plunging and not too early. That's why most fund managers cannot beat the market as most are not allowed to time the market. Buffett had mediocre returns in the last five years – I had warned my readers three years ago in my blogs/books. To me, the 'buy-and-hold' strategy has been dead since 2000. The average loss from the peak for the last two market plunges is about 45%. Most charts depend on falling prices, so you will not save 45% and a 25% loss is my objective.

Fundamentally speaking

The market in 2016 is risky due to the proposed interest rate hikes (as of 4/2015 the Fed indicated only .5% so it would not be a factor), our record-high margin, strong U.S. dollar (as of 4/15, it was weaker) and the high expenses of the wars. Each reason could be a good-size article. Personally I try to maintain 50% in cash and would flee the market if my technical indicator tells me to.

Politically (and statistically) speaking

The election year is the second best for the market, but it may not be this year. We **seldom** have three terms from the same political party. For that, I predict a win by the Republicans. Republicans are usually pro-business, but ironically the democratic presidency has a better track record for a better market performance.

The market has more than recovered since the day when Obama took office. The S&P500 performance under Republicans vs. Democrats since 1926 to 2014 is approximately:

Annualized return under Democratic presidencies: 13%
Annualized return under Republican presidencies: 6%

The market is riskier based on the above statistics. In addition, there is a good chance that we will have either a non-politician president, or a lady president for the first time (more materialized in 4/16). The market usually would not favor this kind of change. Statistics do not mean it will happen but history repeats itself more often than not in investing.

Critical political issue for 2016

On our way back at about 4 pm on a Saturday, the bus was full of Spanish-speaking workers. I bet most are illegal workers working in my suburb such as our malls, the hospital and many restaurants. Why illegals? I bet most legal folks would get welfare instead of working on that shift. If they work, the state would take away the freebies such as health care in many states.

The illegals do not have this option. I do not think the politicians understand this. There is no need to build a border wall but rather punish the employers who hire illegals. Before we do this, we need folks willing to take the jobs that are taken by the illegals today.

What will happen if the politicians allow all the illegals to be legal? There will be nobody doing these low-level jobs I predict. No one in his right mind wants these jobs when it is far easier to collect welfare. Why would politicians make this stupid decision? They want to buy Hispanic votes as evidenced in the last two elections.

In addition, most politicians side with the welfare recipients. Since 40% of the population does not pay Federal taxes, the politicians have to satisfy their needs in order to buy votes.

We should encourage folks to work. Representation without taxation is worse than taxation without representation.

Our high taxes, increasing minimum wage, regulations and strong US dollar dampen our competitive edge.

Some political decisions/regulations that affect the stocks

Beside the presidency and the interest rate hikes, there are many political decisions and regulations that affect the stocks. Just to name a few here:

- The never-ending wars postpone our secular bull market beyond 2020.
- Solar City (SCTY) and this sector depends on a government energy credit.
- My Chinese solar panel stock evaporated when the US banned them from importing them to the US.
- Any gun control measure will affect gun stocks (initially positive).
- When Hillary spoke against bio tech stocks or the coal mines, that sector sank.
- Restrictions on cigarettes if China and Russia follow our bans.
- Our immigration policy and great colleges attract the best from all over the world to come to the U.S. At the same time, we need to limit economical refugees from burdening our entitlement systems.
- France imposes extra taxes on foreign investors.

- Government bailouts on 'too big to fall' companies.
- High corporate taxes boost the exodus of corporate headquarters to tax havens outside the US.
- Infrastructure projects.
- Taking out the ban to export oil would increase the profits for oil companies.
- After the annexation of Crimea, the Congress restricted using Russia's rocket engines and gave some new opportunity to the US companies in this area. Besides political consideration, Chinese rockets are the most cost effective and more reliable.
- China's suppressing corruption affected Macau's casinos. Actually every major change in Chinese policy affects the world and global investors.
- Currently the policy of forcing Chinese banks to take stocks in failing companies makes me stay away from investing in all Chinese banks.
- As of 7/2017, the market has gained a lot since Trump's election especially those sectors fulfilling his election promises. Freddie Mac and Fannie Mac tripled after the election.

Summary

Politics affects the market. I predict a risky market in 2016.

Economy and religion also affect the market. Statistically speaking, the market is ahead of the economy by about 6 months. However, the current market is an exception due to the excessive money supply. The correlation will return to normal.

Religions in the Middle East have caused wars. These huge expenses are consumption-related, not investing. It will not be good for most sectors of the economy especially in the long run.

2 Trade war to military war

The failure of one or more of the following would lead to a military war with China: trade war, our economy (partly due to the Pandemic), resolving the conflict between China and Taiwan and our loss of USD as a reserve currency. From this Pandemic, we know co-operation between countries work. If we sue China on this virus, China would take counter actions and it would spell military conflict.

This time is most likely started by us. China's objective is improving the living standard of her citizens and capturing her status in the world's stage. China has a non-interference clause in her foreign policy.

Why do our leaders want to start a war? It is for short-term gain in their political positions. We never care about the long-term consequences. In addition, WW2 had not been occurred physically in the U.S. country.

We never learned from history
One of the reasons of the breakup of U.S.S.R. was the huge expenses of the war in Afghan.

The French failed in Vietnam before us. Does Vietnam threaten the safety of our country today?

We have never found mass-destruction weapon in Iraq.

All these wars cause us a lot of resources that should be used to improve our economy. We have wasted money in our military expenses, maintaining foreign military sites.

Chances of a war with China

It has been reduced due to the advances in Chinese weapons. It is decades behind. However, it is more than enough to defend herself. The fast missiles could make our carriers sitting ducks though it has not been tested.

If we send the children of our leaders to the front line, there will be no war. The youths should spend their best time of their lives in education and jobs instead of being sent back in body bags. The percent of black soldiers is high and hence it is a kind of social injustice.

We have a lot of hawks in our government. Most are sponsored by our offense industry.

3   The hawks and the doves

I am one of the doves hoping China and U.S. can co-exist peacefully. It would benefit my (and most likely your) wealth and living standard by doing so. For example, by decoupling, all the chicken feet will be dumped to the ocean instead of selling them to Chinese, who treat them as delicacy.

There are many hawks. Many work for the military or are retired from it. Without wars, they do not have jobs. Yes, we need to have a small army to defend the country and I'm grateful for all the arm forces fighting for us. Many work for the defense sector. Without wars, these companies would go bankrupt, even it is good for mankind. Most of our leaders want to flex our military muscle to ensure we are on top and boost their shameless ego. That's why we have endless wars since WW2. Our huge war expenses should be redirected to improve our living standard and improving our deplorable infrastructure.

The media report what you want to hear. They usually demonize China so they can sell more stuffs. The following are my opinions. Take out nationalism for a moment, and determine for yourself which are right or wrong.

The following article outlined Defense Secretary Mark Esper's opinions and I will discuss his points.
https://www.defensenews.com/opinion/commentary/2020/03/19/espers-dark-vision-for-us-china-conflict-makes-war-more-likely/

Mark: It will take to complete the U.S. drawdown (in Afghan).
Tony: Is this the reason we deploy our military to South China Sea?

Mark: And the Air Force described a flight by a nuclear-capable B-52 bomber over Somalia in February as, in part, a warning to China of engagement to come.
Tony: What do you think if China do the same close to one of our coastal cities?

Mark: the United States is in a new 'era of great power competition,'.
Tony: China has not expressed 'great power competition'. In addition, China has a non-interference clause in their foreign policy.

Mark: China that continues to grow its military strength, its economic power, its commercial activity...
Tony: What is wrong to be stronger? Did U.S. at one time was getting stronger and stronger?

Mark: do the things that really undermine our [and our allies'] sovereignty, that undermine the rule of law, that really question [Beijing's] commitment to human rights.
Tony: That is our standard. China has lifted millions from starving to death in the last few decades. Is it the #1 in human rights? In addition, we use double standards. Do you believe Saudi Arabia and many countries have far worse human rights than China? We keep our mouths shut and our eyes closed, as they are supposed to be our 'friends'. Which nationalists did participate in the 911 attack? Is our constant gun shooting at each other a human rights violation?

The article: in illicit business practices, including hacking and theft of trade secrets
Tony: Most if not all countries spy on each other and steal trade secrets. If you believe CIA is a friendly information gathering agency, you believe in fairy tales. Do you believe Microsoft, Google and any major companies do not steal secrets from each other? Should we blame someone for not protecting our secrets, especially those secrets on national security? Guess who is that someone?

The article: But none of it remotely justifies twisting great power competition into a shooting war.
Tony: I agree whole-heartedly.

The article: a U.S.-China war would pose a real threat to the American homeland.
Tony: I agree whole-heartedly.

The article: Our goal with Beijing (and Moscow, for that matter) should be diplomacy, mutual economic benefit and peace — not war.
Tony: This is my goal too.

Do you agree with me more or our 'Offense' Secretary more?

Strategy 16: China

China is number one in global trades. It affects the economies of many countries. Here are a few articles to provide you with the basic information about China. The "One Belt, One Road" Initiative will have impact on many countries including China and the U.S.A. As of 2020, I do not want to invest in China due to the trade war and high debts. One of the most popular ETFs is FXI.

We are falling, while China is rising as evidenced by the two currencies. Our government is trying to stop China's rise. However, when China fixes her problems (most likely before 2025), Chinese stocks would rise. Here are the reasons for the rise: 1. Investing in infrastructure, technologies and education, 2. A skilled and dedicated work force and 3. Huge home market. I have written a book titled "China: Trade War and Pandemic", which has more than 400 pages (6*9).

1   The myths on China

"China as a sleeping lion whose roar would one day shake the world." - Napoleon.

Yes, China is roaring in this decade and the roar is getting louder and louder.

The most successful story in the last two decades

When the USA played the China card against Russia, it took away the embargo. Deng Xiaoping started an economic zone to build infrastructure (electricity, road, etc.) in a fishing village in South China and the rest is history. It is my Coconut Theory that when hard working folks have a chance to sell their 'coconuts', they will prosper. Lifting millions from starving to death is no small task. To me, Deng and Nixon should receive a Nobel Prize. However, since China has dominated the world, except the last three centuries, it is no surprise to me.

The Myths on China

Sam Walton was a patriot. He preferred to make less money by not selling Chinese goods. He estimated wrongly the profits from the Chinese products. When he died, the company turned into stores for Chinese products making his heirs the richest family and many of his investors millionaires.

Investors should not follow these myths that have been spread by TV networks and even professors.

- A TV network advocates "Made in USA" in a series.
- A professor from a prestigious university believed India would replace China as their population is younger.
- A professor from one of our top universities believed colonization is good using Hong Kong as an example.
- China is evil and they are communists.
- They're stealing our jobs, technologies and movies.
- All Chinese products are inferior products.

All the above are wrong or not totally correct and I will dispute them one by one.

Globalization

China is one country in the chain of the global economy which promotes free trade. Buy the product from the country that produces the best product at the least cost. Globalization works and debunks the myths.

- China is moving up the product-value ladder. Some manufactured products, such as garments, will be moved to countries such as Vietnam and Burma with wages lower than China. This TV series "Made in USA" makes you feel good and hence makes it easy for them to sell their advertising.

  In reality, manufacturing in many products will not come back to the USA due to our high wages, regulations, taxes and robots. In a sentence, we're hurt by our own success that leads to higher living standard, protecting our workers, stricter environment controls... We need to give up these industries that we cannot possibly compete in and concentrate our efforts on high-value industries and industries we can compete in.

- Product quality is controlled by outsourcers. Do you find product quality problems in Apple's products with most of them manufactured in China?
- When you have a new technical product, you may want to assemble in South China, where most other components such as cable and battery are available
- In many cases we are copying China's mobile technology where China depends on. China has been in the frontier of several industries.

- From 2013 to September, 2016, China has only one failed rocket launch. It is the cheapest and most reliable launch platform. We cannot use it due to security argument. However, it provides a good incentive for the space station that China is building one themselves. By 2025, China could be the only nation on earth that has a space station. Europeans are learning Chinese.
- China has never wanted to be number one. From Opium Wars to 30 years or so ago, China had been bullied by foreigners helping Brits pushing opium to China. China built the Great Wall to keep the invaders away. They could have colonized many countries in the 1400s, but they did not.
- China is not stealing our jobs, but globalization does. Most companies can outsource all functions of the company to other countries where they can find the best workers at the least costs.
- China is polluting the world. Aside from the pollution from factories producing products for export, energy consumption per capita is far less than ours. China is #1 or #2 in implementing most green energy technologies. Unfortunately, China is blessed with coal, but not blessed with the less-polluting gas and oil.
- China is stealing our movies and intellectual properties. It is the same for most developing countries. China will enforce intellectual properties before it can move up to the next phase to a developed country. Our companies have to protect our secrets. Even the US had been in that stage briefly. Charles Dickens was so angry that he did not want to visit the US.
- China is a closer to a developed country by now. Its previous 10% growth is not sustainable but it has been impressive. China will stay in the 5% range for a while
- Yes, China does have many problems that most countries are facing such as pollution, regulations, corruption...

We can shut ourselves out from all foreign trades, but it will harm us more than help us. We have to enjoy a $100 toaster to start. All the chicken feet, a delicacy for the Chinese, will be dumped into the ocean. Our high-tech companies, farmers, movie industry will suffer.

Communism and China
China is only communist in the second "C" of CCP, China Communist Party. Chinese are more capitalist than us. If you do not work, you do not eat well. This simple rule motivates its citizens to work hard. The safety net is improving, but it is a long way from our social security system; our system may be too generous as it has encouraged too many free loaders and

cheaters (also in the corporation level too). It explains why they have a high savings rate. Most companies in China do not have unions, inconveniences of labor laws and sometimes companies even receive help from corrupt officials. After a taste of capitalism, China will never return to communism, which encourages folks to be lazy.

Human rights and Tibet
When you compare present day China to the China 30 years, 20 years or even 10 years ago, human rights have grown by leaps and bounds. To me, food and shelter come first before human freedom. Human freedom should be allowed gradually and it requires educated citizens that China has but not in the rural areas. Allowing freedom too fast would cause chaos (my thought and is debatable).

Before the 'liberation' of Tibet, only monks could get an education. One-child policy does not apply to Tibetans and other minorities. Their culture is maintained throughout from the experiences in my two visits in the last 10 years.

Hong Kong
Present and past, Hong Kong's wealth depends on its proximity to China, contrary to the colonialism theory a professor had stated. I had bet on the iShares MSCI Hong Kong ETF (NYSEARCA:EWH, an ETF for Hong Kong) at the start of the Umbrella Protest. My order had not been executed due to my low price. The reason that the stock market did not drop further could be the plan allowing citizens in China and Hong Kong to buy stocks from the opposite exchanges. It will materialize soon after they finalize the tax and regulation details. Hence, the Chinese have more investment choices instead of investing in ghost cities.

India
Indians compare themselves with Chinese, but Chinese usually compare themselves with the USA. India will not catch up with China in this decade. It is more corrupt than China, more protective than China, and has more social inequality than China. The Tier I cities in India cannot even compete with the Tier II cities in China when you compare the infrastructure, high rises, subway, airport, etc.

The growing population of India eats up all the limited resources of the country. As a Chinese saying goes, you get rich by making fewer babies and building more roads.

China's advantages

- Huge internal market. The scale of economies is quite obvious.
- An educated and hard-working work force.
- Relatively low wages for qualified engineers and researchers. The wage of an average US engineer is about the total wages of four Chinese engineers from my rough estimate. It is giving some technology companies problems, such as Cisco.
- Government incentives and subsidies.
- Most big projects and major purchases to foreign countries have a clause of technology transfer. If we do not oblige, they buy them from your competitor. The trick is to use the money for research (not bonuses to the management) and hold out the top technology.
- Bitter tough lessons in the past 250 years starting from the Opium Wars to WW2.
- One-party political system is not a bad thing. By the time China connects most, if not all, the Tier I cities with high speed trains, we're still arguing about which political party is on top for the first one.

I'm not naïve to believe that China does not have their problems. For starter, they need to control air pollution, water pollution and food quality sometimes at the expense of jobs. They need to have more regulations to protect their citizens.

The success of China is good to the world
After the last earthquake struck China, Chinese and the overseas Chinese helped to rebuild the disaster region without asking other nations for help. If China is as poor as before, you may have 20% of the world population begging for money.

When you need a drug to cure a terminal disease, do you care whether it is from the USA or from China? It is too expensive to develop a new drug in the USA.

China has rescued many US companies such as GM from go bankrupt. So is Volvo. China will buy many bankrupted US companies if we allow them. Some bankrupted US companies do not have much salvage values, but we argue not to sell them to China based on national security. Most do not make sense.

Vietnam is copying China's model and it is at least 15 years behind. Eventually, many factory jobs will be replaced by robots and countries such as Vietnam with labor cost even far lower than China. It already has attracted many industries such as textile that cannot afford the rising wages in China. The latest riot against foreign factories (mostly from Taiwan) is more political and not against the Chinese. The Chinese there have been more integrated with the Vietnamese than most other SE Asian countries.

Resource-rich countries such as Brazil and Australia benefit from the demand in China. They will return to the normal trade levels when the global economy improves. Macau and Hong Kong have been benefiting from Chinese tourists. With the suppression of corruption, the gambling industry in Macau will suffer. Due to the recent Umbrella Protest, Hong Kong will suffer from fewer Chinese tourists.

China has become number one in tourist spending in France. It is similar to many other countries. Most companies producing luxury products benefit. The myth of an average Chinese citizen making less than $5,000 is debunked by these tourists. First, the median salary is not $5,000 and the size of the middle class is huge. Most countries benefit with the rise of China today, except Japan, which has an islet dispute with China. Philippines, backed up by the USA, has similar problems with China. Hope they will resolve the problem diplomatically by sharing resources.

Not too long we will compete with China on higher-value products as we're competing with Western Europe now. There are many recent examples that worry me more. A Chinese company captures 70% market of the consumer drone that was invented by our military. Chinese military drones cost about one quarter (or half by some estimate) of ours and they have little restrictions to whom they sell to. Chinese has a monster machine to build bridges. They have more than the high-speed rail than all other countries combined. These are a few of many examples. When the average Chinese student spends at least two more hours in studying than ours, they will achieve more in life and catch up fast.

2   One belt, one road

Chinese is building two <u>modern silk roads</u>, one by land (one belt) and one by sea (one road). It has been participated by more than 60 countries. It is a $3 trillion infrastructure campaign funded mostly by China. It would take about five years to complete. The idea is from President Xi and was initiated in 2013.

It is natural for China: use of excessive infrastructure industry, higher wages in China, rising internal demands of foreign products, converting the U.S. treasuries into other assets, and most importantly creating alternate routes for energy / ores as described below in more detail.

- Obama announced "return to Asia" or "refocus on Asia" by sending about two thirds of our naval power to Asia. China realized that it was aimed to them. By blocking the sea route, China's oil supply would be cut. It is a strategic action to find another land route to these resources.

  China and Myanmar have opened a cross-border pipeline into south-east China. It would save a lot of transportation expenses and avoid the blocking in the Malacca Strait.

- China has built up a lot of USD reserve from the trade surpluses with most of her trading partners. It would be less risky by converting this reserve (especially from our U.S. Treasuries) to other investments such as the loans in building infrastructures in foreign countries. In case of a war, their U.S. Treasuries held by China could be frozen.

- Improve transportation of products between China and Europe and resources / energy from Middle East to China.

- China exploits the excess capacity in building infrastructure. China leads the world in building high-speed rail, bridges and tunnels. Japan (with no experience in building rail in hot climate), India (with few successful projects by foreigners) and Vietnam have been experiencing many problems in building high-speed rail that are not built by Chinese.

- Enrich the wealth and living standards of the countries that are in OBOR projects. Even the U.S. and the West would benefit by reducing their foreign aids to these countries.

China's objective is to make the poor countries richer as a responsibility to the world. Most affected regions should increase the GDP by 5% on the average from my rough estimate.

- Eventually most China's higher-value products will catch up with the West and the U.S. When the developing countries are richer, they are the target markets for China.

- China's Yuan has been used as the reserve/trading currency instead of USD though it is a long way to replace USD as a reserve currency. China has set up an exchange for trading energy in Chinese currency. Other commodities will follow if not already done.

- It could reduce some conflicts. Philippines received billions on the loan and has downplayed the islet conflict with China. Hence the chance of Chinese military interference would be reduced.

- It would strengthen the economics, politics and culture ties of China and the affected countries. Western China has not been developed due to the remote and less habitable conditions.

- It would make U.S. very unhappy and U.S. would take counter actions to protect her interests.

Many developing countries and provinces in west China will benefit. Many projects will be financed via Asian Infrastructure Investment Bank (AIIB), which is mainly funded by China. Today most of these projects are financed by IMF and World Bank, which are controlled by U.S.

China may supply most of their services such as building factories or improving ports. However, China will not see their profits from the investments in the short term. Some loans will be partly donated to friendly allies. Many countries may not be able to pay back the loans in cash.

China should concentrate on soft power by promoting mutual respect, understanding local cultures and reducing military conflicts such as islet dispute with Vietnam. All the signed contracts could be overturned when a new governor comes into power. The participating countries should be careful on the ability to pay back the huge debts.

US is not participating in this campaign. We will not benefit from these agreements and we will lose our influences to the developing countries. However, some big projects require advanced technologies and they will be supplied by US corporations such as turbines from GE. Honeywell and Caterpillar will likely benefit. India may not participate due to the road thru a territory claimed by Pakistan.

As in most projects, China will face problems and challenges. Thailand and Indonesia are modifying their original railroad projects. The project is easily accepted in developing countries but not in developed countries such as EU. China is having its own economic problems. Some projects may not pay back and China would end up losing money. China needs to analyze the projects carefully.

It is better to invest in profitable infrastructure projects than selling destructive weapons. Many finished projects such as the major railway in Africa and an empty airport do not benefit China and even the host so far. They need to select those projects that are beneficial otherwise it would be a waste of resources. A train started from a Chinese city to arrive in London and another one to Madrid. In general, it is faster than sea route and less expensive than air fright. Or, it is more expensive than sea route and more time consuming than air fright. Many products such as red wine are suitable to ship by train. It also depends on how far the products are from the closest seaport or railway station. In general west China and their neighbors will benefit more.

China has or will face challenges and problems. The finance would drain China's reserve funds. Many top officers in the countries receive maximum benefits while their citizens are not. Need to resolve them by making more jobs available to common citizens. Some current highways would be abandoned. India will object due to her animosity with Pakistan. Russia may have the own ideas and/or not investing enough in the part of their infrastructure. The southern route would weaken the importance their northern route. The rails among countries are not uniform and that's why they have dry docks to transfer goods from one rail system to another.

There will be reactions from U.S. and Japan who would lose their influences esp. in Africa and S.E. Asia. China have made the ports in Germany and Greece busy and bought in a lot of wealth. China invested in Greece's port when Greece was in deep financial crisis. For a successful project, China would get about 1.8 times the return while the receiving country would get 3 time the return.

Many countries in South East Asia have already been benefited by Chinese investment and infrastructure. There are many conflicts such as corruption by local governments, cultural differences and traditional military conflicts with countries such as Vietnam. Under YouTube, search "Cambodia China Anthony". Here is one of the series.

Iran

Middle East could cause WW3 and Iran could be a strong factor. Iran is rich in oil and gas. In recent history, the oil right was controlled by U.K. and partially by Russia. U.S. and her allies embargo Iran on their terrorist actions (some claim U.S. army are terrorist), and the nuclear development. To me, trading oil not using USD is one of the major reasons. The recent murder of the number two leader did not get the approval of our allies. Iran bombed the U.S. bases to save face. The reason of not a full-fledged war could be due to Russia and China who may not want to do so now. China, a country without sufficient oil and gas, is eager to develop the land route to Iran's energy.

3   Shenzhen

Let's start with a video from Professor X. Click here or type the following in your browser:
https://www.YouTube.com/watch?v=SGJ5cZnoodY&t=923s

Shenzhen has become the Silicon Valley of the East, or in the next decade we would say the US's Silicon Valley is the Shenzhen of the West.

If you bought all the stocks in the Shenzhen Exchange, you could be very wealthy and there is no need to read my books on investing.

For example, it would take 9 months to assemble a new product but only 3 months in Shenzhen as most of the components are readily available next door or in the next street. Shenzhen's advantages are no longer tax credit and cheap labors (but highly-trained Chinese technicians, engineers and researchers). Many tech companies from over the world come to Shenzhen to set up shops in order to be successful.

There are many high-tech products from Shenzhen and they're sold all over the world. Unless you've been living in a cave for the last 10 years or you are blinded by your dumb nationalism, you should know China is catching up with technology, science and infrastructure.

Under Deng's vision, Shenzhen has become one of the (if not the) wealthiest city in China. Your home work is to study the many articles on Shenzhen starting with Wikipedia or enter the following in your browser.
https://en.wikipedia.org/wiki/Shenzhen

Extra credits. There are several other YouTube videos on this amazing city. Why copying the current technology to make it better or using it for a new product is creative and profitable? Any other countries copy Shenzhen's model and will they be successful? Do you agree from the video that open source encourages copying technology without compensation? What does our 9-year old most likely do with no homework? Is it too early for the Chinese 9-year old study electronics and programming? Have a good day, class and no video game today.

4   Decoupling

Trump proposed decoupling with China. It has materialized to some extent as of 4/2020. The U.S. citizens and the two political parties blame China for all their ills. Many jobs will not move back to the U.S. but to Vietnam and India. There will not be a lot of jobs gained and they have to pay higher prices at worse quality as illustrated by banning tires from China. Our corporations will suffer too losing China's educated labor and the huge market in China. It also motivates China to advance to higher-value products and China will not dependent on U.S. such as the computer chips.

China did not want to decouple from the U.S. However, it may not be up to China's choice and China is more frustrated with us. In 2019, China ships about 18% of their total export to us. It is high but not much compared to Hong Kong (14%).

The decoupling may not be totally agreed upon by both countries and that could lead to first a cold war and then a military war. In any case, we will be more isolated except with Canada and Mexico. Iran and Russia already have a strong tie with China.

The following summarizes briefly the consequences.

Affecting both countries
- Our trade deficits with each other will be zero from a total decoupling.
- Chinese stocks will be delisted in U.S. exchanges. It will hurt these Chinese stocks for a few months.
- Our firms such as MacDonald's and GM will be withdrawn from China. Their assets (not including the names and trademarks) will be sold to Chinese companies.
- Citizens of both countries would have a record, unfavorable attitude towards each other.

Affecting us

- In a survey dated 5/2020, 96% of U.S. corporations do not want to leave China even our government pays the moving expenses due to increasing the costs of goods and losing China's huge market. They may not support Trump's election.
- China would sell our debts. It would shake the USD as a reserve currency.

- China would ban exporting rare earth elements to us. There are not too many substitutions and the prices for these elements would skyrocket.
- China would ban exporting active drug ingredient to us.
- There will be zero Chinese tourists. Chinese tourists have the highest spending among all foreign tourists. Coupled with the pandemic, many retail stores would close.
- There will be zero Chinese students. The 370,000 Chinese students in 2019 had been financing the U.S. colleges as most pay tuitions. Coupled with the pandemic, many colleges would be in tough time.
- The Chinese goods will be replaced by other countries. They will cost more and at worse quality. The previous example is replacing tires from other countries when Chinese tires were banned.
- We may not gained a lot of jobs as they will be moved to low-wage countries such as countries in S.E. Asia.
- Huawei will ask Verizon and other companies to pay royalties in using their technology and even worse banning using Huawei's patents in their 5G components. If they refuse, Chinese will freely use the U.S. patents without paying royalties.
- U.S. companies making chips will lose her needed export to China and eventually they would become competitors to Chinese chip makers in the global market.
- Apple would face losing the market and manufacturing capacity in China.

Affecting China

- China's economy will deteriorate for at least 3 years. However, China's government has a lot of cash reserve and Chinese are still happy to go back a decade or two when the country was poorer.
- Many small factories are out-of-business. Many factories are moving to South East Asia. It affects the lower class of workers in South China and many workers have been moving back to farms where they came from.
- Chinese will pay more for farm products that are replaced by other countries.
- China will concentrate more effort on agriculture and farm land. Today Chinese do not really need American farm products. China is close to feed her citizens by her own agriculture, which would be enhanced.

- Chinese high-tech will suffer initially. However, if they can get them from foreign countries other than U.S., they should be fine. U.S. is trying to stop our allies to import these products to China. If U.S. do not or cannot stop TMSC (a Taiwanese company) to manufacture chips for Chinese companies, China should be fine. Huawei's phones and 5G network do not use U.S. chips.

- For the first time for the last 30 years in my memory, there are no Chinese students entering M.I.T. this fall of 2020. The return of Chinese students has been helping China to advance in technologies.

Affecting the world

- The trade war between China and U.S. is taking a break until the pandemic is controlled in the U.S.
- There will be global recession for at least a year.
- World supply chain will be changed.
- De-globalization would make products more expensive.
- Low-wage jobs are being moved to low-wage countries. High-value products are being moved to Japan, Taiwan, South Korea and even U.S.A. Mexico is benefiting for jobs in between.
- Japan, Taiwan, Saudi Arabia, Canada and Mexico would stay with us. EU countries will take side initially and they will side with China for economic reasons. Finally Australia will side with China due to economic reasons; today about one third of their exports to China and Chinese accounts to 15% of the foreign tourists.

Summary

There will be no winner in decoupling. The worst is that it would lead to a military war. We no longer force China to accept our standards and our way to do business. The global order is the same as U.S. order that China does not abide by.

Strategy 17: Contrary investing

1   The contrarian

Contrarians invest in the manner opposite of the crowd. Look for extremes in the market sentiment and investing activities and do the opposite.

However, timing is everything. You want to follow the herd and switch gears when the market or the asset is overpriced.

When an asset or a strategy is overbought, it will return to the normal price. There are one or two exceptions. Gold is one but it is not due to gold alone, but the depreciating USD and the long term depreciating of gold after inflation.

Blindly taking contrarian actions could cost you. You need to analyze and determine whether the herd is wrong.

To illustrate, do you want to move to equities when their prices have been down as of 7/2012? It really depends on the following factors.

- If the long-term trend is down (i.e. moving to a W-shaped recession), we want to wait longer before we move back in.
- If we're heading to the same path as Japan's lost decades, we may want to wait even longer.
- If we're heading to a secular bull market (not today), then waiting too long will be bad.
- The counter argument is the excessive printing of money that could lead to a rising market.

Do we want to buy bank stocks after 2008 or tech stocks after 2001?

- With the rear mirror now, the answer is 'No' even some of these stocks had lost half of their value. As long as the root problems have not been fixed, they might fall further and some companies may even go bankrupt. Do not invest in equities one year after a market plunge and two years in the sector that caused the bubble in general. They are quite correct in the last two bottoms (2000 and 2007). It has more chance to be right than wrong in the future, but as in life nothing is 100% sure.

Individual analysis

Ignore what the media says. A lot of time the 'news' is obsolete by the time it reaches us. It is the group thinking. Sometimes they magnify the news in order to sell their ads. The worst is that the smart money manipulates the news which tells us to trade while they're doing the exact opposite.

Buffett told us to ignore airline stocks. However, many airline stocks made over 4 times their stock prices in the last few years. Popular books are no different. One predicts the Dow at 40,000 and one predicts a market plunge in 2009. As of 2016, they're all wrong. When they are right, they will tell the world.

#Fillers: I wish I have a time machine

After collecting bottles for money, an old lady ordered a bowl of plain rice and ate by herself. I wish I could have ordered a meat dish for her and I was 'ashamed' of being generous.

A well-dressed gentleman offered his just-bought hamburger to a beggar. The beggar refused and asked for money instead – most likely he needed the money to buy liquor. A tale of two citizens.

During a lunch with my fellow tourists, a beautiful girl danced for our entertainment. I did not offer her anything and it had been bothering me for years.

During college, my housemates asked me to apply for food stamps. I had used only a few stamps then as I did not cook. I feel ashamed as this is my only time to collect social welfare.

We have regrets in life and we can only bring them to our graves.

2   Take advantage of experts

Day traders usually unload the stocks by the end of the day. They also unload most of their holdings before the weekend/holidays and they buy back on the next trade day. Take advantage of their routines by trading opposite to what they trade. I have to stress that this is a short-term technique. In addition, when too many investors follow this technique, it will not work.

Links
Contrarian
(http://en.wikipedia.org/wiki/Contrarian_investing
#Filler: Organic growth

The company grows using its own profits - not from the bank loans and/or from the extra stock offerings. My definition only.

3   Institutional investors

Institutional investors include banks, hedge funds, insurance companies and mutual funds. They are important as they move the market, not the retail investors.

You want to follow them closely. When they buy specific stocks, buy the same stocks and vice versa. It is better to be one step before their actions. Due to their large holdings, usually it takes more than a week to finish the trade. Basically this is how day traders make money by jumping onto their wagons. When you see a sudden surge in volume of a specific stock, there is a good chance the institutional investors are trading.

Several sites including GuruFocus.com keep track of the stocks they are holding and their current trades. Finviz.com has similar information. IBD gives higher ratings to the stocks that are held by institutional investors.

Normally the stocks owned by the institutional investors have larger market caps (over 1 billion) and most have stock prices over $10.

Once in a while, their trades are not rational. When you act against them, you need a good reason and be patient.

I took advantage of them using Apple for illustration:

- Recommended in my book <u>Scoring Stocks</u> to buy Apple in June, 2013 (the publish date) while most of the institutional investors were dumping Apple. Apple scored very high in my book then.

- I recommended to sell Apple in my <u>blog</u> in Feb., 2015 when Apple was $132. The profit is about $60 per share from the recommended dates.

  I took advantage of the correction making <u>12%</u> in 2015 for holding Apple for about 2 months.

4   Short Squeeze

When there is a short squeeze (i.e. over shorted), the stock may appreciate due to the shorters unable to find more stocks to short. The candidates can be found in Finviz.com. I use 35%. However, there may be valid reasons for the shorts such as a lawsuit pending, losing sales... Select the stocks with sound fundamentals.

The following are tests (not real trades) and many tests will be added. As of 09/04/15, the returns are:

Stock	Buy Date	Return	Annualized	SPY return
CALM	07/16/15	-3%	-33%	-1%
GME	07/16/15	-1%	-7%	-1%

The following are real trades as of 09/04/15.

Stock	Buy Date	Return	Sold date
CALM	03/11/15	47%	N/A
GME	04/06/15	8%	N/A

CALM, a candidate

Cal-Maine Foods Inc. (CALM) had fallen from over $60 to $46 recently and it was my heavy bet. The opening price on 12/15/2015 was $46.76. Readers might wonder why I still recommended accumulating a falling stock. Simply put, the race is not over and this horse has a lot of potential (i.e. fundamentally sound). The payout would be huge as it has been ignored (the short float is over 55%).

Let me show you my evaluation process, so that you may use it to enhance your strategy if you have one.

Currently, this stock was screened by my Short screen that spots fundamentally-sound companies with short floats over 35%. Most of the screened stocks deserve to be shorted, but I cannot find any justification for this stock.

Technically speaking

First, this stock has been hated as described by the following table with the exception of Finviz's "Recom". Most of the data in this article were derived from the free Finviz.com on Dec. 15, 2015. The 'Conditions' are my personal preferences.

	Condition	Indicate	12/15/2015
Short Float	>35%	Short squeeze	55%
RSI(14)	<30%	Oversold	31%
SMA-20	<0	Short-term down	-13%
SMA-50	<0	Mid-term down	-17%
SMA-200	<0	Long-term down	-9%
Recom.	1 - Buy & 5 – Sell	3 – Neutral	2

Fundamentally speaking

Did this stock deserve this hatred? From the following table, it is a big NO.

	Condition	Indicate	12/15/2015
Forward P/E	>0 and < 20	Favorable	7
ROE	>20%	Favorable	40%
Profit Margin	>8%	Favorable	15%
EPS Q/Q	>15%	Favorable	418%
Sales Q/Q	>10%	Favorable	71%
P/FCF	<15	Favorable	12
Debt / Equity	<.5 (industry related)	Favorable	.05

One or two favorable metrics do not mean a 'Buy' or great fundamentals. However, all these metrics all yell 'Buy'. They are my major fundamental metrics that have recently proven my predictability.

I combined all these metrics and scored CALM in 3 scoring systems plus PEY described below. As of this writing, CALM passed all my scoring systems with flying colors. Actually when stocks exceed the passing score by that much, I have a little concern; I cannot find any problem with this stock.

	Passing Score	Score
P-Score	3	6
Short-term score	15	40
Long-term score	15	24
PEY	5%	23%

Explanation

- P-Score, Pow's Score. It uses the metrics available in the free Finviz.com with the exception of using Fidelity's Analyst Opinion instead of Finviz's "Recom". This score system is described in my book "Scoring Stocks".
- The other two systems use additional metrics and/or scores I subscribe to. I monitor these two scoring systems periodically and adjust the scores accordingly. My Short-Term Score is used for holding stocks for less than 6 months.
- PEY, Pow's Earnings Yield. It is similar to EV/EBIT (5 from GuruFocus or 1/5 = 20% for Earning Yield). Both consider debt and cash. The advantage of PEY is all the metrics are readily available for calculation if using Cash/Share instead of Short-term Liability. PEY also uses expected earnings.

Intangibles

From Seeking Alpha, enter CALM and you should find many articles. I have not found any alarms on CALM. Some farms that are affected by the bird flu will return if not already to production and eat into CALM's market. It is always a possibility that CALM will be infected by bird flu. However, with most chickens staying inside the farm and the extra precautions, the chance is slim. Let me share three scenarios below.

Say if there is another bird flu (not in CALM) that happens, the egg prices would rocket up and also is the profit of CALM.

Let's say if that happens to CALM, it will affect onto the location involved. As I stated, the management (they had been great) should have taken precautions to minimize the chance of a bird flu.

Then what if it happens in Hong Kong or another Chinese city, they would ban chicken from local farms and bring the frozen chickens from the unaffected countries such as the US. It would bring profits to CALM.

The egg price is returning to its normal price. Hence, the EPS will be lowered. With a Forward P/E less than 7 and PEY greater than 23%, the stock price would have to fall a lot to cause any great alarm.

Bonus metrics

From GuruFocus.com (a paid subscription), F-Score was 7 and Z-Score was 8; both are favorable.

From Blue Chip Growth (no longer free), all three grades were "B". That was good but not the best. Not too long ago, most were "A". I do not know the reason for the downgrade as today's stock price is now lower and there is no change in the fundamentals.

Summary

This stock is technically unsound but fundamentally sound. It may still trend downward, but when it shoots back up, it would be like fireworks on display. Most value stocks are swimming against the tide, so we have to be patient for the market to realize its real value.

No one can identify the bottom precisely and consistently. I expect a short squeeze is coming when the shorters cannot find more shares to short. The interest rate hike could trigger some covering of the shorts. The shorters are paying about a 8% dividends; I do not recommend to short high-dividend stocks. With this price, the risk is low and the potential appreciation is high. When one or two institutional investors move in, the price will surge. I bought it on 3/11/15 and sold it on 10/28/15 making a profit of 48% or an annualized return of 77%.

5   Herd theory

When the herd makes money, they think they're a genius. The last one to leave the herd will be the fool of all fools such as the last holders of Lehman Brothers, AIG, Bear Sterns, internet stocks in 2000, etc. The biggest fools are the 'value' buyers when these companies were plunging fast. When a specific stock looked great yesterday and it lost 50% today, it 'must' be super good to some. Wrong! Check out why it plunged. It could be missing some important metric, or something is really wrong with the company that did not show up in the research.

The real genius is the one who makes money all the way up, but leaves before the bubble bursts. Even a genius cannot predict the peak and the bottom, but I'll call him/her a genius if s/he is right better than 60% of the time.

Recently dividend growth stocks have the highest premium in the last 30 years. It is a mild bubble when we've many retired, or retiring folks seeking income. However, the bubble will burst when the interest rates rises. At that time, the long-term bonds with low yields will lose.

Dividend stocks will benefit when the interest rates is low. Bond holders would move to dividend stocks from their low-yield bonds. Long-term bonds lose their value when the interest rates rises, and vice versa.

It is the same for the internet bubble in 2000. I did unload most of my tech funds in early April, 2000. The more I read during that time, the more I got scared. It was partly luck and partly 'genius' to move all these sector funds to traditional industries. At that time, they did not have contra ETFs, so cash, money market fund and bonds would be the best choices.

Filler
Had you responded to the pandemic, which was confirmed on Feb., 2020? If you do, you should have shorted stocks on airline, cruise line and related sectors, or at least bought contra ETS (the market returned after the big dip due to the excessive printing of money). After the excessive printing of money, we would have bought ETFs related to gold such as GLD and RING.

Strategy 18: Special situations

We use the pandemic of 2020 for discussion that was predicted pretty much correctly in the following article.

1   Disasters in 2020?

There are some predictions that the U.S. will suffer a lot in 2020. Some predictions are correct and some including the "world end in 2012" are not. Hence, this article should belong to the Conspiracy Theories. Even with some good arguments, I am **not totally convinced**. However, I would take actions, similar to buying insurance. I would like to invest in gold and foreign countries (but all countries will be on fire if the prediction is correct). I will limit my Chinese stock holdings in 2020 for sure.

Prediction #1 (materialized as of 2/2020). To some, China has a cycle of disasters every 60 years and 2020 is supposed to be the year for disasters. It happened in the last three: 1960 Great Famine (1959-1961 estimated 30 million died), 1900 Boxer Rebellion (1899 – 1901) and 1840 First Opium War (1839 – 1842). I cannot find any major disaster in 1780 and the Sino-Japan War was not in the cycle year. It has 3 rights and 2 wrongs – not a bad bet. If Trump got reelected, it could be China's disaster in 2020. China could benefit if Trump settles the trade war soon.

Prediction #2. Some predictors believe the USD could lose the reserve currency status. It is quite possible as we have been printing too much USD and our national debt is ridiculously high compared to our GDP. The hint today is that some countries are not using the USD for trading. The "One Belt, One Road" is another example, where the participants are trading with Chinese and /or Russian currencies.

Secondly, they also believe there will be an overdue earthquake that would destroy California. Despite of any predictions, it would happen but hopefully not in my life time. It could destroy Silicon Valley and Hollywood, the most important areas for our economy. The stock market could lose most of its value. The Federal government would not likely be able to rescue California in this scale and that could lead California to become independent. It is likely but I do not bet on it.

The two events if materialized would possibly cause a global depression and even civil wars. Election year is traditionally a good year for the market, but we should be cautious with our money this time.

Believe it or not? Another conspiracy theory? But, do not say you were not warned. Personally I do **not believe it,** but I will take some actions just like buying insurance. I hope the predictions are wrong. For more info, check out Billy Meier from the web. He did have some correct predictions but some of his photos were falsified.

It could be the most entertaining article in this book, or the most important one. Even if there is no disaster, it is always better to diversify with gold (about 10% I suggest) and to sell short when the market is risky.

https://www.thebalance.com/dollar-collapse-how-to-protect-yourself-and-survive-3306263
Will update this article on 1/1/2021 if we survive. Written on 8/2019.

Update 1/2020.
There are plagues in years ended with '20' such as 1720, 1820, 1920 and this year 2020. Is it a coincidence?

Update 3/2020.
The virus spreads to Europe and U.S. It could cause a global depression. Hopefully the warmer climate would kill the virus and save our economy.

U.S. tries to solve the financial crisis by excessively printing money. It could cause inflation and the USD will be shaken (Prediction #2). So far, China seems to recover from the virus, and it is the only threat to our USD.

Prediction #3, as of 4/2020
If U.S. asks China for damages, China would likely refuse. If the debt of about 1.07 T is frozen, China would take counter action. This would lead to military war and WW3. Even if it does not happen, consider decoupling. Personally I do not invest in Chinese companies and ETF on China and be careful with companies whose factories and investment are in China. Gold could be a better investment when war happens. I bet the war will be threatened but not materialized. Appropriate trading could be profitable.

Prediction #4, as of 10/2020.

So far all presidents elected in the same year as the disaster cycle (60 years apart as 庚子年) died: William Henry Harrison (elected on 1841, missed by 1 year I guess), William McKinley (1900) and Kennedy (1960). Coincident? In astronomy, it occurs when some planets lie in a straight line.

With the old ages of our president candidates elected in 2020, the chance is quite high this year. Biden's VP candidate has very good signs in Chinese astronomy. I bet she will be the first female president within 5 years.

2   How to prepare for disasters

This article prepares you for some of the predicted disasters in 2020, which may never materialize. [Update 03/2020. Pandemic has happened and the breakout was in China.] However, it also helps you to prepare yourself for any future disasters. The disasters may never happen but your actions are the insurance for protecting yourself. Depending on your risk tolerance, allocate 2% to 10% for this effort. I divide the actions into several categories as follows. As to all my recommendations, you should consult your financial advisor before taking any actions, especially the risky ones like this one.

Preparing for the depreciation of the USD (U.S. Dollar)

As of 5/2020, this has not happened, and I hope it will not happen in my lifetime. The government has been printing too many USD and the economy may not be that rosy as our government has described as of 2019. As a result, the USD could lose the reserve currency status. We know what happened to the U.K. when the pound was replaced by USD. In preparing for a market plunge, we usually accumulate cash, and / or buy safe Treasury Bills. It may not work this time as USD could lose its buying power.

Here are my suggestions on what to buy. Buy gold (GLD, IAU for ETFs, RING for gold miner and gold coins), and silver (SLV for ETF and silver coins). Despite the delisting, I invest in FXI, an ETF for Chinese companies. I bet Yuan, the Chinese currency would appreciate. Most investors should have 5% to 20% in gold investment.

When we have detected a market plunge via market timing, buy contra ETFs for risky investors.

Talk to your financial advisor before taking any actions. I am **not responsible** for your loss or gain. As of 2019, it is too early to prepare for this disaster.

Protecting your lives

Protect yourself from a stage of no government and police protection.

Action
Buy guns or weapons (I'm for gun control with a realistic approach).
Store enough food.
Store enough water.
Store enough wood.
Store enough gasoline and have a generator.

Strategy 19: Sideways but volatile market

When the market is sideways and volatile like during the pandemic of 2020, you buy when the market tanks and sell when the market rises.

Refer to Book 5 for covered calls.

1 Short-term trading

Due to the government rescue, the stock market rose on the date this book was published. It would save us temporarily. I bet we have not be out of the hole yet. The economy would be down for a long while and the excessive printing of USD would shake its status as a reserve currency. I have tried the following strategy briefly but not this time. During this virus, it had worked so far, but it may not work in the future. Again, it is just for reference only and you should seek advices from your financial advisor before you trade. The 5% is arbitrary. Adjust it to your personal risk tolerance.

- Buy SPY (other equivalent ETF is fine) when it is 5% down and sell it when SPY appreciates by 5%. Use stop to limit your loss (5% less than your purchase price is fine).

- Buy SH (contra ETF or equivalent) when it is 5% down (or the market is 5% up) and sell it when SH appreciates by 5%. Use stop to limit your loss (5% less than your purchase price is fine).

Strategy 20: Sector expert

An expert would short the sector when you know it is going down such as the airline and store retail during the pandemic, you short the sector and vice versa.

When you work in a sector, or you're interested in a specific sector, you may want to specialize in that sector for investing. High tech is a popular sector. You need to specialize in a growing sector unless you short ETFs and/or stocks.

With an aging population, health care is a good one. With a growing population, commodities and agribusiness (including water) are good sectors.

Strategy 21: Oil and Saudi Arabia

We use the current coronavirus for discussion that was predicted pretty much correctly in the following article.

1   Falling oil price

When oil price is down below $30, I believe it is a buy to the investors. 3/2020 is the second chance after 1/2016. It may happen again in 2021. We had a chance to buy when the oil price fell almost to zero. The long-term future of oil is not that good. Many countries are switch to green energies. However, it is far less polluting than coal. In Dec. 2020, I found many oil companies had attractive forward P/Es.

The cost of the oil depends on the following factors:

- The ease of drilling. The production cost for most oil ranges from $2 to $20. Most drillers are not profitable when the oil price per barrel is below $50. Most cheap oils (close to the earth surface) have gone except in Saudi Arabia.
- The quality of oil. Most of Saudi Arabia's oil are good quality while Venezuela's oil is heavy and very expensive to refine.
- Transportation. It is least expensive if it is close to the customer. Venezuela has a long way to transport except the U.S.A.
- Competition of shale energy and now the reduced cost of green energy such as solar and wind.

High oil reserve (Venezuela is among one of them) does not mean high production due to the above factors.

#Fillers: I wish I have a time machine

After collecting bottles for money, an old lady ordered a bowl of plain rice and ate by herself. I wish I could have ordered a meat dish for her as I was 'ashamed' of being generous.

A well-dressed gentleman offered his just-bought hamburger to a beggar. The beggar refused and asked for money instead – most likely he needed the money to buy liquor. A tale of two citizens.

During a lunch with my fellow tourists, a beautiful girl danced for our entertainment. I did not offer her anything and it had been bothering me for years.

During college, my housemates asked me to apply for food stamps. I had used only a few stamps then as I did not cook. I feel ashamed as this is my only time to collect social welfare. We have regrets in life and we can only bring them to our graves.

The oil prices for the last 10 years from Nasdaq.com:

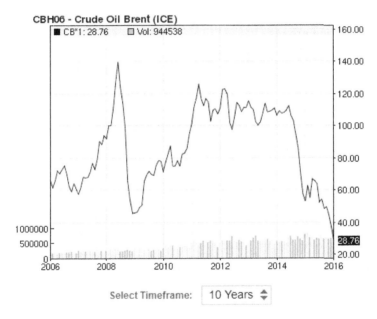

Crude Oil Brent

Latest Price & Chart for Crude Oil Brent

End of day Commodity Futures Price Quotes for Crude Oil Brent

Select Timeframe: 10 Years

Crude Oil Brent Related ETFs: BNO

My predictions

Prediction #1. For the year, it will be in $25 to $40 per barrel. Personally I will not wait for a $25 rate as it may never materialize.

Reasons:

- Global economies have not recovered yet.
- Iran's oil will add more supply.
- OPEC and Russia cannot trim supply as their economies depend on oil export.

Prediction #2. For years later, it will return to $50 per barrel and be on its way to $100.

Reasons:

- Global economies will recover (they always do). But I do not know when that will happen.
- OPEC will trim their supply.
- Supply will be reduced due to the current cut back on drilling and exploration.
- Global population growth.
- Inflation (about 3% per year).
- Historical prices. Recently we had oil prices below $30 and then it went up to $140. Adjusted for inflation, the current price is even far less than $30.
- As a rough estimate (depending on individual oil fields), it takes about $50 to extract, market and explore one barrel of oil (i.e. the cost of goods).

It is better to shut down many of the oil fields such as ocean fields and oil sands at today's $30 range. OPEC cannot cut due to the payments on the loans of many on-going ventures but they should in the future.

To supply the oil with the depressed prices would be the same as spending all the money without caring about retirement.

Summary

It is a supply and demand play. It could also be a case of commodity dumping and the U.S. may try to protect its own energy industry – you may have heard it here first.

The Losers: OPEC. They tried to cut the price to bankrupt the shale energy ventures. You do not want to shake a baby too hard or drop a big stone on your own toe. Many will lose their jobs in energy fields and the railroad industry due to shipping less coal.

The Winners: Investors who buy at low prices now and wait patiently for the long term. I hope we're in this role. As history has shown, the crisis most likely will be a profit potential.

Oil and the market

Today the consumers benefit from low gas prices. Airlines benefit too if they have not hedged on fuels or are not forced to buy at fixed prices from foreign countries. However, the stocks tank with the fall of the oil prices, so the savings in driving for most of us is not worth it.

Some still argue that oil prices will go to $10. If it does, I will keep on buying. As from today's $28 to $10, you lose about $18 or about 65%. However, it has the potential to go back to $120 and that would be more than 400% return from $28 and 1,200% return from $10. I'm buying OIL, an ETN (similar to ETF) that is supposed to float with oil price. UWTI (3X leverage) can triple your money in either direction. I do not recommend UWTI as in one day it could wipe out your entire investment. Ignore the weekly fluctuations due to speculation by traders and look for the long term.

Usually falling oil price would benefit the market in general. However, falling too much as of today is not good for the economy. Usually the market is opposite of the oil price. Today it is an exception due to the oil producing countries including the Saudis and Russia dumping foreign equities to meet their obligations. I predicted that when the oil price is at $85 per barrel, then there will be less dumping of foreign equities and the high oil will affect the market (or the market will be in the opposite direction from the oil price again). The world economies are interconnected today better than before. When the U.S. market suffers, most other global markets suffer too. In addition, when there are major withdrawals from the U.S. funds, the fund managers have to sell their foreign holdings.

China cannot build storage fast enough. They need the oil as they're blessed with polluting coal but not with oil (even oil does not generate a lot of electricity). I recommend that China buys the futures of n years at y price. This will resolve the current fluctuations and bring back the market which would not correlate with the oil price. Some argued that oil prices have reached its peak and its average price is $35 for the last 70 years. He did not consider inflation. It is a big deal for 70 years – I remember I paid $1 for a Big Mac dinner 35 years ago and today it is about $7. He also did not consider all the easy oil has left – the oil that can be extracted without much drilling.

Today the production cost for off-shore drilling or from oil sand is more than $35 per barrel.

There are many articles on this topic on oil. Just google "Oil Price". Here is one: 1.

Update as of 5/2016: Barron's prediction is mostly wrong as oil has passed $45 per barrel. It is due to unexpected events such as the fire in Canada.

I bought OIL in Jan. 19, 2016 (one of my purchases in this period). I expected it to increase in price by 50% as the oil does, but it only increased 25%. What happened to half of my profit? Consider USO as an alternative to OIL.

Expecting the oil price to appreciate, it is better to bet on oil service companies instead of OIL. Here is an article on how to play the oil commodity and a site on energy ETFs. I have the annualized returns of energy ETFs and CVX from Jan. 19, 2016 to May, 12, 2016.

Symbol	Description	Ann. Return
OIL	Crude oil	33%
USO	US Oil Fund ETF	112%
OIH	Oil services	80%
XOP	SPDR Oil & Gas	138%
IYE	iShr DJ US Energy	75%
XLE	S&P Energy	76%
CVX	Chevron	81%
Average		85%
SPY		32%

Exploring uranium

China will have 25 or so nuclear generators on-line by 2020, 4 years away from this writing. I hope it would give this metal a boost. With Japan's problem, uranium demand was at its historical low after inflation adjustment. We need to account for the old (more than 30 years) nuclear generators that will be decommissioned. However, the net gain is still substantial.

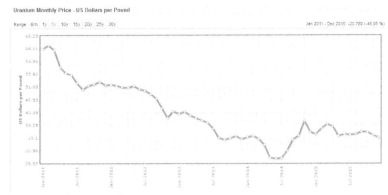

Source: Index Mundi

The price fell from 60 to 27 and rebounded to the current 35. The Monday quarterback would tell you to buy it at 27. Similar with oil, it is not unreasonable to double the price. The question is when. It could be 3 years or as high as 15 years.

Mining could be a different story as they need to survive from this depressed price. URA is the only ETF I can find with uranium and over 100 M. URA has many mining companies included. I will evaluate the companies in the future and at the current time frame, it is too risky for me.

An updated article on uranium.
https://seekingalpha.com/article/4252305-uranium-market-background-potential-investment-cameco

Strategy: Miscellaneous

1   Miscellaneous strategies

- Some **mutual funds** have been losing a lot of money such as during the internet crash in 2000. Buy those funds (usually sector funds) that you expect them to recover. It could be a tax strategy as they will not distribute profits to their fund owners for a while.
- **Inflation**. They are gold (GLD, gold mines such as RING as an ETF and gold coins / bars) and silver. I prefer skipping copper and other commodities including oil unless the economy is trending up. Bonds and CDs are most likely not good investments as they return you with cash that have been depreciated due to inflation.
- Supply and demand. In 2009 and 2020, the Fed prints a lot of money excessively to save the economy. In the long run, our national debts are increased. In addition, it could cause inflation unless the economy recovers due to the simulation as in 2009. There is a lot of money chasing the fixed assets such as gold and stocks. As a result, both of these assets would likely rise especially in the short term. If we have hyperinflation, we would lose the buying power after cashing in the appreciated stocks.
- Almost **day trading**. When the stock is rising in the morning, there is a better chance it would continue the trend and vice versa. Reverse the trade at around 3 pm, and day traders almost never leave their positions open during weekends and/holidays. The chance is improved if both the market and the sector the stock is in are both rising. Take advantage of institutional investors. When they trade, they need days and even weeks to trade a stock. You can tell from the volume of the trade and usually the stock belongs to blue chips. Join the wagon.
- As stated before, some strategies described in this book work better than the others in different conditions of the market. If you can match the right strategy or strategies, you will see firework, and vice versa.
- Index rebalancing. The index such as S&P 500 rebalances at least once a year and some do it 4 times a year. If you buy the stock before it is added to the index, you should make a lot of money. The ETFs that follow the specific index are forced to buy the stocks just added to the index and sell the stocks that have been removed from the index. I do not recommend shorting these stocks, which is risky especially for beginners.

Some indexes provide the criteria to rebalance. Here is my summary from what I guess. It is based on market cap, number of shares floating, the average trading volume (3 to 6 months), how long it has been in the market, profit (better with rising), sales (better with increasing) and any restrictions (such as a foreign stock). There are minor criteria.

I do not have inside information on how any index to rebalance. I tested a strategy based on the above criteria on S&P500 for example. First criteria is the stocks should not be in the index already. So far, the testing has been proved profitable, but the test is too limited.
There are several articles that you can "Google Index Rebalance".

- Positioning strategy. Start with two ETFs: SPY (or any ETF that simulates the market) and a money market ETF for example with even positions (i.e. 50% invested in each ETF). At the end of a period (a week or a month depending on how much time you have for investing), reallocate the ETFs as a percentage of how much the each ETF gains (i.e. the higher allocation for the winner). For better performance, use more ETFs such adding QQQ, GLD, SH (contra ETF to SPY) and PSQ (contra ETF to QQQ).

2   More on strategies

To me, the most important advance for retail investors is the availability of historical data bases at prices we can afford. It shows us the performance of our strategies for the last 10 or so years in an hour or two. The following are my suggestions to make a better use of the findings from these databases and their pitfalls.

- Start with proven metrics as demonstrated by research (the metrics used in this book and other sources such as from SSRN.com) and your own trading.
- Select parameters as close to your trading style as possible. For example, if you only deal with small stocks, select market caps from 100 M to 500 M.
- Some screens perform better in the short term while some perform better in the long term. I recommend testing the performances for 3 months, 6 months, 12 months and 18 months for short-term screens (1 month for momentum stocks). If you believe the strategy is for a long term only, get the performances for 6, 12 and 18 months.
- In 2015 (use a date more current), I start with the year 2000 and end with 2014 for a total of 15 sets. It covers the two market cycles. The market before 2000 may not be relevant as today's market is quite different from that time. Actually I prefer the tests for the last 10 years.
- Run the screen in the first part of the year and test the performance at year end. Repeat the test for the rest of the intervals: 3, 6, 12 and 18 (adding 1 for momentum and 2 years for long term).

- I do not start with an amount (say $10,000) and see the results at the end of a period (say 10 years). It could be misleading when your screen performs exceptionally well (or bad) in the first few years. I call the one I use "window testing" for lack of a better term. To illustrate this, the start date is Jan. 1, 2000 (actually Jan. 2 due to holiday) and end date is Jan. 1, 2001. The next set is Feb. 1, 2000 to the start, the next set is Feb. 1, 2001 and so on.

- I use the next available date if the date falls on a weekend or a holiday for consistency. If you have more time, try another set starting in mid year. For some strategies and when time allows, I test the strategy monthly.
- If my screen makes 10% and the market makes 20%, it is 100% worse off. I compare how much it beats the market.
- For simplicity I use the SPY to simulate the market. No index is ideal. The S&P500 is capitalization cap weighed. In 2015, the bubble stocks dominated this index. The better selection is to choose the index according to the type of stocks that you usually have such as the Russell 2000 for small stocks.
- Consider safety such as the Sharpe ratio, maximum drawdown (peak-to-trough loss) and a winner percent. A winner percent at 55% (target for 52%) is very good. If your strategy has a very high winner percent, most likely it is safe but just not only performing.
- Why your actual performance with real money may be worse than the tested strategy:
  - Survivor bias. Most databases take out the stock when they're bankrupt, merged or acquired. Hence the performance of the screen is better than it really is as there are more bankrupt companies than merged /acquired. From my experience I have at least one such stock in a year. Hence, the test results are not correct if the database does not take care of this bias.
  - Emotions do not allow you to stick with the strategy.
  - The strategy does not work in the current market; that's why we need to test the performance of the last 6 months.
  - There is idle money between trades.

- I use the top 5 stocks (hence sorting is important). In addition, if you do not buy foreign stocks, deselect them. I use the top 2 for some strategies such as sector rotation.
- If you cannot find data in some screens in any month, just leave it blank (actually null), which will not be included in calculating averages / totals. If the market is risky, you may not find any value stocks.
- The most recent tests would resemble the performance of the strategy better. Hence, I have an extra average of performance on more recent tests.
- Return = (B-A)/A, while A is the return of SPY for me. It does not handle the negative numbers. Use (B-A)/ABS(A). In any case, check the results to see they make sense. When B or A is zero or very small number, the results could be misleading. I usually delete the test results on huge returns in both directions.
- Using sector rotation strategy as an example, the holding periods are 1, 2 and 3 months.
- Some strategies work better on different phases of the market cycle such as growth stocks in the market trending up and staple stocks during market plunges.

3 From a guru (technical analysis)

This strategy is from a guru with my modifications.

- Always trade with the trend (buy in upward trend and sell short in downward trend). Again selling short is not for beginners. I use buy for illustration.

  The guru prefers the short-term trend (SMA-20, Simple Moving average from Finviz.com), intermediate-trend (SMA-50) and long-term trend (SMA-200). If the percentages are all positive, it is a buy.

  I prefer the trend for the stock, the sector that the stock belongs to (use the related sector ETF) and the market (use SPY to simulate the market). Hence you have a total of 9 trends. In practice, it is hard to have all 9 trends to be practiced. The trends of the stock is most important, and followed by the sector.

- Average up (NOT average down). You add your bet on the stock that is moving up. Most traders do not do that, as they think they are paying more than before.

- Use trailing stops to protect your trade on rising stocks and regular stops after you place a buy. Close the position when the stock is too risky, your reasons for the purchase are satisfied, or you have a better stock to buy. When you are not sure, sell half of the position.

- Buy back the stock that you just closed, when the conditions are favorable (trends for example).

- Prepare a trade journey. You want to repeat your success stories and avoid your failures.

4   Pointers from short-term gurus

- Develop a trading system that fits your personality, your skill and your timing available for trading. A beginner's trading system is different from a skilled trader's system.
- Start with two or three technical indicators (SMA is my favorite), current events more than fundamentals. Study daily news about the stock you want to trade.
- Even with a win-loss ratio of 50%, you still can make a lot of money by protecting your portfolio with stop loss and your profits with trailing stops. Define and enforce your exit strategy.
- Knowledge is everything, and hence learn from the best traders. There are schools (some on-line) teaching folks how to trade. It is less expensive than paying your tuition via actual trading. This book and most other books are a good start and most cost effective. Many old books (so is this book 15 years later if I do not update it) and old technique may not work today; today we have no commission brokers, and most technical indicators are available free.

- Beginners cannot beat professionals without luck. You do not gain knowledge by paper trading. Start small. Never risk the money you cannot afford to lose.
- Need basic capital for trading and a laptop to start. Plus living expenses for a few months if you trade full time. Prepare your new venture psychologically. Be emotionally detached in investing. Silence is golden, the rule I just violated. Your friends will not share their wins but blames, and it affects your ego and your trading.
  I know many made so much in 2000 and in early 2021 that they quitted their day jobs, and then they found out they had big losses later.

- Diversify but not over-diversify. Most of us can handle about three trades simultaneously, or more if your holding period is longer than a day.
- When the number of new heights exceeds the new lows by a large margin (determined by you as all markets are different), consider sell (the market could be peaking). Buy, vice versa.
- Day traders may close their positions (more long than short) at the end of the day, especially on late Fridays to avoid unexpected events and interests. The exception is when the market is surging. Learn money management – never bet it all in one trade. Do not trade in the first hour of the market.
- When you have three unsuccessful trades in a row, it is time to take a break and/or switch to paper trading. Better double your bet on winning stocks, and not the other way round.
- Record all your trades and the results in a trade journal. Review it and learn from your successes and losses periodically.
- Modify your trade system according to your gained knowledge and the market trend. Test it out with no or minimum money until you are comfortable.

Links: https://www.youtube.com/watch?v=qL7Z7XQ6tPA

5 "To short" or "Not to short"

In my Best Book for 2021 2nd Edition, I had two lists for short-term holding, one to momentum and one for short. Here are the results after a month.

Momentum Stocks (Total count = 7. Date: 02/08/2021. End: 03/08/2021).

Symbol	Name	Return %
ATGE	Adtalem	-1%
ATRS	Antares Pharma	-9%
CMRE	Costamare	11%
REGI	RenewableEngergy	-40%
RIO	Rio Tinto ADR	-6%
SPWH	Sportsmans Ware	-1%
WIRE	Encore Wire	8%
	Avg	-5%
	SPY	1%
	Beat SPY by	-916%

Selling Shorts (Total count = 3. Date: 02/08/2021. End: 03/08/2021).

Symbol	Name	Return %
HYLN	Hyliion	17%
NEXT	NextDecade	29%
RMO	Romeo Power	33%
	Avg	26%
	SPY	1%
	Beat SPY by	3833%

The average of these two lists beat SPY by 1458% without considering dividends and fees. This is the return if you invested evenly in these two lists. Past performances have nothing to do with future performances. The investment in my $20 book was trivial compared to what they would gain.

Initially the results were reversed. The performances depend on the market that rose initially and plunged later. I recommend to trade the list when the trend is with us. If the market is up 3 sessions in a row, it should be trending up, and hence buy the stocks in the momentum list. Close the positions when the trend is down. If the market is down 3 sessions in a row, short sell the stocks in the Selling Short list. It is a mistake to ignore the trend as some may think why s/he buys the stocks that have been up in the last 3 sessions.

Book 2: Technical Analysis (TA)

Technical analysis (TA) is the analysis of the price movements and the short-term trend and possible reversal, while fundamental analysis focuses on metrics such as price/earnings ratio and debts. TA assumes the future stock price behavior can be determined by the patterns of past price behavior – it is true more times than untrue. Traders use TA a lot and can profit by shorting stocks. Investors can use them to find the entry points and exits points and some investors only buys stocks with positive long-term trend (using SMA-200%).

Many times stock analysis based on fundamentals fail when the evaluation is solely based on fundamentals. Technical Analysis (TA) has the following characteristics:

- Most of the time, TA is profitable in the short term (less than 3 months). The weather man is more accurate in tomorrow's weather rather than a month away. TA can also signal the reversals.
- It is too many signals if you have more than three TA parameters. To start, use SMA (Simple Moving Average) and RSI(14); both are available in Finviz.com without charting.
- You can combine TA with fundamentals such as a rising SMA50 with increasing Insider Purchases. In addition, you can use more than one TA indictors.
- For market timing, TA is a huge part, but many fundamentals should be considered too. You can use similar techniques to time the market and time stocks and/or sectors such as Golden Cross / Death Cross.

Technical analysis wins for the following reasons:
- Information such as a new product or a major lawsuit pending is not reflected timely in fundamentals, but rather in technical analysis. It gives us guidance in understanding the trend of a stock or even the entire market.
- Most TAs are based on accumulated data. For example, if RSI(14) is greater than 65, most likely this stock is overbought. If there is no reason for this condition, you may consider to sell it.
- When too many investors follow TA, it would become self-prophecy.
- Do not act against the trend. The fundamentalist may buy a stock when it loses 50%, the TA investor most likely will not buy it. Many times the losing stocks will lose another 25% or so. The TA investor most likely buys it on the way up only or short it on the way down.

An example. NVRO (a stock symbol) has appreciated about 100% from mid Feb. to Oct. in 2016 despite its poor fundamentals. It has a new product that could revolutionize physical healing and eliminating pain that will not be shown in the fundamentals except by the eventual Forward P/E. Technical chart can inform us of the uptrend.

Volume is the confirmation. Institution investors drive the market. When the market (esp. the S&P 500 stocks) is down and the volume is up, there is a good chance institution investors are dumping their holdings. It is obvious when most of the indicators are up but the volume is small.

#Filler: Rocket stocks

As of 6/2017, TSLA, AMAZ, NFLX and AAPL were all over-priced by most fundamental metrics. However, they are the darlings of institutional investors. My advice is not to do anything (not to buy and not to short them) as we cannot fight the city hall and their momentum.

1   Technical analysis (TA)

The basics

Technical analysis (a.k.a. charting) is easier to learn than you might expect. It represents the trend of the market (a stock or a group of stocks) graphically. If more investors are in the market, the market would move upwards until it changes direction. We divide the trends into short-term, intermediate-term and long-term.

The chartists usually do not consider fundamentals as they believe they have already been priced into the stock price and some fundamentals are not available to the public. To illustrate, a new drug has been discovered, the stock price of the company jumps initially by insiders purchases and the informed. Its fundamental metrics do not demonstrate this right away, but many investors are buying to boost up the stock price as evidenced by the technical indicators such as SMA for 20 or 50 days.

The volume is a confirmation. When the stock moves up or down by 10% with a low volume, the trend is not yet confirmed.

The trend of the stock price is not a straight line in most cases. Hence a trend line is usually drawn to indicate the direction of the stock. Many investors believe the stocks fluctuate in certain ranges (i.e. channels) and the chart draws the upper value (the resistance line) and the lower value (the support line). In theory, the price of a stock fluctuates within the resistance line (ceiling for understanding) and support (floor). When it reaches its support, it becomes a buy and vice versa for a sell. Most charts including Finviz.com would display these lines.

When the price passes out of the channel, it is called a breakout. Darvas, one of the oldest and most successful chartists, profited from the breakouts of the resistance line and believed the stock was close to the support line of the new channel. Hence it would be a long way up in theory.

If it were so simple, there will be no poor folks

It works most of the time, but do not place all your money on it. For chartists, 51% is great (the same for playing Black Jack). Some trends reverse very fast such as the bio drug stocks in 2015. You need to hedge your bets such as placing stop orders. Most do not want to spend their lives in watching the trend from a big screen.

Most novices use too many technical indicators and lose in their performances to the professionals. Recently, most chartists were not doing all that great and I did not find many books on their success than a decade ago. It could be due to too many followers in similar setups. I verified it with my recent testing using Finviz.com.

Simple Moving Average

The basic technical indicator is SMA-N. It is the average of the last N trade sessions. When N is 20 (or SMA-20), we classify it as short-term. Similarly, SMA-50 is an intermediate-term and SMA-200 is long-term. I prefer 50, 100 and 250. This trend duration is important. For example, do not want to place long-term purchases using the short-term SMA-50. There are many modifications to SMA such as giving more weight to recent data, but I have not found them any better. Finviz.com includes this information without charting (SMA-20, SMA-50 and SMA-100 in percentages).

Defining the trend periods is rather arbitrary. I use SMA-350 to detect the market plunges and SMA-100 for stocks. Weighted Moving Average weighs more weight on recent price data.

It can be used to determine whether we are in bull, bear or a sideways market using SMA-50 (or SMA-200 for longer term) for the market (using SPY), the sector (using an ETF for the sector and the specific stock. The trend is up when it the price is above the SMA and the reversal of the trend.

https://www.youtube.com/watch?v=jdYNaE5GJ0k&list=WL&index=5&t=609s

The trend is your best friend
Most traders use TA for trending in a short duration. Investors can also use TA to time the entry and exit points for better potential profits. Value investors usually are patient and they do bottom fishing and they search for 'oversold' condition using RSI(14). Again high volume is a confirmation.

Many sites provide charting free of charge such as Yahoo!Finance. Finviz.com provides a lot of technical indicators without charting such as SMA% and RSI(14). It also provides screen searching for stocks that meet your technical analysis criteria.

Hands on

Bring up Finviz.com and enter any stock symbol such as AAPL. You can see the daily prices of AAPL from about nine months ago to today. Three SMAs (Simple Moving Average) are displayed as SMA-20, SMA-50 and SMA-200. The first two are for short-term trends. When the price is above the SMA, it is expected to be trending up. Again, the trade volume is used as a confirmation.

You can also see the resistance line and the support line drawn. In theory, the stock will trade within these lines. When it exceeds its resistance line, it is called a breakout, and vice versa for a breakdown. Sometimes it displays some technical patterns such as Cup and Shoulder and Double Down (both are positive patterns).

Select Weekly data. The Candle chart is better described than the Daily chart. Candles give us better descriptions of the price: open, close, high and low. The green color indicates the price is up for the period (a week in this example) and the red color indicates a down period.

In addition, Finviz.com includes some technical indicators in the metric section such as RSI. Most other chart sites are similar in the basics. Use Finviz's Help and select Technical Analysis for more description. Investopedia has enhanced descriptions on this topic.

TA patterns

There are many TA patterns such as Bollinger Bands and MACD. The patterns are based on the stock prices and many times they prove to be correct predictions especially on stocks with high volume and high market caps. Patterns have been repeating themselves many times as they are driven by investors.

Sites for TA

There are many free sites for charts with explanations of their technical indicators. Popular ones include BigCharts.com, SmallCharts.com and Yahoo!Finance. Fidelity includes some unique features in its charts such as P/E.

Why I do not use TA as a primary tool for stock picking

My investing style is different from a day trader's. I prefer to 'Buy Low and Sell High' instead of 'Buy High and Sell Higher'. I try to find the real bottom price. TA will not find the bottom very easily but it tracks the trend better. As a bargain hunter, I do not expect the stock will rise fast as I'm usually swimming against the tide. However, value stocks could stay in the low price for a long time (i.e. value trap). I like to select stocks that turn around as evidenced by the SMA-20 and SMA-50.

With that said, my momentum portfolio has appreciated consistently and usually has the best performing stocks among all my portfolios. It is based on the timely grade from my subscriptions plus the metrics on timing.

Most chartists would also tell you to buy the stocks that have broken out (i.e. higher than the resistance line) and/or stocks at their highs. Contrary to value investing, you should exit when the trend reverses. The reversal could happen very fast and hence protect your portfolio by setting up stop loss (preferably with trailing stop) orders.

My opinion

I do not want to argue whether TA is good for you or not. You need to find that out. Most likely, the day traders and very short-term traders will profit more from TA than the investors seeking value stocks for the long-term gains.

Random remarks

Even if you do not use technical analysis, you should spend some time in learning it. It is better to marry fundamentals and TA. My random remarks are:

- The Institutional investors (insurance companies, pension funds, mutual funds, etc.) use TA and they MOVE the market. A lot of times it becomes a self-fulfilling prophecy. It is better to join them as most of us cannot beat them.

- Day traders take advantage of the institutional investors by spotting their trends.

- Most TA stocks should be good sized and have large average daily volumes. I prefer to use TA on value stocks to prevent long-term losses.

- I do know some folks making big money using TA, but I know more making good money using fundamentals. Since TA predicts the market better in the shorter term, its practitioners may have to pay higher taxes (in today's tax laws) in taxable accounts.

- Our objective should be making money with the least risk. Once you claim to belong to a certain group of either Fundamental or TA, you will be biased and forget your primary objective in investing.

- TA tracks the last two big market plunges (2000 and 2007) pretty well. The chart will not warn you right away for the upcoming plunge (as it depends on past data) to avoid the initial losses, but they will warn you to avoid bigger losses.

Afterthoughts

- Besides searching for stocks that have potential breakouts, we should check the stocks we owned for potential breakdowns.
  Technical Analysis tutorial.
  https://www.YouTube.com/watch?v=GENBVwV8PMs

  SMA tutorial.
  https://www.YouTube.com/watch?v=Na-ctpPsnks

Links

Fidelity video: Technical Analysis
https://www.fidelity.com/learning-center/technical-analysis/chart-types-video

2   Examples of using TA

I have outlined how we can spot market plunges using TA and I use it to monitor the market every three months or so (I recommend to do it every month and even more frequently when the market is risky). Here is an example of how to use it to trade individual stocks.

I have to admit I do not use TA that much on individual stocks and clearly I am not an expert in TA. If this article stirs up your interest, read more books or attend seminars / classes on TA. However, this book describes the basic and most useful technical indicators. There are many good and free articles from Investopedia on this topic. Personally I prefer to seek fundamentally sound companies at bargain prices and wait for their full appreciation. It has been proven to me many times over.

TA is very useful for momentum and day traders. With the rising volume, you can detect that the stocks are traded by managers of mutual funds, hedge funds, insurance companies and pension funds, and you profit by riding on their wagons.

Some stocks are good for TA. Usually they are larger companies with above-average volumes and are fundamentally sound. Avoid the stocks that are trending downwards unless you're bottom fishing. Let me pick CSCO (a cyclical stock) for an illustration. I bought it several times in 2012. I sold some in 2013 and 2014 making good profits. This is quite different from what short-term traders would use during the following:

The green line is a 50-day simple moving average (SMA) for the following chart using one year data.

If it does not display clearly on a small screen, type the following on the browser in your PC.

http://ebmyth.blogspot.com/2013/05/chart-for-ta-example.html

Buy the stock when it is above its SMA and sell when it is below. Following the chart would make good money based on this simple rule. Also, practice the strategy "Sell on May 1, Buy back on Nov. 1".

Not all stocks follow this profitable pattern. Fundamentalists may try to pick the bottom in late July while chartists enter positions on its upward trend.

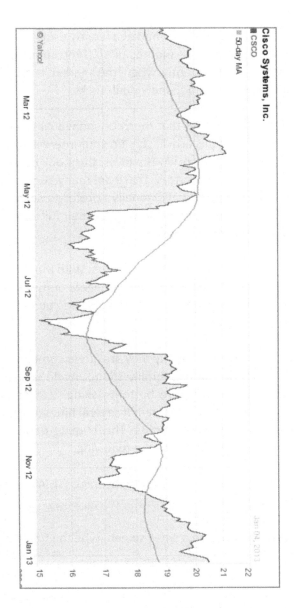

Table: CSCO   50-day SMA   Source: Yahoo!Finance

We can improve the trades by:
- Use different moving average in the number of days (50 in this example) and other indicators such as EMA (a moving average that weighs higher on more recent data). It may improve prediction accuracy and/or cut

down on the number of trades. RSI(14) suggests overbought / oversold conditions.

- Instead of selling the stock for cash, consider selling the stock short. Selling short is definitely not for beginners.

- The accuracy is usually improved by a separate chart for the sector the stock belongs to and another one for the market. For CSCO, you can use an ETF for network companies and SPY (or a similar ETF) to represent the market.

  In theory and in theory only, when both the stock, the sector that the stock is in and the market all move down, the stock price has a high chance that it would move down, and vice versa.

  We use the 50 days (in SMA) for short-term holding of stocks (20 for even shorter holding period and 200 days for longer holding period). Personally I use 30 days for the sector ETF. Again, 'Days' is actually 'Trade Sessions'.

TA is not for most fundamentalists but it should be used

For a bargain hunter like me, TA would not benefit me a lot for picking stocks at their bottoms. I would try to pick up CSCO with prices ranging from 15-17 and all well below the moving average line, but TA would not show me a Buy signal. However, for short-term swing traders TA is a Godsend.

To me, TA is a good indicator for growth, momentum and for short-term trading. Some fundamentalists may use TA for entry and exit point is. Some recommend buying the stock when the price is above the SMA-200 (same as when SMA-200% is positive and that can be readily obtained from Finviz.com).

It is profitable for 'Buy High and Sell Higher' if you can are able to protect your profits effectively. This is also called 'Buy at a reasonable cost'. One's opinion.

In selecting a tool, you have to understand how, and why to use it and whether it fits your investing style. I use TA for market timing for the entire market more than on individual stocks. When I have more time, I probably would use TA more frequently.

Most of us cannot spot the bottom of a stock; I have had some success but most likely they were due to luck. When a stock is moving up from the bottom, there is a good chance it will move further up. TA shows it and the volume confirms it.

Conclusion

Even a fundamentalist like me can benefit a lot by using TA. This book touches on the very basics of TA.

Besides monitoring the fundamentals of the stocks you bought once every 6 months, you should analyze their technical indicators more often (1 month to 3 months depending on your available time). When the market is risky (close to the SMA average), run the SMA chart more frequently (say once a week).

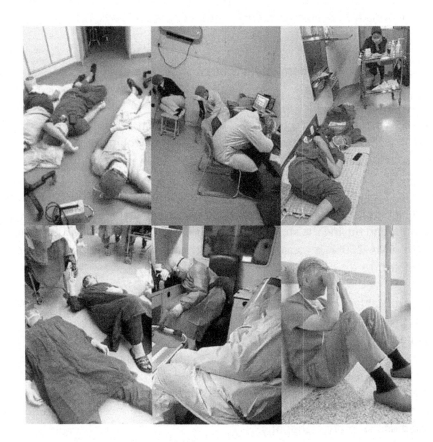

Not taken by me.
They are more important than ALL entertainers and athletes

3 Easy TA without charts

Bring up Finviz.com from your browser. Enter the stock you're evaluating. SMA-200% stands for Simple Moving Average of the last 200 trade sessions. RSI(14)% is the relative strength index for the last 14 trade sessions.

The following is just a suggestion with conservative parameters. Adjust the parameters according to your risk tolerance and requirements. Do not buy the stock with SMA-200% is < 0 (trending down), SMA-200% > 40 (peaking), or RSI(14)% > 65 (overbought).

Filler: Love is blind

The dividend lovers say that when their stocks drop by 50%, they are getting a 50% raise. There was a recent article on this STUPID logic - insulting my intelligence by just reading the title. When the company is bankrupted, they are getting a 100% raise. Should they check in the closest clinic to get their brains examined?

Love is blind and fools are fools and this cannot change the truths in our lives.

---

4 Bollinger Bands

Bollinger Bands have been proven useful for traders. In theory, the stock is traded between the upper band and the lower band forming an envelope. For more info, click the following link.

http://www.investopedia.com/terms/b/bollingerbands.asp

The following chart was drawn by Yahoo!Finance for CSCO from 8/7/2012 to 8/7/2014 selecting Bollinger Bands for the 50 days as a parameter. If you trade more often, use 20 days. If the chart is too small to display on your screen, enter the following in your PC's browser.
http://ebmyth.blogspot.com/2014/08/screen-csco-bollinger-bands-50.html

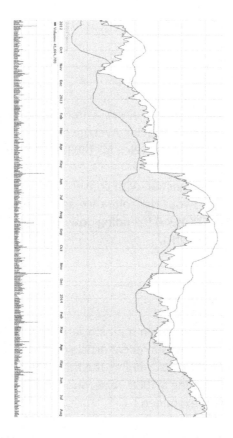

Bollinger Bands 50 Days.   Source: Yahoo!Finance

You buy the stock when the price is close to the lower band and sell the stock when it is close to the upper band.

When the stock price passes the upper band, it is called a breakout. Similar for the stock falling below the lower band.

From the above, we should make some good money.

It is advisable to use at least one more technical indicator. I recommend the RSI(14), which is also accessible from Yahoo!Finance or similar sites. When it is above 70, it is overbought, so I recommend selling the stock. When it is below 30, it is oversold, so I recommend buying the stock. However, fundamentals have not been considered. Some stocks just go to zero and some just surge.

5   MACD

MACD, Moving Average Convergence Divergence, is an effective momentum (i.e. short-term) indicator used by most traders. When the stock price is crossing above the zero line, it is a buy and vice versa. It may give false signals in sideways fluctuation.

###
Again, try to master SMA and RSI(14) first. Using too many indicators usually harms you more than helps you. You can use Finviz.com to search stocks with technical indicators.

6   Other TA indicators/patterns

They are briefly mentioned here. Click on the links or use Investopedia for more descriptions.

Double Bottom is a bullish pattern as the support line is stronger than the resistance line.
Double Top is the opposite and is a bearish pattern. I prefer the price of the second top is less than the price of the first top. It seems there are no enough investment in this stock to break out of the second top.

Resistance and Support. The stock is supposed to fluctuate between an imaginary zone of resistance and support. Short-term traders may sell when the price is close to the resistance line and close any short positions when it is close to the support line. However, breakouts from this zone are possible and many traders trade stocks on breakouts. It is a little similar to 52-week highs and lows. The trend line indicates the trend of the stock.

Cup and handle is a bullish pattern. The stock price peaks and then forms a shape of a cup and handle.

Head & Shoulder is a bearish pattern while the reversed Head & Shoulder is a bullish pattern. It signals that the peak (the head) has been reached and the second top (the shoulder) has failed to reach the previous peak.

Stochastic Oscillator. It is similar to RSI(14). Many traders use this indicator. If it is above 65, it is overbought. If it is below 30, it is oversold. In general, I would trade on an uptrend when the stock is moving from 60 to 85; it depends on how volatile the stock is. It is better to use with other indicators and as a reference.

To illustrate when to buy, one suggestion is to buy when this indicator changes to an uptrend while the price is still going down.

Many traders follow these technical indicators and SMA. They could become "self-fulfilled" prophecies.

Link

Chart patterns. https://www.youtube.com/watch?v=o6hZma0bajE

7   More on technical analysis

This chapter describes some TA indicators that can help us. Click on the following links for a better description.

- Finviz.com.
  It has SMA20%, SMA50% and SMA200% to represent the short-term, intermediate-term and the long-term indicator. SMA stands for Simple Moving Average and n for days for the duration of the average (for example, 20 days for SMA20%).

  If you are a long-term investor, use SMA-200% (or SMA-350%). Using SMA-20% would cause a lot of sells / reentries, which costs more in trading fees.

  Buy when the price is above the Moving Average line and sell when the price is below it. Finviz.com provides the percent of moving above the moving average to indicate just how much the price deviates from the average.

If you hold the stock for an average of 50 days, use SMA50%, and so on. If you hold stocks for an average of 90 days, you have to create your own SMA using one of the many web sites including Yahoo!Finance and specify 90 days for the period.

Try other similar technical indicators such as EMA, which is supposed to weigh more on the more recent data. A weather man can predict tomorrow's weather better than the weather a week away.

- RSI(14) indicates whether the stock is overbought or oversold. RSI oscillates between zero and 100. Traditionally, and according to Wilder (the author of this method), RSI is considered overbought with a value above 70 and oversold with a value below 30 as described in the article.

  When it is oversold, most likely the stock will fall, and vice versa.

  (http://stockcharts.com/school/doku.php?id=chart_school:technical_indicators:relative_strength_index_rsi)

  Click here for another article.
  (http://financial-dictionary.thefreedictionary.com/Relative+Strength+Index)

- Cup and handle is a popular indicator of when the stock price would surge.
  (http://www.investopedia.com/terms/c/cupandhandle.asp)

- Double bottom indicates that the stock will move up.
  (http://stockcharts.com/school/doku.php?id=chart_school:chart_analysis:chart_patterns:double_bottom_revers)

  It shows a double bottom for Apple in 2013.

8   Using Fidelity

Click "Research and News" and then "Stock". Simple charting and advanced charting are both provided.

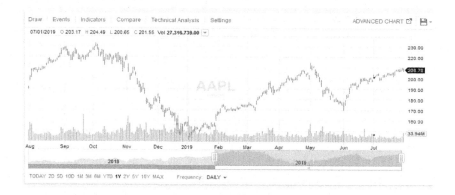

Hints:

● Fidelity provides suggested stops.

● Click on the Support and Resistance under Technical Analysis to display the Resistance Line (upper limit). Click on the Resistance Line and you can get the Support Line (lower limit).

● Click on Advanced Chart and then click on "learn how to use the chart". Under Advanced Chart, select Draw and Trend Line. Select the upper line by touching the highest points and do the same for the lower line.

Summary

This book is lengthy with a lot of information on strategies. I have used some of them based on the current market conditions and my own requirements. I include some I believe they have values to some investors. For just a moment, forget everything you've learned here and elsewhere on strategies and use your common sense to see whether the following makes sense to you.

- Evaluate your requirements and select the strategy or strategies you want. Test them thoroughly on paper before committing real money.

- Need to check recent performance of your screens. There are no evergreen strategies that I know of. This is why many gurus have failed in 2015 (and so far in the first part of 2016) as the market changed.

- Some strategies perform better in up markets and vice versa.

- Stick with my three-step process: Market Timing, Screen Stocks and Evaluate Stocks.

  When the market is risky, do not buy stocks. "Strategy" is the first part of Screening Stocks and the second part is when and why to sell stocks. You need to provide exit strategy such as stop orders to reduce further losses.

  Some strategies perform better for holding stocks short term (3 months or less), while some (most based on value) perform better in the longer term (12 months or more).

Some strategies perform better in a specific stage of a market cycle. Select several strategies for paper trading. Use the one that performs best in the last month or two. It could continue the performance in the coming month. In any case, use stops to protect your investments.

Book 3: Evaluating Stocks

The simple formula to make money is to find value stocks and wait for the market to realize their values. Only buy when the market is not risky. Most successful investors are doing this.

The book value of a stock is simply the net worth of a company (= Assets – Liabilities). When the stock price is higher than the book value per share (i.e. 'Stock Price / Book Price' > 1), it is over-valued. When this ratio is more than 2 or less than 0.5, you have to be cautious. When it is way underpriced, there may be a critical reason.

Intrinsic Value includes the intangibles such as patents. However, both the Book Value and Intrinsic Value have not been convincing predictors from my tests. I briefly describe some basic but important metrics here.

- Expected Earning Yield (E/P). The future appreciation depends on future earnings and the current price of the stock (you do not want to overpay). I prefer a range from 5% to 30%.
- Growth of Earnings and growth of sales. Compare them to their numbers in the same quarter of last year. I prefer 10% or higher.
- How good is the management? Measured by ROE. I prefer 10% or higher.
- How safe is the company? Measured by 'Debt/Equity'. I prefer less than .5 (same as 50%). However, some industries are debt intensive.

These are the ratios readily available from many sites including Finviz.com except reversing P/E for earning yield. In most cases there is no need to dig into the complicated financial statements to start with. However, ensure they are up-to-date. For example, when a stock has a one-to-two split, the price is updated but may not be the Earnings per share, Book per share... to give erroneous info.

The predictability of most metrics changes according to the current market conditions. Monitor their performance and act accordingly. I prefer E/P but Earnings/Sales had better predictability in my last test.

How to start
Check out the Simplest Way to Evaluate Stocks in the Common Tools section.

First we filter stocks from about 7,000 selected stocks available; the number is variable from different web sites and/or services. To start with, skip stocks not in the three major exchanges, market caps less than 50 M or daily average volumes less than 10,000 shares.

We have a simple procedure to evaluate stocks for beginners and couch potatoes by using other folks' research in the Common Tools section. Furthermore, refer to Scoring Stocks to evaluate stocks using a scoring system. Some chapters have been duplicated here so you do not have to bounce back and forth.

1   Simplest way to evaluate stocks

Beginners should trade ETFs only. This chapter is for the readers who are ready or getting ready to trade stocks. In general, ETFs are diversified, less volatile than trading stocks. However, stocks offer higher profit but higher risk.

Many stock researches have already been done recently and some are available free of charge. I have no affiliation with Fidelity except I retired from it. You can open an account with them with no balance. Their Equity Summary Score is one of the best indicators; I check out **value** stocks with score higher than 8. Concentrate on fundamental metrics such as P/E for long-term holds, and momentum metrics for short-term holds. Add criteria to limit the number of screened stocks. Finviz.com is a free screener.

Several sources

The popular ones are Morningstar, Value Line, The Street and Zacks (currently free for rankings of individual stocks). If they are not free, check out whether they are available from your local library. I have 3 simple ways to evaluate stocks starting with the simplest. In addition, read the articles on the selected stocks from Fidelity, Finviz, Seeking Alpha and many other sources for further evaluation.

Fidelity

Select only stocks that have Fidelity's Equity Summary Score 8 or higher. There are tons of information about a stock. Once a while I did not agree with the score such as SHOP and ZM that scored high in August, 2020. Include the following for your analysis.

A modified stock selection based on a magazine article

Most metrics are available from Finviz except EV/EBITDA.

1. Forward P/E (expected earnings and not based on the last twelve months). It should range from 5 to 15 (10 to 25 for high tech stocks). EV/EBITDA (from Yahoo!Finance) is a better choice as it includes the debts and cash than P/E; it would be more effective if it uses forward earnings. If you do not use EV/EBITDA, ensure Debt/Equity is less than 0.5 except for the debt-intensive industries.

2. ROE (Return of Equity) measures how well the company uses the capital. I prefer stocks with ROE greater than 5%.

3. Volatility. Conservative investors should select stocks with a beta of less than one (i.e. less volatile).

4. Insider Transactions for sales (i.e. negative) from should be less than 5%. If it is -5%, most likely the insiders are dumping it.

5. Compare the metrics such as P/E and Debt/Equity to its five-year average and its competitors (available in Fidelity).

6. Momentum. Check out the SMA-50 (actually SMA-50%) and SMA-200. Ideally they should be positive. SMA-50% is especially important for stocks you do not want to keep for a long time.

7. Check out articles on the stock as some recent events (for example a new lawsuit) have not been included in the metrics.

8. Compare the trend of the sector this stock is in. Under Finviz, enter the related sector ETF.

Summary
The sources are Fidelity (Equity Summary Score and various comparisons), Finviz and Yahoo!Finance (for EV/EBITDA). Value stocks should be held longer.

Category	Score / Metric	Value /Momentum
Score	Fidelity's Equity Summary Score	Both

Value	EV/EBITDA	Value
	P/E cheaper compared to 5-year avg.	Value
	P/E cheaper compared to its sector.	Value
	Insider Purchases	Both
Safety	Debt/Equity	Value
	Compare it to its sector.	Value
Momentum	50-SMA%	Momentum
	200-SMA% (for long term holds).	Value
Articles	Check out latest events	Both
Market	No purchase if market is risky.	Momentum

A simple scoring system using Finviz

Bring up Finviz.com and then enter the stock symbol.

No.	Metric	Good	Bad	Score
1	Forward P/E[1]	Between 2.5 and 12.5, Score = 2	> 50 or < 0, Score = -1	
2	P/ FCF[1]	< 12, Score = 1	>30 or < 0, Score = -1	
3	P/S[1]	< 0.8, Score = 1	< 0, Score = -1	
4	P/ B[1]	< 1, Score = 1	< 0, Score = -1	
	Compare quarter to quarter of last year			
5	Sales Q/Q	> 15%, Score = 1	< 0, Score = -1	
6	EPS Q/Q	> 20% , Score = 1	< 0, Score = -1	
			Grand Score	
	Stock Symbol Date[2]	Current Price	SPY	

Footnote

[1] Negative values for Sales (due to accounting adjustments), Equity and Book are possible but not likely.

[2] The last row is for your information only. SPY is used to measure whether it will beat the market by comparing the return of this stock to the return of SPY.

The Score

Score each metric and sum up all the scores giving the Grand Score. If the Grand Score is 3, the stock passes this scoring system. Even if it is a 2, it still deserves further analysis if you have time. You may want to add scores from other vendors. To illustrate on using Fidelity, add 1 to the score if Fidelity's Equity Summary score is 8 or higher. Monitor the performance after every 6 months or so to see whether this scoring system beats the market.

Very basic advice for beginners

Beginners should stick with U.S. stocks with Market Cap greater than 800 M (million), Debt/Equity less than .25 (25%) except for debt-intensive industries such as utilities and airlines and Forward P/E between 5 to 20 (25 for high-tech companies). These metrics are all available from Finviz.com, which is free.

Do not have more than 20% of your portfolio in one stock (unless it is an ETF or mutual fund) and do not have more than 30% of your portfolio in one sector.

For more conservative investors, buy non-volatile stocks whose beta (available from Yahoo!Finance) is less than 1. Beta of 1 represents the market (the S&P 500 index). For example, a stock with beta 1.5 statistically fluctuates more than 50% of the market and hence it is very volatile.

Try paper trading to check out your strategy and your skill in trading stocks. If your broker does not provide one, use a spreadsheet to record your trades or check the availability of simulator.investopedia.com.

#Filler: Silence is golden

I am glad I did not give advice to a friend who had to decide whether to take a lump sum payment or an annuity. The correction in March, 2020 would wipe out a lot of his portfolio if he took the lump sum payment. No one would share his profits when the predictions are correct, but the blame if it does not materialize.

It is same in investing that nothing is certain. With educated guesses, we should have more rights than wrongs especially in the long run.

2   Finviz parameters

Most metrics are described in Finviz (via Help), Investopedia and/or Wikipedia and my chapter on P/E. The following are my personal comments and why I feel some metrics are more important than others. Compare the ratios to the companies in the same sector and also its averages from the last 5 years.

From your browser, enter Finviz.com. Enter a symbol (I used ABEO for discussion). A chart is displayed with the prices and volumes for the last nine months. SMAs (Single Moving Average) are displayed sometimes with other technical indicators. Intraday, Daily and Weekly options are available.

Besides the metrics described next and the chart, it describes what the company does, analysts' recommendations (I prefer Fidelity's Equity Summary), insiders' trading and articles that are good for qualitative analysis. "Financial Highlights and Statements" are materials for more in-depth analysis and they were more important decades ago when most financial ratios had not been calculated for you.

The following metrics are roughly based on the flow of Finviz from top to bottom and left to right. I skip those metrics that I believe are not too important. You can also place your cursor on the metric to have the description from Finviz. Some metrics are left blank to indicate they are not applicable (zero, negative or not available). For example, the Debt/Equity of YRCW in 1/2019 is blank (same as null) due to Equity being negative. From Yahoo!Finance, it has a total debt of 888M.

- **Index**. Most of us trade stocks in the three major exchanges in the USA. Stocks listed in over-the-counter are too risky for most of us. Skip the stocks in local exchanges and foreign exchanges if you are not an expert on these stocks. I screen the stocks and then ignore the stocks that are not in the Dow, NASDAC and Amex. Other screeners may let you to select a group of exchanges.

- **Market Cap** (MC). To me, stocks below 50M are risky even they could be very profitable. Ensure the Avg. Volume is at least 10,000 shares and / or your order is less than 1% of the average volume. Some small stocks are controlled by the owners and have small volumes. In this case you cannot sell your stock easily.

Float = Outstanding shares – Insider shares.

Usually it does not matter as they are typically the same. However, it does for small companies with large insider shares. Most of these owners do not want to sell their family businesses and hence they reduce the chance of being acquired entirely or partially for good prices.

- If **Forward P/E** (a.k.a. Expected P/E) is not provided, use the P/E which is based on the trailing last 12 months (TTM). Alternatively, calculate the E by using the E from P/E and multiplying it by its growth rate. It may not be seasonally adjusted. I prefer Expected P/E (or called Forward P/E) as it provides a better predictability power from my limited research.

  Finviz.com leaves the P/E blank (same as null) if the earnings are negative. In this case, I would check out Yahoo!Finance's EV / EBITDA, which also considers taxes and interests. It is similar to the blank on some metrics, if the Asset is negative even they seldom occur.

  Earnings Yield is equal to E/P and True Earnings Yield (my term) is EBITDA / EV. It is easier to understand. Compare it to the annual dividend yield of a 10-year Treasury which is quite safe. It is also useful in screening and sorting the screened stocks. If you use P/E instead of E/P, in most cases you need to screen or sort stocks with a clause "P/E > 0".

  Compare the P/E or Forward P/E with the average P/E for the sector and its average P/E for the last 5 years that are available from Fidelity.com. Some sectors have high P/Es. If the sector is cyclical, the earnings could be affected.

- **Cash / share**. It is used to calculate Pow P/E and Pow EY when EV/EBITDA is not available. To illustrate, if the stock is $10 and it has $10 cash / share without debt (i.e. Debt/Equity = 0), most likely it is underpriced as you can get the whole company for nothing. You should find out why the price is so low. It could be the market ignoring the stock, or there is a serious event happening such as major lawsuit.

- **Dividend %** is useful for income investors. The payout ratio should not be more than 30% except for matured companies.

- **Recs**. Select stocks with 1 or 2. Do not base your stock selection on this recommendation alone. There have been many bad recommendations that could cost you a fortune in losses. Use Fidelity's Equity Summary Score instead.

- **PEG** is a measure of the growth of P/E and hence a growth metric. The lower value is better as long as earnings are positive. If earnings are negative, then the reverse is true. It is a defect in using P/E and PEG and that's why I recommend EY (Earnings Yield) and EYG, earnings yield growth.

  If there are two companies with the same P/E, the one with a better PEG ratio is better. If two companies have the same E/P, the company with higher Earnings Growth (EPS Q/Q) would be better.

- **P/B**. Book value (= Total Assets − Total Liabilities) may not include intangible asset such as patents. Do not trust it 100%, so is ROE which is based on book value. Negative equity is possible when Total Liabilities is more than Total Assets.

- **P/S**. If two companies are unprofitable, this ratio can be used. I prefer profitable companies.

- **P/FCF**. I prefer it to be greater than 0 and less than 50 for value investors. Most metrics can be manipulated easily, but not this one.

- **Sales Q/Q** reduces the seasonal deviation. To illustrate, retail sales for the Christmas season should be compared it to the same season in prior year.

- **EPS Q/Q**. Same as above. I prefer the growth of EPS over Sales. Both of these Q/Q ratios are growth metrics. When a company terminates its unprofitable product(s), its Sales Q/Q could be down but its EPS Q/Q could be up. In 2000, many internet companies had great Sales Q/Qs but negative EPS Q/Qs.

  Q/Q comparison (quarter to quarter) takes out the seasonal variations.

  When the company buys its own shares, EPS could be misleading as E is fixed and the number of shares is reduced. In most cases, the fundamentals of the company has not changed.

- Positive **Insider** Transactions are favorable. Sometimes, they are misleading. Need to scroll to the end of the screen and check out more info there. If the transactions are outdated such as 3 months or so ago, and or they are buys in a similar amount than the sells a while ago, they are not important. Insiders know the company better than us. So is Institutional Transactions as institutional investors move the market.

- Insider Own, Shares Outstanding and Shares **Float** determine the number of shares that are available for trading. A small Float with a high Insider Own limits trading and the stock should be avoided in most cases. Compare your trade position for the stock to the Avg. Volume.

- **Profit Margin**. I prefer it over Gross Margin and Oper. Margin which does not include interest expenses and taxes. When you sell software, the Gross Margin is high as it does not include development, support and marketing, etc. A retail store has low Gross Margin. It all depends on the industry, and hence it is better to compare companies in the same industry.

- **Short Float**. I prefer it to be less than 10%. If it is greater than 10%, the shorters could find something wrong with the company. If it is over 25%, I would check the fundamentals. If they are good, I would buy expecting a short squeeze potential. It has been risky but proven to be profitable for me.

- Technical metrics: SMA-20, SMA-50 and SMA-200. Finviz expresss them in convenient percentages. If they are all positive, it means the trend is up. SMA-20 is short-term trend and SMA-200 is a long-term trend. If you are short-term swing investor, stick with short-term trend and vice versa. The first two are momentum grades. Many long-term investors do not buy stocks when their SMA-200% is negative.

- **RSI(14)**. If it greater than 65%, it is overbought. If it is under 30%, it is under bought for me. Some use 5% up or down than mine. Use it as a reference. Most stocks making new heights are always overbought, and many of these stocks keep on rising. I recommend use trailing stops to protect your profit.

- **Beta**. A volatile stock fluctuates a lot. It is good for short-term traders. A beta of 1 means the stock would fluctuate with the market and more volatile if it is higher than 1. For volatile stocks (higher than 1), the stops should be higher. For example, if your stops are normally 5%, you may want to use 7% or even higher.

- Management performance is measured by **ROE**. It is also judged by **Analysts' Rec.** and Institutional Ownership (except for small companies). The confidence of their own ability, the company and its sector is measured by Insider Ownership and Insider Purchases.

  ROE = Net Income / Average Shareholder's Equity
  According to Investopedia, a normal ROE for utilities should be 10% while high tech companies should be 15%. Compare this ration and many other ratios with its peers that is available from Fidelity.

- Avoid all bankrupting companies at all cost. Debt/Equity, P/FCF, Cash/Sh., P/B, Profit Margin, Forward P/E, Short Float, RSI(14), SMA20% and SMA50 would give us hints. Need to summarize all the info and study many other factors such as obsoleting products (including drugs).

- Unless you have concrete information, do not buy stocks a week or so before the Earnings Date.

More useful information:

- The price chart. It has a lot of features such as the resistance line. Some charts include technical indicators such as double top (a bearish warning) and double bottom (a bullish sign).
- Description under the symbol. It briefly describes what the company (sector and industry) does and its country of registration. You want to buy a stock within a sector that is trending up. For example according to Finviz, Apple is in the Consumer Goods sector and the Electronic Equipment industry.

  If you do not want to buy foreign stocks, skip it if it is not listed in the US exchange.
- Articles on the company for qualitative analysis.
- Insider trading. Pay more attention to the insider purchases at market prices. Use common sense.
- The last line lets you open Yahoo!Finance and other sites.

Your broker's web site

Your broker web site should have plenty of tools to analyze stocks. As of Dec., 2018, Fidelity lets you use their extensive research free by opening an account with no position restriction. I describe some of their metrics that should be beneficial to your research.

- Equity Summary Score. Potentially good buy when it is 7 (8 for conservative investors) or higher. With some exceptions, you should avoid or short stocks if the score is 3 or below. The stocks ranking from 4 to 6 could be turnaround candidates if they are supported by good Q/Q Earnings and/or good news.

- The 5-year averages are good yardsticks. For example, in Dec., 2018, C's P/E is about 9 and the average is 14. Hence it is a value buy.

Other sources

If you have other sources (most require a subscription or being a customer), skip the stocks that have one of the failing grades. The exceptions are a new positive development and increased insider purchases.

Vendor	Grade	Fail
Fidelity	Equity Summary Score	< 7
IBD	Composite grade	< 50
Value Line	Proj. 3-5 yr. return. Also its composite rating	< 3%
Zacks	Rank	5
Vector Vest	VST	< 0.7

You may be able to find Value Line and IBD in your library. Try out the free stock reports from your broker first. Finviz and Seeking Alpha should have articles (now fewer free articles from Seeking Alpha) on stocks and earnings conferences, which could have important information after separating from the "welcome" and garbage talks.

Yahoo!Finance has good info. "EV/EBITDA" is better than "P/E" as it considers debts and cash. Most use Earnings from last 12 months, which has poorer predictability than Forward Earnings to me.

When negative values such as Equity in Finviz.com, we need to adjust many related metrics or do not use them at all.

MarketWatch.com has many articles on the market in general and personal investing.

If the stock is closed to the Earnings Date (found in Finviz.com), you should avoid trading the stock; as earnings could have a big swing for the stock price. Consult Zacks' ranking which is currently free for individual stocks.

Gurus

It is nice to know how gurus would rate the interested stocks. GuruFocus is a good source. NASDAQ is a simplified version, but it is currently free. Bring up Nasdaq.com from your browser. Select "Investing" and then "Guru Screeners". On the third selection, enter the stock symbol such as THO. Click "Go". You will find how 10 or so gurus would evaluate this stock in theory. Click "Detailed Analysis" for each guru.

Quick and dirty

Many times we need to evaluate a stock fast such as taking action due to some development. Refer to my other article "Simplest way to evaluate stocks". The following should take a few minutes. Bring up Finviz.com and enter the stock symbol.

Using SWKS on 6/10/16 to illustrate, Forward P/E is about 11 (fine between 3 and 25), Debt/Eq. is 0 (fine less than .5), ROE is 30% (fine greater than 5%) and P/PCF is 31 (fine if not negative).

Also, check out Market Cap, Avg. Volume, Dividend, Short Float (fine between 0% and 10%), Country and Industry. Judging from the above, it is a buy.

If you have more time, check out the following: Recom. (Ok if less than 2.5), P/B (fine between .5 and 4), Sales Q/Q (fine if not negative), EPS Q/Q (fine if not negative), Cash/Sh (compare it to Debt/Sh) and Profit Margin (fine >5%). Check some articles described for this stock.

5-minute stock evaluation

It takes even less time than the above "Quick and Dirty". However, I recommend you should spend more time in researching stocks.

- From Finviz.com, enter the stock or ETF symbol. Look at the number of reds in metrics. If there have more than greens, most likely it is not a good stock.

- It should be fine if Fidelity's Equity Summary Score is greater than 8.

If you have more time, I recommend you to check the following:

- Check out Forward P/E (E>0 and P/E < 20), Debut / Equity (< 50%) and P/FCF (not in red color).

  If time is allowed, replace Forward P/E with True P/E (same as "EV/EBITDA"), which is available from Yahoo!Finance and other sources.

- SMA20 (or SMA50 for longer holding period). If SMA20 is > 10%, it is trending up.

- It is fine if the Insider Transaction is positive.

- Be cautious on foreign stocks and low-volume stocks.

- If most of the above are positive, it is likely a buy. As in life, nothing is 100% certain.

Links
PEG: http://en.wikipedia.org/wiki/PEG_ratio
Short %:
http://www.investopedia.com/university/shortselling/shortselling1.asp#axzz2LNDvpemo
Openinsider: http://www.openinsider.com/
Finviz: http://Finviz.com/
terms: http://www.Finviz.com/help/screener.ashx
Insider Cow: http://www.insidercow.com/
Current Ratio: http://en.wikipedia.org/wiki/Current_ratio
How to find quality stocks.

http://seekingalpha.com/article/2381395-how-to-identify-quality-stocks-and-is-there-really-alpha-to-be-had

3   Intangibles

I give a score for each stock I evaluate. Occasionally some stocks with poor scores have great returns and vice versa. In general, the scoring system works. It has been proven statistically and repeatedly from my limited data. I stick with high-score stocks with some exceptions.

Once in a while I change my scoring system to adept to the current market conditions. To illustrate, the market bottom phase and early recovery phase of the market cycle favor value more than momentum/growth. Here are some of my recent experiences and strategies:

- I double or even triple my stake on stocks with high scores. In the longer term, they are consistently better winners than the average with some minor exceptions. Besides the score, look at the intangibles described in this article.

- Watch out for the stocks with outrageous metrics such as P/E of 4 or less. It could be a big lawsuit pending, an expiration of some important drugs, etc. Also, be careful with scores in the top 5%. From my statistics they do worse than the average. Their problems may not show up in the current financial statements.

- The technology of a tech company cannot be ignored even though the company's P/E is high, that I set a limit of 25 instead of 20 for other stocks. The value of the company's technology and patents will not be shown in the fundamental metrics except from the insiders' purchases at market prices.

  For example, IDCC rose about 40% in 2 days. There was a rumor that Google was buying the company and/or Apple was bidding on it too for its mobile technology. Charts usually would flag this kind of event. For non-charters, use the SMA-20% from Finviz.com. They could be a little late as the charts depend on rising prices.

- There are more acquisitions during a market bottom (same as early recovery). The companies with good technologies are bargains and the larger companies especially those in the same sector understand their values better than most of us. These potentially profitable companies will not be shown by their scores explicitly. When corporations have a lot of cash or the credit is cheap, they are looking for smaller companies to acquire or invest in. The candidates are usually small, beaten up, low-priced and having valuable intangible assets such as technologies, customer base and/or market share of the industry segment. 2009-2012 was just the perfect environment and the before that was 2003. I had at least one stock in each of these periods and they appreciated a lot.

- The opposite is Netflix, Chipotle in 1/2012 and Amazon in 1/2013. They are over-priced by any measure. However, the mentioned companies are investing in the future. The shorters (not for beginners) are having a tough time in making money on them. When their P/Es are higher than 40, watch out. Some could be OK in the mentioned companies, but usually they are not. Do not follow the herd and your due diligence will verify whether they will still go up.

  Use reward/risk ratio. It is based on experiences. To illustrate, if the company has the equal chance to go up 50% and go down 25%, then it is a buy and the reverse is a sell.

- The retail investor just cannot possibly know about some events until they actually happen. For example, ATSC dropped 15% due to losing its second primary customer. Fundamentals cannot predict this kind of events. Charts can signal this event, but usually they are too late unless you watch the chart all day long.

- After a quick run up, TZOO plunged due to missing some negligible earning expectations. It seems the original climbing prices already had the perfect earnings growth built-in.

  I do not understand why a company loses 10% of its market cap when it missed by 1% of the expected earnings. It could be driven up and down by the institutional investors. Evaluate the stock before you act. Acting opposite to the institutional investors could be very profitable for the right stocks. Avoid trading before the earnings announcement dates (about 4 times a year for most stocks).

- The following are not easily found in financial statements: industry outlook, patents, good will, market share, competition, product margins, management quality, lawsuits pending, potential acquisition, pension obligations, advertising icons, etc. That is why we need to read articles on the stocks in our buy list or our purchased stocks.

- The financial data could be fraudulent or manipulated. I do not trust small companies in emerging markets. I have been burned too many times. Check the company names such as foreign names, ADR and their headquarter addresses (from the company profile in most investing sites).

  Earnings can be manipulated with many accounting tricks. A jump in earnings from last year may not be as rosy as it looks. Check the footnotes in the accounting statements. I usually skip financial statements unless I have big purchases in mind as my time in investing is limited.

- Cash flow cannot be easily manipulated. It is good information whether the company will survive or not, but to me it does not prove to be a consistent predictor in my tests, but an important red flag for companies on their way to bankruptcy. Examples abound.

- Repeated one-time, non-recurring and extraordinary charges are red flags.

- Stay away from the companies where the CEOs are over-compensated. As of 7- 2013, Activision's CEO raised his salary by more than 600%, while the stock lost its value in double digits.

- Value stocks. Need to know why they become value stocks (i.e. fewer investors want to own) even they are financially sound. For example, there are two primary reasons for the downfall of a supplier to Apple: 1. Apple is declining in sales and 2. Apple is switching suppliers to replace their product. Technology companies are continually building better mouse traps. They could turn around in a year or so with better products.

Conclusion

Buying a stock is an educated guess that its stock price will rise. Fundamentals do not always work, but they work most of the time:

1. When we buy a value stock, we're swimming against the tide. Hence, we need to wait longer (usually more than 6 months) for the market to realize its value. The exception is the Early Recovery phase (see the

Market Cycle chapter) and it has faster and larger returns than most other stocks from most other stages of the market cycle.

2. Some metrics are misleading. Book value could be misleading for an established company such as IBM. The image of the cowboy in a tobacco company could be a very important asset that is not included in its financial statement.

3. The market is not always rational.

Afterthoughts

- Brand names of big companies are one of the most important intangibles. Here is a strategy to buy big companies in a down market. It has been proven that it works. However, do not just buy these companies without analysis.
http://seekingalpha.com/article/1324041-buying-brand-names-in-a-bear-market-can-make-you-rich

- The reputation of a company takes a long time to build but a bad incidence to destroy in the case of GM such as the delay in recalling the killer switches.

#Filler: Carrie Fisher, another sad American story

Unless drug addiction is part of the culture now as evidenced from the legalization of certain drugs, we're in a permissive society! Brits pushed opium as a nation when they had nothing better to trade. Opium killed millions of Chinese and bankrupted China. When we do not learn from history, we will repeat history. It is another sad story of fame and money and then losing it all. I bet she would be happier in a normal life instead of being born in a privileged class. Same can be said for many celebrities such as Presley, Houston and her daughter. RIP.

4   Qualitative analysis

This is the last analysis to evaluate a stock fundamentally. Then the next is technical analysis which is used to find an entry point (also the exit point) for the stock.

Where quantitative analysis fails and why

I find that some stocks with high scores fail and some stocks with low scores succeed as indicated by my performance monitor. The scoring system still works statistically for the majority of my stocks.

- Reasons why stocks with low scores perform in addition to the described in the last discussion:

  o   Over-sold. The institutional investors (fund managers and pension managers) dump them first, and then followed by the retail investors. These big boys will buy these stocks back when they reach a certain price range. RSI(14), a technical indicator described in the Technical Analysis article, is useful to detect these over-sold stocks. This metric is readily available from many sites including Finviz.

  o   The falling price (P) improves all fundamental metrics that have the stock price such as P/E and P/Sales. However, the trend of the price is down.

  o   The company has turned around after fixing its problems and/or the market has changed for the better.

  o   The current problems have been resolved but not known to the public. It includes resolving a lawsuit, a new product, a new drug, or a new big order, etc.

  o   Heavy purchases by insiders. The company's outlook is not shown in its financial statements. Sometimes the insiders hide them so they can buy more of their companies' stocks for themselves.

- Reasons why stocks with high scores plunge in addition to the described in the previous discussion:

o The company's fundamentals and its prices have reached or closed to the maximum heights. They have no way to go but down. It is particularly true when the stock's timing rating is at or close to the highest point. TTWO that I gifted to my grandchildren had been 5-baggers in the last few years before it plunged in 2018.

o It has reached its potential value (or a target price) and it is time for many investors to take profits.

o Sector (or stock) rotation, particularly by institutional investors who drive the market.

o The outlook of the company, its sector and/or the market is deteriorating.

o The stock price may be manipulated. There are many reasons to pump and dump the stock. Shorting is not recommended for most investors. However, some experienced shorters make money consistently when they find valid reasons to short stocks.

o It could be due to a new serious lawsuit, a new competing product or drug, canceling a major order, etc.

o Downgrade by analysts. They could spot some bad events such as product defects, violations of regulations or accounting errors / frauds. The downgrades are more important than the upgrades that could have conflict of interest.

o The financial statement had been manipulated. The SEC may ask for an investigation.

o Does not meet the consensus in earnings announcements, which have been over-acted by many investors.

Qualitative Analysis

We need to do further analysis after the quantitative analysis and the intangible analysis. Check out the company's prospects. Check out the date of the article and any potential hidden agenda items from the author. Older articles may not have much value.

Be careful on 'pump-and-dump' manipulation written by authors with a hidden agenda. It has happened especially on small companies before even SeekingAlpha.com has its share. Here was an article that tells you to sell NHTC. There was another article to tell you to buy ARTX. They fit into this category.

The sources are:

1. Seeking Alpha.
   Type the symbol of the company to read as many articles on the company as you have time for. Today this site and many other similar sites require you to be a paid member. If you cannot find too many good articles, check out the articles from Finviz.com.

   Recently, I read an article on AMD and it said it may have good profits in the next two years with the game consoles. The outlook of a company is not shown by any fundamental metric which are far from favorable.

   Following a well-known writer, I bought IBM without doing my due diligence (my fault). It went down more than 15% quickly. You can learn from my mistakes.

2. Research reports from your broker. If you do not find many, open an account with one that provides such reports. Some subscription services such as Value Line provide such reports.

3. Yahoo!Finance board. Most comments are garbage. However, once in a while you find some great insights. Usually you cannot find any info from other sources on tiny companies.

4. The most recent company's financial statements. They are usually available in the company's web site.

5. 10-Ks from Edgar database (www.sec.gov/edgar). Check out new products and its potential competition, key customers, order backlog, research and development and pending lawsuits.

6. Check out the outlook of the sector the company is in and the company itself.

7. Check out its competitors.

8. Some companies are run by stupid people. I received information via my email saying that my mutual fund account could be treated as an abandoned property. I have been cashing dividend checks every year and why it would be considered as an abandoned property. I called them right away to close my account.

The tall and handsome guy presented articulately how he would turn around JC Penny on TV. I could tell you right away that all his tricks had been tried by other companies such as Sears, and most did not work. The intelligent investor does not care about how handsome, how articulated, how rich his family is and how many advanced degrees from prestigious colleges he possesses. If he does not make sense, do not buy his preaching and his company's stock. [Update. As of 5/2020, J.C. Penny filed for bankruptcy protection. If you had this stock and my book, you would have saved a lot of money minus $10 for my book!]

9. Check out its business model. Some business models do not make business sense and some do. Here are some samples.

- Giving razors makes sense, as the customers have to buy the blades eventually and keep on buying blades for life.

- Supermarket M lowers prices on common merchandises such as Coke and it works. They make money by providing inferior (but profitable to them) products that you cannot compare prices easily such as meat and seafood.

  Eventually there will be a supermarket in my area to satisfy me both in price and quality or at least make a good tradeoff.

- Last week it had been brutally hot. I went to a Barns & Noble's bookstore to enjoy reading the updated books and enjoyed the air conditioning. When there are more free loaders like me than customers, this business model does not work.

- Market dumping works to capture the market. Microsoft used to do it with their new Office and Mail products that could not compete with the established products at the time. Google is following the same model to dump its equivalent products to compete with Office. Now, Microsoft is taking a dose of the same medicine.

- ## **Bonus**

1   Adaptive Stock Scoring System

No.	Metric	Good	Bad	Score
1	P/E (use expected P/E if available)[6]	Between 2.5 and 12.5, Score = 2	> 50 or =< 0, Score = -1	
2	Price / Free Cash Flow	< 12, Score = 1	>30 or < 0, Score = -1	
3	Price / Sales[1]	< 0.8, Score = 1	< 0, Score = -1	
4	Price / Book[1]	< 1, Score = 1	< 0, Score = -1	
5	Analyst's Opinion[2]	> 7, Score = 1	< 4, Score = -1	
6	Short % (check reason for high %)	Between 30% & 40%, Score = 1[4]	Between 10% & 20%, Score = -1	
7	Insider Purchase[3]	Score = 1		
8	Profit Margin[3]	> 25%, Score = 1	< 5%, Score = -1	
	Compare Q to Q last year for #9 and # 10			
9	Revenue Growth[3]	> 15%, Score = 1	< 0, Score = -1	
10	Earning Growth[3]	> 20% , Score = 1	< 0, Score = -1	
11	Intangibles	Positive, Score = 1	Negative, Score = -1	
			Grand Score	
	Stock Symbol Date[5]	Current Price	SPY	

Footnote.

[1]   Negative values for Sales (due to accounting adjustments), Equity and Book are possible but not likely.

[2]   It is from the Fidelity web site. If you have no access to it, use Finviz's Rec.: Score =1 if Rec=1 and Score = -1 if Rec = 5.

[3]   This metric can be found from many sources. They may use different terms for the same data.

[4]   A short squeeze could be coming when a stock is over-sold. If the critical problem of the company cannot be recovered easily, change the Score from 1 to -1.

[5]   The SPY in the last row is for your information only. SPY is used to measure whether it will beat the market by comparing the return of this stock to the return of SPY.

[6]   Earnings yield E/P (the reversal of P/E) should be between 8% and 40%.

Score

Score each metric and then sum up all the scores giving the Grand Score. If the Grand Score is 3 (I use 2 for my passing grade), the stock passes this scoring system. Even if it is a 2, it still deserves further analysis if you have time.

For some reason I do not know why and how to explain, the top 10% (15% for long term and 5% for short term) of the stocks we score and why they do not perform better than the passing grade. It happens in two of my scoring systems. Be cautious on them as it has happened more than once. The stocks scoring in the bottom 10% are consistently poor performers and that's good. To simplify the usage, ignore the stocks that have scores greater than 7.

The metrics from #1 to #6 are yearly metrics based on the last twelve months except the 'expected P/E'. These are popular value ratios.

Metric 9 and 10 are quarterly comparisons of the same quarter last year. They are readily available from Finviz.com.

Some metrics such as the Analyst's Opinion can be obtained directly from Fidelity. If you do not have access to it, use Rec. from Finviz.com.

Metric

For more information, search the metric in Wikipedia or any financial site.

- P/E.
  Price to Earning is a primary value ratio. The Expected Earning has better predictive power than the one from the last two months.

- Price / Cash Flow (same as Price / Free Cash Flow).
  Cash Flow is one of the few metrics that cannot be manipulated. It is a red flag when it is increasing fast. Statistically, it is not a good indicator for the long term but it does add safety.

- Price / Sales.

Different industries have different averages for this metric. A supermarket business should have a very low ratio. Adjust it according to the industry the stock belongs to.

- Price / Book.
  Usually it is not a good indicator for matured companies such as IBM.

- Analyst's Opinion.
  Fidelity has a good handle on this metric. It is based on the past predictive accuracy of the analysts.
- Short Percent (= Shares being shorted / shares outstanding).
  The stock buyers who short the stocks frequently are right more times than they are wrong. The percent between 10% and 20% is high to me.

  However, when it is too high, a short squeeze may be coming. When there are too few shares to sell, the stock price could boost up due to supply and demand. You need to find out the reason why it is so high. If the reason is valid to short the stock, stay away from this stock no matter how high the stock scores. Any scoring system is not sacred and it can be ignored for many situations such as a pending serious lawsuit.

- Insider's Purchase
  When the insiders purchase their company's stock at the market price, most likely the company is doing well. No one knows the company and its sector better than the officials of the company. Ignore options. Ignore the purchases after the insiders selling. Insider purchases explains why some lowly-scored stocks appreciate fast. Hence, ignore the low scores for stocks with heavy insider purchases and include them for further analysis.
- Profit Margin.
  Ignore or relax this metric during a recession. For those industries that do not have gross margin, use operating margin instead.
- Revenue growth.
  Ignore or relax this metric during a recession.
- Earning growth.
  Ignore or relax this metric during a recession.
- Intangibles.
  The outlook of the company, its industry and the stock market.

For simplicity, each outlook scores -1 for poor and 1 for good. Add up the three scores. There is more to it such as serious lawsuits pending, new products, sector rotation, changing market conditions....

Analyze the high-scored stocks further. If a red flag surfaces, skip the stock. Red flags can be detected from or not from the financial statements. When you use financial statements, ensure they are the most updated ones that usually can be found in the company's web site.

Holding Period

The performance monitor uses the holding period of 6 months. After six months, some metrics may change. Hence, evaluate the bought stocks again at that time using the same scoring system. In my last monitor, the metrics did not lose the predictive accuracy, but in the long run it should.

Check out your tax rates for long-term and short-term capital gains. For non-retirement (same as taxable) accounts, you need to make more adjustments such as selling the losers/winners before/after the required holding period for long-term capital loss/gain (as of 2016, it is 366 days to qualify for long-term capital gains).

Fundamentalists are swimming against the tide. It takes time for the market to realize their values. Hence, selling too early (3 months or less) without good reasons is not recommended. When a stock passes the profit target, consider selling it even if it has been bought just over several days ago.

Variations

Enter your changes to this scoring system to suit your investing style and/or different market conditions. The current system uses fundamental metrics. For growth investing, add the appropriate metrics such as PEG, price momentum, etc. This described scoring system **will not work on momentum strategies** (holding stocks less than a month) and day trading.

2 Trading plan

You should have a trading plan and it should include the following basics:

1. Your overall objective.
2. When to buy, what stocks and how many.
3. When and what stocks to sell.
4. When and how to monitor your trading strategies.

The follow are my suggestions. Adjust them according to your personal requirements.

Be disciplined

Being disciplined will provide better results in the long run and save you time. Following the trading plan will not allow your emotions to take over.

To illustrate, you have a specific day (Monday or the first day of the month) to check the value of your portfolio. By checking it several times a day, it becomes a waste of time and energy. It could cause harm to your emotions.

Set your objective(s)

Set up your objective and requirements first. Your objective could be seeking the highest profit, profit at the least risk, protecting principal, generating income or a combination. Beating the market should not be your primary objective.

For example, a better objective is making more than 5% per year in the next 10 years with the least risk. Why 5%? I estimate that we have a 3% inflation rate and 2% taxes. The higher risk you can take, the higher the return it would be.

You can be conservative and aggressive at the same time by setting up two accounts, one for each objective. In addition, you may want to define the maximum investment amount for each account.

I have three objectives and they usually fall into different accounts and different holding periods.

- Non-taxable account. Profit at the least risk. Buy value stocks. Review purchased stocks every 6 months.
- Roth account. Buy momentum stocks seeking for the maximum short-term (1 month) profits.
- Conservative investing in all accounts. Define a larger safety net. Conserve my cash. Move all to stocks only when the market is the most favorable.

Contrary to the above, most investors' or traders' tend to have an objective in beating the market by a specific percent. It is fine also to measure how you perform against the market. For ultra conservative investors, not losing money may be your primary objective. In any case, consider safety.

If you made 10% and the market was up by 20%, you under-performed the market. However, do not blame yourself if your primary objective is conserving wealth. Most likely you may have had a high percent of your portfolio in cash and/or safer investments which do not appreciate a lot but they conserve your wealth.

Be flexible

Every one's trading plan is different. You should start with a simple one and add features that would be useful for you. Keep it simple as you will not likely follow a complicated one.

Other features are: how to screen stocks, your average holding period, tax consequences, performance monitoring, etc. This chapter shows you the very basics of a trading plan and you should start one if you do not have one.

You can refer to any chapter of this book in your trading plan. To illustrate, refer to the chapters when to sell a stock and spotting market plunges.

You can change your objective. When the market is risky, you may want to be more conservative for example.

Disciplined but adaptive

Stick with your plan consistently unless you have a good reason. When your previous strategy that has worked but it does not work now, you should still stick to it. It is a common mistake for traders switching different technical indicator when the current one does not work. It explains why most of the beginner traders lose money.

It should be adaptive. When the current market favors growth, stick with a growth strategy.

A sample trading plan

You can review what stocks to buy and sell once a week or once a month depending on how active you are in the market. List the criteria you buy stocks. Define your average holding period for a specific objective. Also define when and why you want to sell a stock.

Personally I prefer to have two sections: Common Tasks and Specific Tasks. Common Tasks include 4 categories: **Weekly Tasks, Monthly Tasks, Quarterly Tasks and Yearly Tasks**. Evaluate stocks to buy on Tuesday on every week for example. Update the portfolio and check out the chart on marketing timing on the first week of every month. Review the performance of your portfolio quarterly (or half a year). Perform year-end tasks.

Specific Tasks include tasks we have to do on specific dates such as filling tax return, transferring stocks to my children and renewing investing subscriptions.

Weekly Tasks:

Mon	Covered calls
	IBD-50 review.
Tue	Finding momentum stocks.
Wed	Sell Momentum stocks held over 2 weeks.

Monthly Tasks:

Mon	House keep all stock transactions.
	Review market timing and any corrections.
Tue	Find stocks using selected strategies.
	Find stocks using screens.
Wed	Evaluate stocks
Thur.	Buy stocks
	Review sector rotation.
Fri	Evaluate any stocks to sell.
Any	Monitor momentum performance.

Quarterly Tasks:

1	Monthly tasks.
2	Monitor performance.

Year-end Tasks:

1	Tax adjustments for taxable accounts including selling losers in non-retirement accounts.
2	EOY purchases.
3	Fully invested on Dec. 15-Jan. 15 esp. on 2nd year of the presidential cycle.
4	Monitor performance of screens.
5	Review Dogs of the DOW.
6	Optional. Gift appreciated stocks to your heirs.

Review your performance and your trading plan

If you do not know what you did, how will you know where you're going? Review every trade transaction and monitor their performances.

Learn from your losses. Did you stick to the trading plan? If you lose too many times and/or take too much risk (evidenced by many losses and/or big losses), you may have to modify your trading plan. However, the trading plan may not be good in the current market (for example trading growth stocks in the bottom of the market cycle).

If you have to let the winners get away too often, review what went wrong. Sometimes, a lesson is not a lesson but just bad luck.

Learn about yourself

Learn about your risk tolerance, how mentally prepared are you for big losses and big wins. If you have more money than you can use for the rest of your life, conserving wealth should be your primary objective.

To illustrate with a portfolio of one million dollars, your average stock position is $100,000 if you only have time to follow 10 stocks.

To many, a portfolio with 10 stocks is quite risky. You may consider having 10 stocks of $50,000 each and invest the rest ($500,000) in ETFs, mutual funds and/or bonds. Ensure that no more than three stocks (some prefer 2) are in the same sector.

Prepare for some losses. Reduce the average loss to only small amounts. I prefer to use 25% maximum loss for volatile stocks and 20% for other stocks. Some prefer using stop loss orders of 10% to 15% loss. Today's market is too volatile to stop losses less than 15%. My opinion. You should have some big winners but you may let some get away by selling them too early. One way is to use stop orders (10% less than the market price) and adjust the stops periodically (say a month) for the appreciating stocks.

Summary

Write down your objective and what tasks you do every week, month and year in the inside back cover of this book (hard copy only). If you don't do it now, you never will.

Trade journal

Keep a journal of your trades along with your ideas. Review it from time to time and look at why you bought a specific stock. It is far better than trying to recall the experiences from memory.

Your journal should be part of a trading plan. You use it to monitor the performance of your trade and how the current market conditions affect your performance. When you use a screen that is for short term, you want to exit the trade accordingly. When the screen does not perform, it may mean the market is not favorable to this screen and you should skip using it with actual money. Here is a screen shot of mine. I group the trades under different screens.

	A	B	C	D	E	F	G	H	I	J	K	L	M	N	O	P
1	Performance			Prce		S						Date		Return		Status
2	Stock	QTY	Account	B.P.	S.P.	Buy $	Sell $	Profit	Curr P.	% better	Buy Date	Sell Date	Days		Ann. Ret	
3	LAKE	2,000	401K	10.93	13.99	21,860	27,975	6,115	9.45	48%	07/15/15	11/24/15	132	28%	77%	S
4	ABTL	1,500	ROTH	16.60	18.50	24,900	27,750	2,850			07/16/15	09/10/16	422	11%	10%	B
5	ELMD	5,000	401K	4.01	4.22	20,054	21,095	1,041	4.81	-12%	03/17/16	04/07/16	21	5%	90%	S
6												00/10/10				

When using an excel spreadsheet, the formulae is:

B.P. (Buy Price) =IF(B3="","",IF(D3="","",D3*B3))
% better =IF(I3="","",(E3-I3)/I3)
Days =IF(K3="","",L3-K3)
Return =IF(D3="","",(E3-D3)/D3)
Ann. Ret =IF(N3="","",N3*365/M3)

Add any columns you want such as Account.

3   Order prices

Market orders
It is simply trading the stock at the prevailing market price. Place market orders only when it is necessary as stocks price can easily be manipulated especially on stocks with low trading volumes. To avoid manipulations, do not place market orders after hours.

However, in a rising market, many fast rising stocks can only be bought via market orders. Many winners never take a breather on their way up. In this case, you can only buy the stock via market orders.

Consider bid and ask. A 'bid' is the price a potential buyer would like to buy while the 'ask' is a potential seller would like to sell. Your market price is usually the worst price in either case, but it is a guarantee that you would trade the stock. A large spread would mean that it would take a longer time to use a limit order and/or the trade volume of the stock is small.

In my momentum portfolio on 11/2013, I placed a sell price for GERN far higher than the market price. Surprisingly I sold it for this price making an annualized return of 1,176% for holding it for 21 days. When there are few or no other sellers for the stock, the market price would be the price you set. If I cannot sell it in the next 9 days (30 days is my holding period for momentum stocks), I would set it lower. Update: One year later, GERN lost 29%.

Sensible discounts
I prefer to buy the stock at the price closest to the last trade price (to most it is the market price) via a limit order. I seldom lose buying these orders. Sometimes I use the day's lowest price to buy (or the highest to sell) plus a penny (or minus a penny for sell prices to sell).

My other purchase strategy is using 0.15% or 0.25% less than the current prices for stocks I really want. For some promising stocks, I buy them at almost the market price and then place another order on the same stock at 0.5% less than the last traded price (and sometimes 2% depending on the current market trend).

We all want to buy less and sell at higher prices. However, if the trade price is too far away from the current market price (such as 5% from the market price), these trades may never be executed. I have had a long list of buy orders that were not executed and turned out to be big gainers. Learn from my bad experiences.

Use a good discount (such as 10% from the market price) if you believe the market, the sector or the stock will dip by 10%. After you bought the stock, you place a sell order 10% more than the price you paid for it hoping the stock will return to the original price and you pocket 10%. Wishful thinking! However, it has happened to me several times primarily due to temporary market dips.

It works when there is a correction and/or the stock is very volatile. It is usually within the 5% range to take advantage of these situations, not the 10% as described. For a 10% plunge, it usually is due to some serious problem of the company surfacing. One common reason is not meeting its earnings expectation and in this case it usually continues its downward trend.

Larger discounts on a falling market
During a falling market (or a mild correction), 3% less than the current prices for buy orders may be fine for some stocks (use 5% for volatile stocks). To illustrate, I placed about 10 of these orders over the last two months during a market dip. Most of the orders were filled. When the market is plunging, do not buy any stock.

Caterpillar and Cisco were some of my buys at these discounts. They were in my watch list to buy. Initially these shares often fall even lower as the trend was downward. As of 12/18/12, CAT earned me from 3% and 14% (bought in 6/12 and 7/12) and CSCO bought in 7/14/12 returned about 34%. My original objective: Buy deeply-valued stocks, wait and sell them when the economy returns.

When you predict the market will dip by 5%, set your buy orders accordingly. Again, predictions are just educated guesses. From my experience, they work most of the time but not all of the time.

On the day of the earnings announcement, the fluctuation of the stock is usually high. Check any change in the earnings estimate before the announcement and act accordingly. Zacks is supposed to be a useful tool to predict earnings estimates. Do not leave orders during the earnings announcement dates, which can be found in Finviz. When the earning turns out to be good, the stock price surges and your order will not be executed.

When the earnings are bad, the stock price will plunge usually and you most likely over-payed.

Option expiration dates usually cause more volatility. Retail investors do not have to be concerned except you may use wider stops. In theory, dividend days have little effect on the stock price as it will be lowered by the dividend amount.

High volume of a stock could mean opportunity

High volume usually increases the stock price volatility. If the volatility of a stock increases substantially (such as doubling its average daily volume), there could be important news on the company, recommendation changes from a major analyst or trading by the institutional investors. It usually takes the institutional investors a week to trade a stock with their sizable positions.

Many times it is started by the insiders who know about the breaking news of a stock before it is publicized. Some investment services / sites specialize in identifying the increasing volumes on these stocks.

Because day traders do not want to leave any open positions overnight, higher volatility occurs at the end of the day. It is the same on the day (usually on Friday) when the options are expiring.

Monitor your trade prices
You cannot tell whether you are paying a fair price without keeping a record. To illustrate, you're paying 1% less than the market prices in buying stocks. You may have missed buying some winners. If the 1% you saved is smaller than the appreciation of the stocks you would have bought at market prices, then you should adjust the buy prices to 0.5% less than the market price and monitor again.

Market trend makes a difference too. When the market is trending up, buying any stock would most likely be profitable and usually the purchase orders with higher discounts will not be executed.

Follow the same logic on sell orders. Need to have at least 25 stock purchases (and potential purchases) to make the conclusion meaningful. If you do not trade a lot, you will not have enough data to verify. As described, I prefer not to place an order during the earnings announcement dates which can be found in Finviz.com. If you cannot buy the stock, consider to use market order the next day. With most brokers offer no commission trades, the "All or none" option is not valid.

Good prospects

When you find gems especially those stocks that are followed by analysts, buy them at market prices and consider doubling the bet if you are really sure you have a winner. From my super stock screens, I spotted NHTC. I placed several bets and one market order. All of them were NOT executed except with the market order. At the end of the day NHTC is up 18% and my executed order is up 14%. I did not have the best buy but made a good profit. NHTC was on its way to a huge appreciation and I sold it too early. I have earned not to sell a winner and protect the profit with a stop.

Lower the buy for risky stocks (if the beta from Finviz is greater than 1 for example) even if they have good fundamentals.

Quality over quantity

If your time is limited, spend all the time on researching one stock one at a time. However, you need to own at least 3 stocks (more stocks for a large portfolio) for your diversification purposes.

Double your normal purchase position on stocks that look great after the research. For risky stocks that look good, you may want to halve your normal purchase position to cut down on the risk. If you are less risk tolerant, do not buy risky stocks at all. My results are not conclusive on risky stocks but I do get a good sleep.

A recent example

Recently I sold EA with $1 more than my order price but $2 less than the current price of the day, which was the earnings announcement day. I do recommend not placing orders right before the earnings announcement day for the stock. If the earnings are good, you do not get all the profit as in this real example; my broker did get me $1 more. If the earnings are bad, you will not sell it any way. It is the same for buying stocks.

Afterthoughts

- Besides luck, the smart investor never sells at the peak but usually within 10% of the peak. No one can predict the peaks consistently.

- I made mistakes like most of you. One time my buy price was higher than the last price executed. Luckily my broker adjusted it to the right price but I may not be that lucky next time. Several times I switched the buy price and sell price by mistake. One time it was due to my boss coming by that forced me to enter my order hastily. Try to avoid the first hour of a trade session.
- Some experts do not suggest their clients to buy stocks on the way down. With respect, I offer opposing arguments.

  o It is fine to buy them on the way down, if you have the conviction that the company or the economy will recover.
  o No one knows where the bottom is, but averaging down could be beneficial if the company or the economy can recover. Check why its stock price is falling and whether the company can fix its problems. Some major problems are only temporary or easy to fix.
  o Most of my big profits are made by buying close to the bottom prices on stocks that have a good potential to recover.
  o Many value stocks are on sale when the market dips. The most favorable time is in the Early Recovery, a phase in the market cycle defined by me.
  o Most experts agree that: The best time to buy is when there is blood in the street. It is demonstrated by the year 2003 and 2009.
  o Contrarians never follow the herd, but you need to have a good reason to be contrary. I recommended Apple in 2013 when every institutional investor was dumping Apple.
  o Stocks are manipulated via selling shorts. When the shares of a stock to short (like over 30% of shorts) are running out, there is a good chance for a short squeeze. Ensure the company being shorted heavily is not heading into bankruptcy.
- Make good money when you are right only 45% of the time by: 1. Limit your losses via stops and 2. Place higher stakes on stocks with higher appreciation potential.
- Some make money on earnings announcement (found in Finviz.com). Earnings would amplify the stock price by at least 5%. Once in a while, there are exceptions. In the last quarter of 2015, Disney posted great results, but the stock dropped. It could be that the market even expected better results or the market is not rational. I believe the later in this case.

Links
Selling short:
http://en.wikipedia.org/wiki/Short_%28finance%29

4   Stop loss & flash crash

You can limit your stock loss with stops. There are some incidents where you do not always want to use a stop loss.

- Flash crash (May 6, 2010 also August 2015).
  It would turn your stops into market orders that could be substantially lower than your stop prices. Some brokers offer stop limits, but they do not guarantee the orders will be executed.

  The better way is a "mental stop" (my term). You do not place a stop order but place a market order to sell when your stock falls below a pre-defined price. During flash crashes, you do not want to place the market orders to sell but place orders to buy from your watch list.

  I bought some stocks at more than 10% discount during the flash crash (actually I could buy them even at better discounts) and within a week most had returned to the prices as before the flash crash.

  Placing buy orders with huge discounts to the market prices works better for volatile stocks. You should cancel the unexecuted trades before the weekends / holidays and reenter them afterwards to avoid unexpected events that may affect the stock prices.

  Avoid trading drug and bio tech companies with huge differences to the market prices. High tech is a good sector for this purpose and fluctuating 10% in this sector is more of a norm than an exception. Buying an ETF at 5% discount is a better bet than buying specific stocks from my experience.

- My experience with 911.
  I sold many stocks due to stop orders during 911. The market came back in the next three days and I missed the recovery from the stocks that were sold and did not buy back them in time.

- If your stocks are rising, you need to adjust the stop loss prices accordingly. To illustrate- in maintaining a 10% stop loss, your stop is at 90 when the current price is 100. When the stock price rises to 200, it should be adjusted to $180 (10% less than the current price). It is also called a trailing stop. Need to review these rising stocks, and change the stop price periodically (one week to one month depending on how volatile is the stock)).

Most brokers allow you to enter most trades "Good till Cancelled". Even for that there is an expiration date such as 6 months for Fidelity. Fidelity's trades for Short Sell expire by the end of the trade session. Check your broker's current policy.

- Risky markets.
  When the market is risky, you may want to use a stop loss. To prevent another flash crash, you may want to use a 'mental' market order. It is not perfect, as it requires constant watching of the market.

  There are many investing services and sites that give you the 'right' prices for a stop loss. Basically it depends on how volatile are the specific stocks. The chartists will tell you under normal conditions stocks are trading between the resistance line and the support line. Use the stop loss just below the resistance line to avoid the stop order from being executed due to the volatility of the stock.

  For simplicity as I have too many stocks in my portfolio, I use a percent. In the old days, it was recommended 8% or so below the prices you paid. In today's volatile market, I recommend 12%.

- Risky stocks.
  A stop loss is the only way that you can limit your loss for big drop (such as 25%). Affimax lost 85% of its stock value in one day with the news that three of its patients died.

- Low-volume stocks.
  The market order could drive the prices right down as there are few buyers in low-volume stocks. If there is only one buyer, he will buy with the best price for him (or the worst price to the seller).

  Unless I have good reasons, I would skip the low-volume stocks. I define low-volume: If my buy amount is higher than 1% of the average daily amount (= average daily volume * stock price).

- Beta.
  Stocks may be more volatile than the market. Beta is used to measure its volatility. The market can be measured by the S&P500 index. If the

beta of a stock is 1, its volatility is the same as the market. If it is 1.2, it is 20% more volatile.

Set a lower stop loss for volatile stocks to prevent stocks from selling due to regular fluctuations.

Afterthoughts

Let me show you my bitter experience. The following are 5 stocks I wanted to buy and the average return was quite good.

Stocks	Return
URI	63%
GMCR	572%
MTW	186%
PII	-74%
TSCO	-127%
Avg.	124%

I placed buy orders at 5% less than the market prices as most 'bargain' investors do. I bought both of the two losers but no winners. The winners never took a breather on its way up, but the losers went down. I did buy GMCR via a market order in my momentum strategy in a separate account.

5   Selling short

This article describes the advantages, disadvantages and how to avoid the pitfalls in selling short. Next we describe the procedures.

Advantages

You consider short selling (same as shorting) when you believe the stock and / or the market is going down. It is easier to make money via selling short than buying stocks especially in a plunging market. Many mutual funds cannot short stocks, and consequently they spend less time in searching for poor companies. The other factor is psychology: Most retail investors do not want to sell losers.

You should start paper trading. Commit a small amount of money gradually when you have proved to yourself your strategy (i.e. what and when to short sell, and exit) is profitable. Consult your financial advisor first and read my Disclaimer under Introduction.

Beginners should try to short the sectors by buying contra ETFs. The major advantages are: 1. Less volatile, 2. Can trade in retirement accounts (some brokers have some restrictions), 3. Do not lose more than your initial trade position, and 4. Fees and dividends are handled for you. Short selling stocks is risker but more profitable than a group stocks in ETFs.

Disadvantages and some suggestions

- Short stocks when the market is plunging and limit your shorting positions when the market is rising. The market rises more than falls, and hence be careful. However, when the market plunges, it is fast and steep.

- Could lose more than 100% of the investment.
  Actually, in theory, there is no limit. If the price of the shorted stock rises by 10 times, the loss is well over 10 times the money of the short position. The 2015 example was Weight Watchers. The price boosted up by more than 170% when Oprah took out a position on them. Fundamentally this stock was not sound and it should be shorted. No stock pickers without insider information (that is illegal) can predict that. Use stops to protect your trade (i.e. cover your short when you lose a percent specified by you).

- Need to pay dividends and interest for the shorted stock. The higher the dividend rate for the stock, the more you have to pay. Investors should avoid high-dividend stocks when shorting unless the expected shorting period is only brief.

  In addition, you need to pay interest for 'borrowing' the stocks to sell. Brokers charge interest rates differently and it could be huge savings to shop around if you short stocks a lot.

- Need both fundamental and technical analyses. From my experience, technical analysis is more important than fundamentals in shorting especially for short holding periods.

- If shorting a stock is successful and closed within a year, the gain is usually subjected to the short-term capital gains taxes which are typically higher than the long-term capital gains taxes. Check the current tax laws and consult your tax lawyer.

- Not all of the stocks can be shorted. Your broker may not have the stock you want to short. It is also possible that your broker can close out your short positions for various reasons; they need to protect their 'loans' to you. Check the margin status with your broker.

- Selling short is not allowed in retirement accounts as of 2020. However, you can buy contra ETFs for a group of stocks to bet against the market or a specific sector, but not on a specific stock in retirement accounts.

- The following sectors are riskier: the drug, mine, bank (unless you know the quality of their mortgages) and insurance sectors. An approval of a drug could drive the stock price up by more than 25% in one day. The same for earnings announcements. It could drive the stock more than 10% in either direction.

- Your screens may find many stocks in bio tech companies. These companies especially with a market cap of less than 1B may have the worst fundamentals. However, when they have a new discovery, the stock prices could rocket. Do not short them when insiders are buying (Insider Transaction in Finviz.com) and high SMA-20% or SMA-50% (from Finviz.com).

- There is no perfect timing. Some stocks fluctuate a lot with no rational reasons, or the prices are driven by institutional investors. Some stocks could be manipulated. The shorted stocks could move up for a long time until they finally crash. Hence, do not short against a rising stock, a sector or a market. When the market is rising, shorting a rising stock in a rising sector is dangerous, and the opposite could be profitable for shorting.

- The best time to short is when the market is plunging. At that time, the best sectors to short are those sectors that are plunging. Hence, find the worst stocks in a worst sector in a plunging market.

- A bad company could be acquired by another company due to a good buy; it could boost its stock price. It is same when the major problem of a company has been fixed.

- Use mental stops (i.e. set a price you can afford to lose and when it reaches the specific price, place a market trade to exit the shorted shares. You do not want to make 5% several times and lose 50% in one trade.

- You may not want to short companies that are fundamentally unsound but with a good momentum (i.e. trending up). They may have good prospects such as improved profit, being turned around, settling a lawsuit and/ or new products are being legalized and/or approved. If you do, then use mental stops to protect your trades.

- Never short sell the stocks that are rising even they are not fundamentally sound such as FAANG in 2015 to 2020. Tesla has gained many times and you have to pay the gains, not limited to your short position.

- I have turned some short selling candidates into buying due to the high insiders' buying and/or high short squeeze potential.

- Watch out for short squeezes when the short percentage approaches over 25%. In a nut shell, the stock is running out of shares to be shorted. As a result, it would rise in price especially on any good news. As of 8/2015, I expect short squeeze for PPC and SAFM (CALM in 12/2015) for the following reasons:

1   The shorting has no bases. It is most likely from one or two hedge funds.
2   Fundamentally sound.
3   Beef will be replaced by a lot of healthier and cheaper chicken if not already, esp. during the drought in California.
4   In Hong Kong for example, they do not allow live chickens imported from China during the bird flu breakout, but they did allow frozen chicken from the USA if there was no political game going on.

What to buy & how

Refer to the chapter on screening short candidates. If Fidelity's Equity Summary Score for the stock is below 4, it is a short candidate.

The following are my suggestions on shorting stocks that have the potential to go down. Basically these stocks are both fundamentally unsound and technically unsound. Many sites (some require paid subscriptions) provide a composite grade for fundamentals and technical. Finviz.com. a free financial site, does provide most of these metrics and many of them are discussed here. If you do not hold the shorts for a long period, technical (the trend) parameters are more important. Parameters for short candidates are:

- Fundamentals

  - The price is more than four times the book value.
  - EY (= 1 / (P/E) is negative. Negative PEG is another consideration.
  - High debts (Debt/Equity > .5) except for industries that require high debts such as utilities.
  - Insiders are unloading their company's stocks. They do this for many reasons. But, when they are buying, do not short the stock as they may know some positive events that we do not know.
  - Bad intangibles such as losing market share and/or a major lawsuit(s) is pending.
    Read articles on the company from Finviz, Fidelity, Seeking Alpha, etc.
  - Do not short stocks that are on their uptrend. It includes the current marijuana stocks that most have no fundamental values and/or historical data.
  - Do not short small stocks with a small market cap or float. I usually short stocks with a market cap or float > 200M (100M for riskier investors). Use higher values for conservative investors.

The stocks with small floats may be controlled by the owners; if they do not sell, the stocks available to trade will be limited. Another indicator is the Avg. Daily Vol. Personally it should be 100 times higher than my bet.

- Technical metrics:

  - Be careful on stocks that have plunged more than 15% recently (Finviz's last quarter performance gives us some hint). It could mean the bottom has been reached.
  - Overbought (RSI(14) > 65). There may be a reason, so it is only a secondary consideration. Most stocks to be shorted may have RSI(14) less than 30.
  - The momentum metrics such as SMA-20 and SMA-50 are important too. SMA-20% and SMA-50% from Finviz.com should be negative (i.e. trending downwards).
  - Some sites especially the paid sites may give you a momentum grade. Select the stocks with a bad momentum grade (a.k.a. timing grade). However, if it is the lowest grade, be careful, as it has nowhere to go but up.

Trading considerations
- Do not trade in the first hour (first half hour for me) as there may have new developments overnight.
- I use subscription services. I do not trade on Monday or the day after a holiday, as the data is at least one day late.
- Your broker may limit your short trade (limited order) to be valid for the day; check this with your broker.
- Your broker may need to approve whether you can short stocks based on your experiences.
- When you sell short and are using limit orders, enter a sell price higher than the last trade price just like selling a stock.
- Close the short position when your trade loses a pre-defined percentage which depends on your personal tolerance.
- Put Option is similar to shorting a company. It is not for beginners.

Margin
Margin should not be used extensively. It is expensive and most brokers try every trick they can to squeeze profits from all transactions to subsidize their

low-commission incomes. Usually you can borrow up to 40% of your current position and the rules and the margin rates vary among brokers.

Many investors had losses during the last two market plunges. However, many including myself had made a killing in 2003 and 2009 using margin. I use it for the following reasons.

- For convenience in placing buy orders that exceed my cash position in my taxable accounts.
- I can pay back my outstanding margin loans from my home equity loan (check the current tax laws) as it is far, far lower than my broker's margin interest rates. However, I do not recommend this for conservative investors.

Random case

- As of 7/2013, shorting Amazon, Netflix and Tesla as a group was not beneficial. It is best to stay away from shorting, except during the plunging (from peak to bottom) in the market cycle.
- Did you watch 60 minutes on Lumber Liquidators in 2015? That's how you do shorting. Find out why the company boosts its profit and stock price in such a short period. If it has been proven to be fishy, place a short position. However, when the news becomes public, it could be too late for us to act.
- As of 1/15/2015, GME had a short squeeze. The stock was up by 10% with a decent earnings announcement. I am surprised that the short % was over 45% for a decent stock with a decent P/E. It had low debts and decent cash reserves. The shorters (same as short sellers) must be losing their shirts. Even for the fundamentally sound Netflix and Tesla, the shorters (one by a famous hedge fund manager) would lose a fortune; Tesla was at one time 11 times its lowest price.

Links & Articles
Introduction
https://www.youtube.com/watch?v=oMnmTV5HF5Y&list=WL&index=3&t=605s

Tilson
Put Options.http://en.wikipedia.org/wiki/Put_option
Fidelity Video: Options.https://www.fidelity.com/learning-center/options/finding-options-strategies/options-analysis-tool-video
Fidelity Video: Selling short.https://www.fidelity.com/learning-center/trading/selling-short-video

6 Covered calls

For basic descriptions on a covered call from Wikipedia, click here or enter (http://en.wikipedia.org/wiki/Covered_call) in your browser.

It is like collecting rent from the apartment you bought. The difference is that the renter has an option to buy the apartment at a preset time and price.

The rent is quite substantial if you do good planning. To start with, you want to buy stocks that have a market to sell. Usually they are large companies with high trading volumes.

Since one contract is for 100 shares of a stock, you cannot sell a covered call on 50 shares of a stock. On the other hand, when you have 1,000 stocks, the commission of 10 contracts would be more than the cost of 1 contract depending on your broker's schedule.

It is time consuming to keep track of the covered calls but it is well worth your time and effort. If the stock price exceeds the strike price of your covered call, you may want to buy the same shares back, so you would not miss any further appreciation of this stock.

However, if it is in a taxable account and you have a loss in a forced sell, do not buy it back otherwise the tax loss is not allowed (i.e. a wash sale) for the year as of 2016. When the contract expires, you may want to start another contract on the same stock if the stock has not been sold.

Covered calls do have their disadvantages such as higher commission rates and sometimes forcing you to sell at a higher tax rate for short-term capital gains in taxable accounts. It is avoidable by using covered calls on stocks that are qualified for long-term capital gains. In addition, you need to buy them back when they increase in price beyond your strike price or lose its potential to appreciate further. Using another put could keep you from not losing any gains beyond the strike price. However, I prefer to use my time in more productive ways and this insurance is not cheap. One's opinion.

One company advertises their techniques using covered calls which could give their users 3 to 6% monthly returns. If you believe in this fantasy, you do not need this book. There is no free lunch.

My recent experience

I sold Netflix covered calls with the strike price about 2% higher and a 3% premium (from my memory) but the price shot up 12% higher in one day, so I was potentially losing 7% profit. However, it turned out to be a good experience as Netflix went downhill later (8/2012).

Normally I prefer to sell covered options for stocks with a quantity from 100 to 600 shares (i.e. 1 to 6 contracts) for the longest time (about 2-3 months). Some non-volatile and small stocks are not candidates to write covered calls on. Some stocks are not optionable. Typically high-tech stocks have a higher premium to be collected as their stock prices fluctuate more. The right stocks can generate 10% or even more a year in addition to the fluctuations of the stock prices.

In general, if I feel the market will be down for the period, I use covered calls especially for stocks holding over one year (unless I have short-term loss to offset any short-term gains) in taxable accounts. Watch out for any tax change that may affect your total return.

Recently I attended a sales pitch on a 3-day training course on a strategy for making 24% per year and it is quite possible especially with the S&P 500 returns about the same. I wish it were available to me 15 years ago. It seems to be too good to be true.

How to sell covered calls

First you need to open an account with your broker and apply to trade options including covered calls.

Check how your broker charges commissions. Ask how much they charge for one contract and 10 contracts of a stock.

The covered call is an agreement to sell the rights to the buyer of the stock at the strike price for a specific date range (a.k.a. expiration date). Typically options expire on Fridays.

You need to write covered calls on the stocks you already own. One contract is 100 shares of stocks. Check out the option chain to select the price, expiration period and the strike price. Normally, the strike price should be higher than the current market price. You may want to have an expiration date 2 weeks or longer. When the contract is expiring in a few days, the contract has little value and most likely the small 'rent' is not worth the risk and the commission.

When the covered call is sold, you receive the 'rent' immediately and any dividend during the 'rental' period.

When the option is 'called' due to a price rise above the strike price, your stock will be sold and you will have to pay the regular commission.

At this point, evaluate the stock to check whether you want to buy it back. If the stock surges, you may have to pay a higher price – thus losing the extra appreciation. In addition, you may have to pay a higher capital gains tax if it is held less than the required period for long-term capital gains in a taxable account.

Note. Notice that some stocks are not optionable and/or not practical to write options on. Most brokers charge a flat rate for the first contract (such as $7) and an incremental fee for each additional contract. Shop around as the fees vary if you write a lot of covered calls.

The best stocks for covered calls are large US companies with a large average volume. The option (a.k.a. the 'rent') pays better for volatile companies such as high-tech companies. From my rough estimates for illustration purposes, the annualized return on covered calls for AAPL is 25% and C is 12% after commission.

#Filler: Double standard
We set up our standard in everything and the entire world has to follow our standard. Shooting citizens at each other, separating children from the illegals, and police brutality are fine according to our standard.

7   Selling a winner

Let the profit rise and at the same time protect your profit. Tesla quadrupled its value in 6 months. Examples abound such as Amazon and Yelp.

You do not want to sell these rocket stocks even if their fundamentals do not make sense. Buffett does not touch these stocks and he usually misses these big gains. However, many of these rocket stocks such as BRRY (Blackberry) will eventually fall losing most of their value. I bet the institutional investors move the market in either direction and usually they read the same analysts' reports. You profit as a contrarian if you have a good reason to act against the herd.

The following example uses a 10% trailing stop. Set the stop at 10% of the current price (i.e. 10% less than the current price), not the purchase price. You need to change the stop when the price rises but do not change it when the price falls. Review your stops every month or more frequently if time allows.

To illustrate, when the stock price rises to 100, set the stop at 90. When the stock price falls to 90, sell the stock at the market price. When the stock price rises to 200, change the stop at 180.

The stop should also be set according to how volatile the stock is. Some stocks are more volatile than others. Most charts show the resistance line. This line assumes the stock price should not fall below this line in normal fluctuations. Set the stop at 2% below this line so your stock will not be stopped out in theory.

To avoid flash crashes, do not place stop orders. Instead, do it mentally (mental stop is my term). When you see that the stock falls below your stop with no sign of a flash crash, sell the stock using a market order.

Of course, there is no bullet-proof scheme. This one should work in the long run. This is my suggestion only, so examine whether it works for you. Small cap and/or stocks with small average volumes fluctuate more.

Examples
I have too many bad examples of selling the stocks too early and sometimes holding them too long.

I made over 40% in a few weeks on ALU, but it went up more than 300% in the next two years. It was acquired in early 2016 by Nokia paying a good premium. I was right that ALU had a lot of valuable patents and I was wrong to dump it when I found out Cisco did not have any intention to acquire it – a big mistake by Cisco and the U.S.

FOSL is another example to teach us to use mental stop loss. FOSL was priced at $33.70 on 1/4/2010. Its fundamentals were just fine with an expected E/P (expected earnings yield) at 6% but decreasing earnings. It gained 115% later in 2010 - not expected.

On 1/3/2011, the expected E/P was still at around 6% and improving earnings. It gained 9% for the year – a little disappointing.

On 1/3/2012, the expected E/P was 7% and a huge earnings growth. Now, we expected a better performance for the year and it did by gaining 20%.

On 1/3/2013, the expected E/P was about 6% and the earnings gain was respectable. It gained 28% to $121. So far, so good.

On 1/2/2014, the E/P and the earnings growth were about the same as in 1/3/2013. However, it lost 7% for the year while SPY (an ETF simulating the market) gained 12%. There was no warning. Did the institutional investors lose the interest of this stock?

On 1/2/2015, the E/P was 7% and the earnings growth was about the same as the previous year. It lost 69% (vs. SPY's 0% return with dividends)!

From 1/4/2010 to 1/3/2016, the annualized return of FOSL is 0% (vs. SPY's 13%). Actually, after dividends, SPY should have an annualized return of about 15%. The lessons gained here are:

- Fundamentals (using EP and earnings growth in this example) may not always work. Otherwise, 2015 should have the same gain as 2014.

- The rosy outlook of the stock may be priced in already. When the outlook fails to materialize, the stock tanks.

8   Tax avoidance

Tax avoidance is a good way to save some money legally. Tax laws change all the time. Check Wikipedia on current investment taxes. Consult your tax lawyer as my knowledge in taxes is limited, and the tax laws are always changing.

In general for Federal returns on your taxable accounts (as opposed to IRA, Roth IRA, IRA-Rollover and 401K), you have to pay taxes on dividends either at the ordinary income rate or at a qualified rate which is usually lower. If the stock that was held longer than a year, you pay long-term capital tax (max. 20%). The short-term capital tax rate at the ordinary income rate up to 37%. In addition, you may have to pay state and local taxes. Currently, you can offset $3,000 or up to your total losses from your regular income.

Do not implement what I did as tax laws change frequently and every one's situation is different. Here is what I did and I hope it will be applicable to you.

- Sold most profitable stocks that I held more than a year in taxable accounts in 2011 to qualify for long-term capital gains. Usually they have more favorable tax treatments than the short-term capital gains, which are treated as ordinary income. I bought some back. I maintained a 15% tax bracket, so the tax bill from Uncle Sam is virtually 0 (not exactly due to more tax on social security and Medicare as a result of the trades). I still had to pay state tax. As a retiree, I can control my income.

- Converted part of my Rollover IRA to Roth in 2012 and 2013. I paid taxes today. However, the Roth conversion gives me tax-free appreciation for the future trades in this account and it will lower taxes and my minimum withdrawal requirement in the future. Check whether it is still available.

- The taxes from dividends in the retirement accounts are deferred but eventually they will be treated as regular income when they are withdrawn. Very few people have higher income during their retirement. If you are the lucky few due to the successful investing in your retirement accounts, you may end up with a higher tax bracket during your retirement, particularly when you are forced to withdraw at age 70 ½.

- Gifted some appreciated stocks to my children. The current price of the gifted stock is used in calculating the total cost allowed, not the price you paid for them. I prefer the value stocks that have potential for long-term appreciation. It is good for them and not good for Uncle Sam. You can gift up to $15,000 (in 2019) for each spouse to each child <u>without paying</u> any Federal tax. For a family of four, you and your spouse can gift up to $60,000 (= 15,000 * 4) a year.

The link: <u>https://www.irs.gov/businesses/small-businesses-self-employed/frequently-asked-questions-on-gift-taxes</u>

The cost basis of the transferred stock is quite complicated. Check out the current tax law. The cost basis of the appreciated stocks are carried to the receiver, so it would lower your capital taxes as most of us are in higher tax brackets than our children.

From my experience, the cost basis of the depreciated stocks after the transfer is the market price on the transfer day as of 2016. I do not understand it enough to comment but just to tell you what I have experienced. I tried to offset my son's unexpected short-term capital gain by transferring a losing stock and that does not work.

- My lawyer set up trusts for me including my house. They will avoid probate hopefully. From the current tax law (as of 2016), the cost basis of your stocks will be stepped up or down to the stock prices on that day you pass away. Ask your heirs to keep a business paper for the stock prices or tell your brokers to adjust the cost basis on the day you pass away. Of course, you have to tell your heirs now to take care of these tasks. Again, ask your tax lawyer for details.

Make sure you specify the beneficiaries in your and your spouse's accounts to avoid probate. Check your local state laws. Some states take more than a year to finish the probate process for a house. As of 2014, my state (Mass.) has an exemption of 1 million, not portable to your spouse, and they calculate the entire estate when it exceeds the exemption. There is no estate tax if my estate is a million dollar. I have to pay a rate on 1,000,001 if it just exceeds it by one dollar. That's why we should move 30 miles north to New Hampshire.

I estimate that it takes about three years for the average estate to be distributed. You want to cut down the duration by having a will to start with, so you do not want to pay extra for your lawyer.

- At age 70 ½ (as of 2016), you are required to withdraw them in a schedule and it could put you in higher tax bracket. Roth withdrawal is not counted in the mandatory withdrawal for a person's lifetime as of 2016.

- Roth IRA if qualified could be the best deal for most. However, you have to use after-tax money to fund your Roth IRA.

- I simulate my next year via my tax preparation software and adjust my income accordingly.

- Most oil partnerships and many MLPs require you to file special tax forms for non-retirement accounts in 2017. I avoided most of them as my time is limited. Some ETFs require you to file the complicated K-1 (vs 1099) in your tax return. You can find this requirement in ETFdb.com. You can avoid them by not buying these ETFs; I prefer to buy them in my non-taxable accounts (i.e. retirement accounts). Usually the taxes on these dividends are lowered as they are treated the return of investment after depreciation.

- Avoid wash sales in your taxable accounts
  http://en.wikipedia.org/wiki/Wash_sale

  You cannot claim the loss for the year if you buy back the stock within 30 days. Before I buy, I check whether I sold this loser in the last 30 days. Before I sell a loser, I check whether I bought it in the last 30 days.

  I placed one order to sell a loser at a higher price and another one to buy it back at a lower price. When there is a big swing in price for that stock, both orders were executed within 30 days. I cannot claim the loss of the sold stock for that year. However, the loss can be adjusted to the cost basis of the newly-acquired stock as of 2013.

  There are many ways to avoid it. Try not to buy it back within 30 days (check the current regulation) and this is the best way. IRS has more restrictions and it is better not to push it to the limit. Buy a similar stock in the same sector. Buy it in your children's account. Again, check the current tax laws.

Afterthoughts

- Tax audit signs.
  http://money.cnn.com/gallery/pf/taxes/2014/03/14/tax-audit/index.html?iid=HP_LN
  Your business would be treated as a hobby if you do not have a profit in three out of the last five years. Day traders and businesses can deduct all the trading expenses. Some form an investing company in some Caribbean island to avoid paying taxes. Again check the current tax laws.

- As of 2013, the dividend tax is at 20% max. Do not believe it is no tax in tax-deferred accounts. When you withdraw, it will be treated as a regular income and it can be as high as almost 40% (as of 2013). Your dividend tax rate depends on your income.

- When you trade 5 times or more a week, investigate whether you're eligible to trade as a business by the current tax rule. A business allows its owner to deduct business expenses.

- Fidelity: Investment tax.
  https://www.fidelity.com/learning-center/mutual-funds/tax-implications-bond-funds

  ETF Taxes on Foreign Stocks:
  http://seekingalpha.com/article/2491465-foreign-withholding-taxes-in-international-equity-etfs

Links
Tax Avoidance:
http://en.wikipedia.org/wiki/Tax_avoidance
Tax Law:
http://en.wikipedia.org/wiki/Income_tax_%28U.S.%29
Without paying (gift tax):
http://en.wikipedia.org/wiki/Gift_tax_in_the_United_States#Gift_tax_exemptions
http://www.irs.gov/Businesses/Small-Businesses-&-Self-Employed/What%27s-New---Estate-and-Gift-Tax
AMT: http://en.wikipedia.org/wiki/Alternative_minimum_tax
Estate planning fun. http://tonyp4idea.blogspot.com/2014/08/estate-planning-101-for-me.html

9   Coming decades

An aging population and technology advances are the major factors affecting the stock market and specific sectors in the coming decades. These sectors may not rise or fall in a straight line.

The aging population is due to the baby boom after WW2. It is happening now. It gives rise to health care and medicines tailoring to the growing need. The gene modification technology is interesting.

If the seniors start to withdraw their savings, then the market would tank. However, the market has been rising for the last 10 years and the drug companies were not doing well in 2018. The population is rising but in developing countries such as in Africa and India where the GDP is low.

Technology such as robots and artificial intelligence will make many jobs obsolete. The internet would make newspapers obsolete as the readers can find articles for free. If they do not adapt, they will perish. So are brick-and-mortar retailers to some extent. Most big chains have on-line stores. Mobile pay would replace credit cards. When more electric cars (many with full or partial driver assistance) are manufactured, the gasoline price would be reduced and many gasoline stations will have battery chargers.

5G technology would make some sectors prosper while some would become obsolete. Driver-less cars would be one that benefit. After 2030, China would be the main force in the global economy. It has been slowed down by the trade war as of 2019.

There are some predictions that the U.S. will suffer a lot in 2020. Even they have good arguments, I am not totally convinced. However, I would take actions, similar to buying insurance. I would like to invest in gold. China has a cycle of disasters every 60 years and 2020 is supposed to be similar to the great famine of 60 years ago. [Update 2021. Both have been materialized.]

First, the predictors believe the USD would lose the reserve currency status. It is possible as we have been printing too much USD and huge our national debt is ridiculously high compared to our GDP. The hint today is some countries are not using USD for trading.

There are many companies that have been replaced by new companies with new technologies such as Blockbuster by Netflix, many department stores by Amazon, etc. The taxi industry is threatened by Uber, so is the hotel industry. Artificial intelligence will replace a lot of Wall Street and legal staffs.

10   Future trends

We're at the cross roads in many areas. Let me outline some of my thoughts. Check it out in five years and see how many have materialized.

Economy
1. Today the market is fundamentally unsound but technically sound. When the technical goes down, it could be the time to exit the market.
2. FAANG as a group of stocks is very risky it seems to me. Netflix is the riskiest fundamentally.
3. Oil prices will take a break before its upward trend. When the oil price was at $30, I bought some oil stocks. When the oil price was at $50, I sold most of these oil stocks. I expected there to be fierce correction and at that time most sectors including oil would go down. Why did I expect an uptrend on oil after that? It is a simple supply and demand at work. Today drilling, exploration... are not economically feasible. Hence we should have less oil in the future and oil is still competitive and environmentally friendly.
4. China's "One Belt, One Road" Initiative will have impact on the world economy. It will benefit the participating countries and provinces in west China. Even many American companies including GE and Caterpillar will benefit by providing heavy equipment that China does not build today.
5. The world should benefit from the rise of China if China does not create wars.
6. From my estimate, only one job will be gained from 10 returned jobs from Mexico and China due to automation.
7. The wealth gap will be widened due to robots and the advance of artificial intelligence. It could have the biggest impact since the internet.
8. Europe will finally recover despite the rising of terrorism.

U.S.
1. The U.S. is declining but we're still leading in many sectors. We spend too much effort on being a world policeman while China is concentrating their efforts in improving the economy.
2. Trump may not be re-elected. Will it be the trigger to bring down the market? Only time can tell.
3. We used to be a nation of problem solvers, but have become people avoiding problems. Trump did that by dissolving his committee of business leaders. So is Yahoo!Finance. I miss many nice features from this site that are no longer available.
4. We need the H-1B program to attract the world's best programmers and scientists to make us more competitive. We need to monitor and enforce the program to ensure that there are more benefits than that could harm.

11   Disrupting innovation

New technologies may change our lives. It would profit our prosperity by investing in the right companies that would profit from these technologies and divesting from the companies that these technologies would harm them.

There have been many disruptive technologies in the past. Roughly I divided into the following phases in our recent history: Phase 1 (electricity and steam engine), Phase 2 (computer), Phase 3 (internet) and today's Phase 4.

Many technologies converge or are implemented in one sector such as 5G and battery technology into self-driving cars. With the exceptions of 5G and Blockchain that are too wide a topic to summarize here, the following will be described briefly and several links are available to further your research. Some are materializing today in 2020 and they should affect us for the coming decade. Most are fundamentally unsound by our metrics.

- Electric cars. Eventually they will outsold combustion cars. Companies: Tesla and battery research companies. Badly affected companies: auto companies that do not adapt and oil.
- Energy renewable technology. Eventually, cost per energy unit would favor them compared to oil.
- Robots would affect jobs.
- Fintech. Almost all Chinese consumers are using phone as the wallet and it will not be too long for U.S. to accept mobile payment. Companies: Paypal and Square. Retails and restaurants could harm their profits in 2020. Badly affected companies: banks that do not adapt.
- Cryptocurrency. Eventually there will be less than 5 and most are issued by bank and country with good record.
- Gene modifying companies. It has fixed many and continues to fix many diseases by re-programing bad genes. Companies: CRIPR. Badly affected companies: drug companies that do not co-operate with CRISPR, Editas Medicine and Intellia Therapeutics.
- AI, artificial intelligence. We have good research but our privacy restriction limits our implementation. Companies: many Chinese companies in this sector.

Links:
Cathy Wood. https://www.youtube.com/watch?v=eE6u67Ph768

12   Testing strategies

You can use the free screener in many sites including your broker's web site and Finviz.com. However, most do not provide a historical database for back testing. Some include historical data for technical indicators such as SMA (Simple Moving Average) and/or P/E.

Here are some services that have historical data for back testing: Vector Vest, Zacks and Portfolio 123 at low prices. This article outlines some of the hints for evaluating their services. You should list your requirements. They are expensive and time-consuming to learn. However, they should give you valuable tools if they are properly used.

- Price. Most would charge $500 and up for a yearly subscription. If you cannot afford it, use Finviz.com which is free. It does not have a historical database for fundamental data and you need to save the test results.
- Most sites do not compensate for survivorship bias by taking out the unlisted companies. There are more bankrupt companies than merged or acquired companies hence making your strategy looking better than it is actually is. If you take out Enron and/or Lehman Brothers, your test would look better.

  Since more small companies bankrupt than large companies, try to include companies with a market cap greater than 500 million (100 million for strategies for small companies) to reduce this bias.
- I prefer the historical database which starts from year 2000 so we have two full market cycles from 2000 to 2019.
- I prefer dividing the test periods into phases of the market cycle. Some screens perform better in the down market than the up market for example.
- Most have a comparison to the S&P500 index or SPY for simplicity. In the last few years (as of 2019) SPY has been doing great because SPY is weighed by market cap with a lot of high-flyers. If these high-flyers fall, this index and SPY would fall accordingly. Use related ETF for comparison. For example, if you are testing a strategy on dividend stocks, your yardstick should be one related to dividend stocks and most likely you need to add dividends to your results and the ETF. Personally I would buy SPY for the money left over, and hence SPY is a logical choice for me. Do not use DOW index: 1. It has only 30 stocks, and 2. It is price weighed that is not practical.

- I prefer to enter the filter parameters via 'click-and-select'.
- It is easier to understand annualized return; a 1% return per month is equivalent to 12% in a year especially for short-term trades. However, if the period is less than 15 days, the annualized return would be amplified too much.
- Most do not include dividends and it is fine when you do not include the same in your benchmark such as the SPY. For screens specialized on dividends, add the extra dividends to the performance.
- Many vendors group several parameters such as P/E and Debt/Equity into a value score. The other popular score is momentum score with the simple moving average for example. The combining of these two scores is a summary score. There are many other scores such as a safety score using beta.
- Determine that whether the search is for value stocks or momentum stocks. You need to hold value stocks longer (one year for me) and momentum stocks shorter (1 month for me). Then do the same for testing.

  To illustrate, SMA-20, Sales Q-to-Q and Earnings Q-to-Q are momentum parameters while P/E, Debt/Equity and P/B are value parameters. If you test a value strategy, the holding period should be more than 6 months.

- Some screens find more volatile stocks than others. It is measured by the maximum drawback, which is defined as the loss from the recent peak. For stocks from volatile screens, use a higher stop loss otherwise they would be stopped out during stock price fluctuations.
- Read the evaluations of the service you are interested in by googling it. It could save you a lot of money by learning from others' experiences.
- A screen has many criteria such as P/E. My basic parameters are: in one of the 3 major exchanges, U.S. stocks, Market Cap within a specified range, Earnings Yield > 5% and Stock Price > 1. Vary it for your requirements for the specific screen.
- Sorting. You may want to sort Earnings Yield (E/P) in descending order.
- Testing. You may want to test the top 5 stocks according to your sort specified.
- Testing period. For value screens, you may want to hold the stocks for 6 months or a year.

The following uses the Year-End screen as an example. You have the following start date: 11/1, 11/15, 12/1, 12/15, 1/15 and 1/30 and hold the screened stocks for 1, 2, 4 and 6 months.

The number of simulations from 2007 to 2017: 10 years * 6 start dates * 4 (1, 2, 4 and 6 months holding) = 240 simulations. For each sort variation, you double the number of simulations to 480.

Adding every variation to the screen such as Market Cap > 1000 would again double the number of simulations to 960.

It is a time-consuming process. Some sites may have strategies simulating what gurus such as Buffett would buy.

- In reality, after you have found a handful of stocks, be sure to start further research using Debt/Equity, Q-Q sales / earnings, short % and Insider Transaction from Finviz.com; also use Fidelity.com's Equity Summary Score and average 5-year P/E and Yahoo!Finance.com's EV/EBITDA.

- If you have found too many stocks, restrict your criteria and vice versa for too few stocks.
- Ensure the calculations are correct. When you compare the returns to SPY, the negative values could give you wrong interpretations.
- Define your tests according to the phases of the market cycle. Market Peak (a phase defined by me) should have different strategies rather than Early Recovery.
- The last 5 years is better than the last 10 years as it is more similar to the current market.
- A spreadsheet is the tool to summarize all your test results.
- There has been no evergreen strategy, which is defined as a strategy that works well in all market conditions. High Insider Purchases is close to one. Recently, the following was the actual averages for my six strategies. I interpret that the period "2007 to 2014" does not favor stock pickers.

	Beat SPY by
From 2000 – 2006	490%
From 2007 – 2014	-96%
From 2000 – 2014	180%

13   More on strategies

A strategy tells you how to find a stock and when to sell a stock. The most important task is how to screen potentially profitable stocks to limit your selection and then evaluate each screened stock.

Today, there are many pre-defined screens available and we can define our own screens. Most of the financial ratios such as P/E have been defined for us to reduce the need of the time-consuming task of finding them from the financial statements. There are certain items in the financial statements that we should be concerned with after the initial evaluation.

To me, the most important advance for retail investors is the availability of historical data bases at prices we can afford. It shows us the performance of our strategies for the last 10 or so years in an hour or two. The following are my suggestions to make a better use of the findings from these databases and their pitfalls.

- Start with proven metrics as demonstrated by research (the metrics used in this book and other sources such as from SSRN.com) and your own trading.

- Select parameters as close to your trading style as possible. For example, if you only deal with small stocks, select market caps from 100 M to 500 M.

- Some screens perform better in the short term while some perform better in the long term. I recommend testing the performances for 3 months, 6 months, 12 months and 18 months for short-term screens (1 month for momentum stocks). If you believe the strategy is for a long term only, get the performances for 6, 12 and 18 months.

- In 2015 (use a date more current), I start with the year 2000 and end with 2014 for a total of 15 sets. It covers the two market cycles. The market before 2000 may not be relevant as today's market is quite different from that time. Actually I prefer the tests for the last 10 years.
- Run the screen in the first part of the year and test the performance at year end. Repeat the test for the rest of the intervals: 3, 6, 12 and 18 (adding 1 for momentum and 2 years for long term).

- I do not start with an amount (say $10,000) and see the results at the end of a period (say 10 years). It could be misleading when your screen performs exceptionally well (or bad) in the first few years. I call the one I use "window testing" for lack of a better term. To illustrate this, the start date is Jan. 1, 2000 (actually Jan. 2 due to holiday) and end date is Jan. 1, 2001. The next set is Feb. 1, 2000 to the start, the next set is Feb. 1, 2001 and so on.

- I use the next available date if the date falls on a weekend or a holiday for consistency. If you have more time, try another set starting in mid year. For some strategies and when time allows, I test the strategy monthly.
- If my screen makes 10% and the market makes 20%, it is 100% worse off. I compare how much it beats the market.
- For simplicity I use the SPY to simulate the market. No index is ideal. The S&P500 is capitalization cap weighed. In 2015, the bubble stocks dominated this index. The better selection is to choose the index according to the type of stocks that you usually have such as the Russell 2000 for small stocks. Russell 1000 has 500 more stocks than S&P500, and hence the first 500 should be the same as S&P500.
- Consider safety such as the Sharpe ratio, maximum drawdown (peak-to-trough loss) and a winner percent. A winner percent at 55% (target for 52%) is very good. If your strategy has a very high winner percent, most likely it is safe but just not only performing.
- Why your actual performance with real money may be worse than the tested strategy:
  - Survivor bias. Most databases take out the stock when they're bankrupt, merged or acquired. Hence the performance of the screen is better than it really is as there are more bankrupt companies than merged /acquired. From my experience I have at least one such stock in a year. Hence, the test results are not correct if the database does not take care of this bias.
  - Emotions do not allow you to stick with the strategy.
  - The strategy does not work in the current market; that's why we need to test the performance of the last 6 months.
  - There is idle money between trades.

- I use the top 5 stocks (hence sorting is important). In addition, if you do not buy foreign stocks, deselect them. I use the top 2 for some strategies such as sector rotation.
- If you cannot find data in some screens in any month, just leave it blank (actually null), which will not be included in calculating averages / totals. If the market is risky, you may not find any value stocks.
- The most recent tests would resemble the performance of the strategy better. Hence, I have an extra average of performance on more recent tests.
- Return = (B-A)/A, while A is the return of SPY for me. It does not handle the negative numbers. Use (B-A)/ABS(A). In any case, check the results to see they make sense. When B or A is zero or very small number, the results could be misleading. I usually delete the test results on huge returns in both directions.
- Using sector rotation strategy as an example, the holding periods are 1, 2 and 3 months.
- Some strategies work better on different phases of the market cycle such as growth stocks in the market trending up and staple stocks during market plunges.

14   Sample portfolio

It is a suggested sample. You need to tailor it to fit your personal requirements and your risk tolerance. In general, you should have an emergency fund for at least 3 months (6 months preferred). Many of our generation have one or even no layoff. However, I estimate the current generation will have 3 layoffs in their work life. It is due to automation, artificial intelligence, global economy, etc.

The rough estimate of stock holding in distribution between stock and bond is equal to 100 − Your Age. To illustrate in the following three portfolios, I use a 30-year old, and hence he should have 70% in stocks and 30% in bonds (including gold, CDs and cash).

In addition, some sectors are better than others according to the market conditions. The following three portfolios are for regular, todays' market and one during market crash. I use low-cost ETFs exclusively. ETF is exchange-traded funds. They are traded similar to stocks, but most are more diversified; their fees are usually lower than mutual funds.

ETF	Normal	Today (2/2021)	Crashing[5]
SPY[1]	40%	30%	0%
QQQ[2]	5%	10%	0%
ARKK[2]	5%	0%	0%
VTIAX[3]	20%	5%	0%
LQD[3]	15%	20%	5%
GLD	5%	15%	15%
CD	5%	0%	0%
Cash	5%	20%	60%[6]
SH[4]	0%	0%	5%
PSQ[4]	0%	0%	15%

[1] VOO is a low-fee alternative for SPY.

[2] QQQ has more tech stocks, while ARKK is active managed ETF specializing in 'disruptive technologies'. During market crashes, avoid them.

[3] VTIAX is an ETF for global companies. LQD is an ETF for corporate bonds.

[4] SH and PSQ are contra ETF to SPY and QQQ. They are shorting the corresponding index. When the market is recovering, switch them back to SPY and QQQ.

[5] Need to balance the allocations about two times a year as ETFs can grow or shrink. When the market crashes, rebalance it right away. All market will crash, and the last two (2000 and 2008) have an average loss of about 45%. Refer to the chapter "Simplest marketing timing".

[6] Today's low interest rate does not benefit us for CDs. I would leave the cash not invested and wait for the recovery to move back to stocks.

Of course, everyone's situation is different. If you are conservative, do not buy SH and PSQ. If you are afraid of inflation (especially due to the excessive printing of money), allocate more on GLD, a gold ETF.

Do not listen to financial news. They are used by institutional investors / analysts to manipulate the market. Many times they act the opposite from what they preach. This is the primary reason retail investors do not do better. With the GameStop incident, do not invest in most hedge funds. Buffett has proved the hedge funds with their high fees cannot buy an indexed ETF such as SPY.

The above is my recommendation. In the long run, it should work fine. Consult your financial advisor before taking actions.

#Filler: Simple measures to reduce net security.
Do not click any links from unknown sources. Some seems to be ok but not. MalwareBytes, for checking viruses, is free for download (they do not pay me).

Personally I use a Chromebook for my financial transactions and a two-factor logon for my stock trading.

#Filler "How to make a 50% return"

https://www.youtube.com/watch?v=eEto5nEkf1Y

#Filler Buffett, the person.
https://www.youtube.com/watch?v=w-eX4sZi-Zs

15   Lessons from my trading in 2019-2020

2020 is a miserable year with the pandemic, but reasonable well for the market. Again, I am too conservative and had not followed by own advice illustrated in my books. If you followed my SMA-350 (Simple Moving Average for the last 350 sessions), you should have done amazingly well. Technical chart (SMA in my case) worked far better than the fundamental in 2020. Tesla made about 6 times even the P/E was over 1,000 at one time in 2020.

I made many financial mistakes along with some good decisions in 2019. I have explained how to avoid some mistakes in my books and I did not follow my own preaching.

In the last two months of 2019, I started buying contra ETFs betting the market would go down while the market has been making new heights. The market is financially unsound but technically sound. Lesson #1: Follow the simplest market timing described in this book. Lesson #2: Never bet against the market on the year before election.

There are always two sides on the opposite views of the market. I studied them and believe 2020 could be a disastrous year for the market. No one is sure unless s/he has a time machine. Again follow Lesson #1.

I did well in buying GLD/SLV, and basic materials including IYW and two copper miners. I will unload some copper miners. Lesson #3: Every portfolio should have a small portion in gold (GLD/or similar ETFs, gold coins and an ETF for gold miners).

Stay away from Chinese stocks for the entire year. I may buy a contra ETF on Chinese stocks. The trade war and the explosive debts will drive China's economy down for a few years.

I had 50% profit in one month using my year-end strategy in 2018. From my memory, I made about 100% on YRCW and lost about 30% on another buy on the same stock. Lesson #4: "Year-End Strategy" works at least so far. Lesson #5: Sell the stocks bought using this strategy within 2 months, and hence I should use retirement accounts for this strategy.

I made some money in trading energy stocks that have been beaten down badly. The outlook of energy stocks is not good. Lesson #6: Buy low and sell high. Lesson #7: Buffett's "Be greedy when everyone is fearful and vice versa" is correct thinking.

There are many 'great' traders making millions and losing most. Lesson #8: Avoid big losses by using stops. Lesson #9: Do not speculate and be a turtle investor.

Sold METC and REI in early 2020 for 14% gain (172% annualized) and 35% (508%) respectively. They were screened from my year-end strategy in early Dec., 2019 and profited due to the daily news (Iran). Lesson #10: Combine different strategies.

I have saved the most important lesson for last. If you spend all day long trading, you will not enjoy life and it is bad for your physical health and mental health. Wish you a healthy and prosperous 2021!

#Fillers:

How messed up our welfare system?

It encourages our citizens to be lazy and let the government bail them out. It encourages more children and teenage mothers.

Do you take a job when you lose all the goodies and free health care?

Many take care of their old parents and get paid handsomely.
One divorced his wife to boost the SSI, and then married a foreigner lady who gave him $30,000 plus free sex.

One of the best sellers in Taiwan is "How to retire comfortably with no work".

The middle class is being squeezed by the rich (who do not pay much taxes) and the poor.

#Filler: Ghosts

I proof there are no ghosts. If they were, the Chinese ghost and the American ghost should act and look the same.

#Filler: Communism to capitalism

China and Vietnam changed from communism to capitalism in recent history. They are both prosperous. Cuba and N. Korea stick to communism, and are still poor. India has been capitalists for a long while, and is still poor. The governance is more important in most cases.

16   Predictions for 2021

The following is from a Bloomberg article with my comments. Most will not happen. If it starts to materialize, consult your financial advisor before take actions accordingly. Again, I am not liable for any actions. This article is written in 12/2020.

https://www.bloomberg.com/news/articles/2020-12-15/if-2020-wasn-t-enough-stanchart-has-eight-big-risks-for-2021

1. We will find soon whether the U.S. Senate would by dominated by Democrats with the result of the Georgia's seats. If the democrats control the senate, then "Technology shares plummet and U.S. Treasury Yields surge on supply fears".

   My comment: It is easier to pass the proposed laws without fierce opposition. I prefer the opposition party gives reasons of rejecting and/or how to amend any proposed laws instead of just saying "No".

2. "U.S. and China find common ground". Yuan would appreciate.

   My comment: It would likely to happen as Biden is less confrontational than Trump. Yuan's appreciation would cause the U.S. consumers and Chinese exporters. If they take out the bans on Huawei, actually it would be good for the U.S. chip suppliers to China in the long run. It is explained in the co-prosperity chapter (one of 4 outcomes in this trade war) in my book "China and US: Apocalypse or Co-Prosperity".

3. "Monetary and fiscal stimulus drives strongest recovery... Copper rallies 50%".

   My comment: It also adds to our national debt. It would have inflation, lower our competitive edge and shaken our USD as the reserve currency. Most investors should have 5 to 20% in gold ETFs and/or gold miners.

4. "Oil prices fall back to $20 barrel".

My comment. $30 is my estimate if it happens. Many oil companies have good forward P/Es. In some locations, green energy is about the same price as oil. OPEC has not been united.

5. "EUR/USD falls to 1.06 by midyear". No comment as there are too many other factors.
6. "Dollar crashes 15%". It is likely to me. That is why we should use gold and metal as a hedge.
7. "Emerging-market debt defaults… equities fall 30% by second quarter".

   My comment. Likely, as they have been overly extended. China may forget some debts in building their infrastructure. Avoid this risky market as the "potential reward / risk" is not justified.
8. "Biden steps down…Sharp correction in the U.S. equities…dollar decline accelerates".
   My comment: I predicted the same in my article "Disaster in 2020". I also predicted the VP will be the first woman president within 5 years for many reasons including Chinese astronomy:

   - Due to bad health; not a surprise for his old age.
   - Unable to unite the divided country.
   - Poor economy leading to high unemployment and poor stock market. '

I also add my own prediction here. China will recover better than most other countries. Korea and China would be the only developed countries that have a positive GDP in 2020. U.K. may have another year of depression due to the new strain of the virus, exit from EU and China's revenging actions similar to Australia.

China recovered from this pandemic in less than 90 days and the factories started to return to normal in April, 2020. The bottleneck now is lack of ships and containers to export their products. If it continues in 2021, China's GDP could be back to 7% (some even predicted 20%). With "One Belt, One Road" and expanding economy, their digital currency would challenge our mighty USD. Despite of the U.S. delisting, I expect Chinese stocks will gain in 2021.

Epilogue

I've received a lot of good responses and thanks. The 3nd Edition incorporates a lot of your feedbacks and my recent updates. Some complaints are not valid though and some could be from my competitors.

- The primary objective of this book is helping you make money, not improving your English skill. Based on the techniques here, I had 50% cash (should be 100% if I followed my charts) before the correction of August, 2015.
- As described in Introduction, charts and tables can be displayed in the full size of your reader by selecting it. I also provide links to the more important charts so you can display them on the large screen of your PC.
- I have my annuity increased by 4 folds using the techniques described in the book over the years.

There are many reasons you should write a review on this book: (http://www.amazon.com/dp/B01BQQYZYI)

- As of this writing (12/2015), I do not know any reviewers on all of my books. Some reviews were obviously written by friends and family members.
- How can a 50-page book have far more and better reviews than my 285-page book on Sector Rotation?
- I bet some reviews were written by my competitors or ones with strong bias against me being an Asian. I beg you to write an honest review.
- A best seller tells us to exit the market in 2009 when my book told you until recently using simple charts for similar period. They had so many excellent reviews from celebrities. If you followed this author, you would have lost a lot of money.

There are 15 strategies described in this book. Try out the first three strategies first. Paper trade your strategies before you commit with real money. If your bet is high, subscribe a newsletter on this subject. There are many to choose from. A current event such as interest hike, a new president…would change the sector performance.

Summary why sector rotation fails

- Not using stop orders. For simplicity, use 5% for most stocks and 8% for volatile sectors. I prefer stops less than the support line to reduce the chance of stopping out due to normal stock price fluctuation. Recommend trailing stops (based on current price) for winning stocks.

- Not timing the market. Include SH or any contra ETFs but not as good as timing the market.
- Not considering different phases of the market cycle. Some sectors are more favorable than others in different stages of the market cycle.
- Not disciplined. If you stick with a proven strategy, it will work in the long term.
- When a sector is in full value, it will be switch to another one with less value. Beware, the market is driven by institutional investors.

Learning from an expert

Andrew McElroy, writing articles on this topic in Seeking Alpha, said, "Great stuff, Tony. It's great to meet experienced traders such as yourself. I had a browse through the book and think your method is a little more refined than mine."

On the next day, he said,
"Your strategy is very rules based and solid. I sometimes envy people who have developed something like this.
That said, if I tried to copy it I would make a dog's dinner of it. There's no way I can undo the way I see the market now. It allows me to make incredible trades, but is also open to errors. No trade is quite the same and I couldn't write down my exact system and rules."
http://seekingalpha.com/article/4029288-sector-rotations-december-update

Final notes

Thanks for reading this book and I hope it will be beneficial to your financial health. If so, comment on it on Amazon.com or the place you bought this book. I will be very grateful.

I believe the readers are getting a very good deal in reading this book. To benefit more, you have to try out the techniques described in this book and paper trade them thoroughly until you are successful.

I have put everything I know on investing in this lengthy book. I do not expect you to buy another of my books if it is about 275 pages long as they will have many duplicated chapters. However, the following book will have recommended stocks: "Best Stocks to buy in 2021" available after Dec. 15,

2020. This book is in the planning stage and there is no promise that it will be published.

I had 50% in a month return in the 2018 year end using year-end strategy and many good picks before. It will include less than 20 books for better picks. A very popular book in 2019 recommending 100 stocks did not even beat the market.

Appendix 1 – All my books

- Complete the Art of Investing (highly recommended combining most of my books on investing). The Kindle version has over 850 pages (6*9).

- Sector Rotation: 21 Strategies and another book Shorting (highly recommended for short-term investors) have more specific chapters on the topic and share many articles with "Complete the art of investing".

- Best stocks for 2021 2nd Edition. Not a promise: Another "Best stocks" books available on July, 2021 and Dec., 2021, and every year hopefully.

- China: "Apocalypse or Co-prosperity (highly recommended). Trade War (most popular in this category). Trade War & Pandemic. Rising China. A Nation of No Losers. Can China Say No. Global Economies. Pandemic.

- Books for today's market: Profit from Coming Market Crash.

- The following books are in a series: Finding Profitable Stocks, Market Timing and Scoring Stocks. Alternate book Using Fidelity.com.

- Books on strategies: "Profit from bull, bear and sideways markets" (Rotation + Momentum + ETF Rotation + trend following), Trading System (similar to printed version of Complete), Swing (Rotation + Momentum), ETF Rotation for Couch Potatoes, Momentum, SuperStocks, Dividend, Penny & Micro Stock, and Retiree.

- Books for advance beginners: Be an expert (highly recommended), Introduce, Investing for Beginners, Beat Fund Managers, Profit via ETFs, Buffett, Ideas, Conservative and Top-Down.
- Miscellaneous: Lessons in Investing. Investing Strategies. Buy Low and Sell High. Buy High and sell Higher. Buffettology. Technical Analysis. Trading Stocks.
- Concise Editions and Introduction Editions are available at very low prices and are competitive with books of similar sizes (50 pages) and prices ($3 range).

Most books have paperbacks. Links and offers are subject to change without notice.

Appendix 2 – Complete the Art of Investing

Instead of buying 16 books, why not buy one book (Complete the Art of Investing) consisting of 16 books? Besides saving money and your digital shelve space, it gives you quick reference and concentration on the topic you're currently interested in. It covers most investing topics in investing excluding speculative investing such as currency trading and day trading.

The Kindle version has about 850 pages (6*9), about the size of three books of average size. With the cost of $10 and at least 850 investing ideas, it is about one cent per idea. Most other books have only a few ideas in the entire book

The 16 books

This book "Complete Art of Investing" is divided into 16 books as follows. Click for the link to the book described in Amazon.com. I squeezed more than 3,000 pages into 850 pages by eliminating duplicated information such as evaluating stocks.

Book No.	Amazon.com
1	Beginner & Billionaire
2	Finding Stocks
3	Evaluating Stocks
4	Scoring Stocks
5	Trading Stocks
6	Market Timing
7	Strategies
8	Sector Rotation
9	Insider Trading
10	Penny Stocks & Micro Cap
11	Momentum Investing
12	Dividend Investing
13	Technical Analysis
14	Investing Ideas
15	The Economy
16	Buffettology

The book links are subject to change without notice.

"How to be a billionaire" is for beginners and couch potatoes, who can use the advanced features of this book in the simplest and less time-consuming techniques. Most advance users can skip this section unless they want to use some of the short cuts described.

We start with the basic books Finding Stocks, Evaluate Stocks, Trading Stocks and Market Timing. You can select and start with one of the many styles and strategies in investing such as swing trading and top-down strategy. Many tools are described in other books such as ETFs, technical analysis, covered calls and trading plan.

Many books start with "Why" to lure you to read more and are followed by "How" and then the theory behind the book.
If the book you're reading is beneficial to you, imagine how it would with 850 pages.

\#

Most readers' comments are on "Debunk the Myths in Investing", which this book is originally based on. As of 2018, I did not know any of the commentators on my books.

"I skipped ahead to his chapter book 14 (of "Complete the Art of Investing"), Investment Advice just to get a feel of his writing style. His research is phenomenal and doesn't overwhelm with big words or catchy "sales-like" tactics.

I truly believe this ordinary man, Mr. Tony Pow, has a gift of explaining his experience as an investor without the bull crap of trying to make you buy his stuff. He seemingly just wants to share his knowledge, tips, and clarity of definitions for the kind of folks like me who want to understand something FIRST before jumping in with emotions of trying to make a boat load of money. I like the technical analysis side he brings.

Mr. Tony Pow talks about hidden gems in his book; well....quite frankly, he is a hidden gem. Thank you and I will also post my comments about this author to my Facebook page!" – JB on this book.

"Excellent book, recommend to all investors... great knowledge. It has fine-tuned my investing strategies... Your book is hard to set aside, as I read it all the time learning good techniques and analysis of stocks, ETF... Since I purchased your book in March, I have underlined, highlighted and placed tabs on top of pages for quick reference." – Aileron on this book.

"Tony, I just finished reading your 2nd edition. It's my pleasure to report that I found it most interesting. You're welcome to use this blurb if you like:

Debunk the Myths in Investing is an all-encompassing look at not only the most salient factors influencing markets and investors, but also a from-the-trenches look at many of the misconceptions and mistakes too many investors make. Reading this book may save not only time and aggravation but money as well!"

Joseph Shaefer, CEO, Stanford Wealth Management LLC.

"Tony, Great work!" from James and Chris, who are portfolio managers.

"'Debunk the Myths in Investing' is a comprehensive book on investing that deals with many aspects of this tense profession in which with a lot of knowledge and a bit of luck (or vice versa) one can greatly benefit...

Therefore 'Debunk the Myths in Investing' is an interesting book that on its 500 pages offer a lot of knowledge related to investing world and many practical advice, so I can recommend its reading if you're interested in this topic."
- Denis Vukosav, Top 500 Reviewers at Amazon.com.

"490 pages (Debunk) of a genius's ranting and hypothesis with various theories throughout, written light-heartedly with ample doses of humor...Yes, the myth of not being able to profitably time the market is BUSTED...

One might ask... Why is he giving away the results of his hard-earned research for only $20? He states that his children are not interested in investing and wants to share his efforts with the world." - Abe Agoda.

"Excellent book, recommend to all investors... great knowledge. It has fine-tuned my investing strategies... Your book is hard to set aside, as I read it all the time learning good techniques and analysis of stocks, ETF... Since I purchased your book in March, I have underlined, highlighted and placed tabs on top of pages for quick reference." - Aileron on this book.

"Great stuff, Tony. It's great to meet experienced traders such as yourself. I had a browse through the book and think your method is a little more refined than mine."

"Your strategy is very rules based and solid. I sometimes envy people who have developed something like this."

Making 50% in one month

I claim to have the best one-month performance ever for recommending 8 or more stocks without using options and leverage. My following return is 57% in a month or 621% annualized. They are slightly different as I calculated the average from the averages of three different accounts. The average buy date is 12/26/18 and the "current date" is 01/28/19.
The performance may not be repeated. I will use the same screen for the coming years and even the expected 10% (or 120% annualized) is very good.

I used the same screen for searching stock candidates. I spent a total of about 20 hours from Dec. 15, 2018 to Jan. 5, 2019.

Stock	Buy Price	Sold or Current Price	Buy date	Sold or Current date	Profit %	Profit % Ann.	Status
CHK	2.13	2.99	01/03/09	01/18/19	40%	982%	Sold
MNK	16.41	21.45	01/03/19	01/25/19	31%	510%	Sold
MNK	16.43	21.45	01/03/19	01/25/19	31%	507%	Sold
NNBR	5.68	8.58	12/26/18	01/28/19	51%	565%	
NNBR	5.72	8.58	12/26/18	01/28/19	66%	727%	
ESTE	4.35	6.45	12/26/18	01/18/19	48%	766%	Sold
LCI	4.61	8.29	12/21/18	01/28/19	80%	767%	
MDR	8.01	9.13	01/08/19	01/28/19	14%	255%	
YRCW	3.29	5.78	12/21/18	01/28/19	76%	727%	
YRCW	3.26	5.78	12/21/18	01/28/19	77%	742%	
ASRT	3.56	4.18	12/26/18	01/28/19	17%	193%	
UTCC	7.13	11.00	12/26/18	01/28/19	54%	600%	
YRCW	2.92	5.78	12/26/18	01/28/19	98%	1083%	

Best one-year return

I claim to have the best-performed article in Seeking Alpha history, an investing site, for recommending 15 or more stocks in one year after the publish date without using options and leverage.

Best stocks to buy for 2021 2nd Edition

We care about performance only. The last book beats the market (SPY simulating S&P500 index) by wide margin. The new edition has another list of recommended stocks. Click here for the book or type the following for more info on the book.
https://www.amazon.com/dp/B08W3KQY42

Performance of the book "Best stocks to buy for 2021" (1st Edition)

List (#of stocks)	Return	Annualized	Beat SPY[1]
Primary list (4)	10%	67%	83%
Primary list without GLD (3)[3]	14%	92%	152%
Secondary list (6)	29%	185%	406%[2]
Year-End list (5)	8%	49%	34%
Secondary list for Year-End (5)	10%	65%	78%
Secondary list without foreign countries (2)	34%	215%	486%[2]

[1] "Beat SPY by" = (Return – SPY Return) / SPY Return. Again, dividends & fees are not considered.
[2] Not a typo.
[3] Gold is optional and it is used for safety.
As in most if not all performance calculations in this book, dividends and fees are not included. The date range is from 12/10/2020 (the publish date) to today, 02/06/2021 (almost two months later). The date could be 1 day off.

Performance of my last book "Best Stocks to buy from August, 2020".
The performance is the returns from 07/28/2020 to 12/07/2020. The average of the 14 recommended stocks beats SPY (an ETF simulating S&P500 stocks) by 29%. There are 13 winners and 1 loser. Dividends have not been included. CMCSA and FDX are big winners profiting from the pandemic. The stocks are ABBV, ABT, CHE, CMCSA, FDX, GTS, JNJ, MCK, MSFT, SCHN, SMCI, UFPI, UNH and ZBRA.

Symbol	Name	Sector	True EY	Return[1]	Ann. Return[2]
Avg.				19%	53%
			SPY	15%	41%
	Beat SPY by				29%

[1] Rounded up for easy reading, but not in the calculation in "Beat SPY by".

Appendix 3 - Our window to the investing world

The paperback version of this chapter can be found in the following link.
http://ebmyth.blogspot.com/2013/11/web-sites.html

- **General**
  Wikipedia / Investopedia /Yahoo!Finance / MarketWatch / Cnnfn / Morningstar /CNBC / Bloomberg / WSJ / Barron's / Motley Fool / TheStreet
- **Evaluate stocks**
  Finviz / SeekingAlpha / MSN Money / Zacks / Daily Finance / ADR / Fidelity / BlueChipGrowth / Earnings Impact / OpenInsider / NYSE / NASDAQ / SEC / SEC for 10K and 10Q (quarterly) reports required to file for listed stocks in major exchanges.
- **Charts**
  BigCharts / FreeStockCharts / StockCharts /
- **Screens**
  Yahoo!Finance / Finviz / CNBC / Morningstar /
- **Besides stocks**
  123Jump / Hoover's Online / FINRA Bond Market Data / REIT / Commodity Futures / Option Industry
- **Vendors**
  AAII / Zacks / IBD / GuruFocus / Vector Vest / Fidelity / Interactive Brokers / Merrill Lynch /
- **Economy.**
  Econday / EcoconStats / Federal Reserve / Economist /
- **Misc.**
  Dow Jones Indices / Russell / Wilshire / IRS / Wikinvest / ETF Database / ETF Trends / Nolo (estate planning) / AARP /

Appendix 4 - ETFs / Mutual Funds

What is an ETF

ETFs have basic differences from mutual funds: 1. Lower management expenses, 2. Trade ETFs same as stocks, and 3. Usually more diversified but not selective than the related mutual funds such as NOBL vs FRDPX.

The major classifications of ETFs are 1. Simulating an index such as SPY, QQQ and DIA, 2. Simulating a sector such as XLE and SOXX, 3. Simulating an asset class such as GLD and SLV, 4. Simulating a country or a group of countries such as EWC and FXI, 5. Managed by a manager(s) such as ARKK, 6. Betting a market or sector to go down such as SH and PSQ, and 7. Leveraged (not recommended for beginners).

Fidelity: Index ETFs (https://www.fidelity.com/etfs/overview).

Wikipedia on ETF (http://en.wikipedia.org/wiki/Exchange-traded_fund).

List of ETFs

ETF Bloomberg
http://www.bloomberg.com/markets/etfs/
ETF data base
http://etfdb.com/
ETF Trends
http://www.etftrends.com/
A list of ETFs. Seeking Alpha.
(http://etf.stock-encyclopedia.com/category/)

Fidelity's commission-free ETFs. Check current offerings and whether they are still commission-free.
(https://www.fidelity.com/etfs/ishares)

Fidelity Annuity funds with performance data.
http://fundresearch.fidelity.com/annuities/category-performance-annual-total-returns-quarterly/FPRAI?refann=005

A list of contra ETFs (or bear ETFs)
http://www.tradermike.net/inverse-short-etfs-bearish-etf-funds/

Misc.: ETFGuide, ETFReplay (highly recommended).

Other resources
Your broker should have a lot of information on ETFs and many offer commission-free ETFs.

Most subscription services offer research on ETFs. IBD has a strategy dedicated to ETFs and so does AAII to name a couple.

Seeking Alpha has extensive resources for ETF including an ETF screener and investing ideas.

Not all ETFs are created equal
Check their performances and their expenses.

Small but well-performing ETFs
Here is a list.
http://finance.yahoo.com/news/small-etfs-pack-big-punch-195430875.html

Guggenheim Spin-Off ETF (CSD) looks interesting. The ETF tracks corporate spinoffs. It has beaten SPY for a long time; check the current performance. Not a recommendation.

When not to use ETFs
I prefer sector mutual funds in some industries but you need to do extensive research. They are drug industry, banks, miners and insurers.

Half ETF
Taking out half of the stocks that score below the average in an index ETF could beat the same full ETF itself. I call it HETF (half the ETF). You heard it here first.

To illustrate, sort the expected P/E (not including stocks with negative earnings) in ascending order and only include the stocks on the first half. Add more fundamental metrics. It will take a few minutes.

Disadvantages of ETFs
- When you have two stocks in a sector ETF one good one and one bad one, the ETF treats them the same. Stock pickers would buy the one that has a better appreciation potential.

- The return is better than the actual return due to stock rotation. To illustrate this, on August 29, 2012, SHLD was replaced by LYB in a sector fund. SHLD was down by 4% and LYB was up by 4% primarily due to the switch. Unless you sell and buy at the right time (which is impossible), your return would not match the ETF's returns due to the replacement.
- Ensure the performance matches the corresponding index, but will most likely not include dividends.

Advantages of ETFs

- We have demonstrated that you can beat the market by using market timing. Between 2000 and Nov., 2013, you only exit and reenter the market 3 times and the result is astonishing.
- It is easy to rotate a sector vs. buying/selling all of the stocks in this sector. It makes sector rotation the same as trading a stock.
- The risk is spread out and your portfolio is diversified especially for a market ETF or buying three or more ETFs in different sectors.
- Eliminate the time in researching stocks.

Leveraged ETFs

I do not recommend them. Some are 2x, 3x and even higher. They're too risky. However, when you are very sure or your tested strategy has very low drawdown, you may want to use them to improve performance. I recommend skipping all leveraged ETFs.

My basic ETF tables

I use a list of selected ETFs and commission-free (check the details) ETFs from Fidelity for my purpose. I include some mutual funds in Fidelity's annuity. Some of these may be interesting to you. I use ETFs for sector rotation and parking my cash when the market is favorable and I do not have stocks that I want to buy. ETFs and funds come and go. Some ideas and classifications are my own interpretation.

#Filler: Honey, my book can play music.
https://www.youtube.com/watch?v=HxGT5z6d-GA&list=PLMZa6mP7jZ2b1otqG4tfbgZpLEdh6YiNF

It may cut down commercials by casting it to TV.

Made in the USA
Monee, IL
13 August 2021